MATLAB Symbolic Algebra and Calculus Tools

■ ■ ■

César Pérez López

Apress®

MATLAB Symbolic Algebra and Calculus Tools

ISBN-13 (pbk): 978-1-4842-0344-6

ISBN-13 (electronic): 978-1-4842-0343-9

Managing Director: Welmoed Spahr
Lead Editor: Jeffrey Pepper
Editorial Board: Steve Anglin, Mark Beckner, Gary Cornell, Louise Corrigan, Jim DeWolf, Jonathan Gennick, Robert Hutchinson, Michelle Lowman, James Markham, Matthew Moodie, Jeff Olson, Jeffrey Pepper, Douglas Pundick, Ben Renow-Clarke, Gwenan Spearing, Matt Wade, Steve Weiss
Coordinating Editor: Melissa Maldonado
Copy Editor: Barnaby Sheppard
Compositor: SPi Global
Indexer: SPi Global
Artist: SPi Global
Cover Designer: Anna Ishchenko

Distributed to the book trade worldwide by Springer Science+Business Media New York, 233 Spring Street, 6th Floor, New York, NY 10013. Phone 1-800-SPRINGER, fax (201) 348-4505, e-mail orders-ny@springer-sbm.com, or visit www.springeronline.com. Apress Media, LLC is a California LLC and the sole member (owner) is Springer Science + Business Media Finance Inc (SSBM Finance Inc). SSBM Finance Inc is a Delaware corporation.

For information on translations, please e-mail rights@apress.com, or visit www.apress.com.

Apress and friends of ED books may be purchased in bulk for academic, corporate, or promotional use. eBook versions and licenses are also available for most titles. For more information, reference our Special Bulk Sales–eBook Licensing web page at www.apress.com/bulk-sales.

Any source code or other supplementary material referenced by the author in this text is available to readers at www.apress.com. For detailed information about how to locate your book's source code, go to www.apress.com/source-code/.

Contents at a Glance

Contents

About the Author

César Pérez López is a Professor at the Department of Statistics and Operations Research at the University of Madrid. César is also a Mathematician and Economist at the National Statistics Institute (INE) in Madrid, a body which belongs to the Superior Systems and Information Technology Department of the Spanish Government. César also currently works at the Institute for Fiscal Studies in Madrid.

Also Available

- *MATLAB Programming for Numerical Analysis,* 978-1-4842-0296-8
- *MATLAB Control Systems Engineering,* 978-1-4842-0290-6
- *MATLAB Differential Equations,* 978-1-4842-0311-8
- *MATLAB Linear Algebra,* 978-1-4842-0323-1
- *MATLAB Differential and Integral Calculus,* 978-1-4842-0305-7
- *MATLAB Optimization Techniques,* 978-1-4842-0293-7

CHAPTER 1

■ ■ ■

Symbolic Variables and Functions

1-1. Symbolic Variables

MATLAB deems as symbolic any algebraic expression whose variables have all been previously defined as symbolic; variables are declared as symbolic using the command syms. For example, if we want to treat as symbolic the expression $6 * a * b + 3 * a^2 + 2 * a * b$, in order to simplify it, we need to declare the two variables a and b as symbolic, as shown here:

```
>> syms a b
>> simplify(6*a*b + 3*a^2 + 2*a*b)
```

```
ans =

8 * a * b + 3 * a ^ 2
```

As we will see, the command needed to transform a numeric expression to symbolic is sym. For example, if we want to simplify the numeric expression $2/5 + 6/10 + 8/20$, we need to first transform it to a symbolic expression with sym(2/5+6/10+8/20), performing the simplification as follows:

```
>> simplify(sym(2/5+6/10+8/20))
```

```
ans =

7/5
```

The variables of symbolic expressions must be symbolic. Some of the commands for working with symbolic and numeric variables are detailed below:

syms x y z... t **makes the variables** x, y, z,..., t **symbolic.**

syms x y z... t real **converts the variables** x, y, z,..., t **to symbolic variables with real values.**

syms x y z... t unreal **undoes the previous declaration, so that the variables x, y, z,..., t may now have non-zero imaginary parts.**

syms **lists all symbolic variables currently in the workspace.**

x = sym('x') **declares the variable** x **as symbolic (equivalent to** syms x**).**

1

x = sym('x', real) **converts** x **to a real symbolic variable.**

x = sym('x',unreal) **enables the symbolic variable** x **to have non-zero imaginary part.**

S = sym(A) **creates a symbolic object from A, where A may be a string, a scalar, an array, a numeric expression, and so on.**

S = sym(A,'option') **converts the array, scalar or numeric expression to a symbolic expression according to the specified option. The option can be** f **for floating point,** r **for rational,** e **for estimate error, or** d **for decimal.**

numeric(x) **or** double(x) **converts the variable or expression** x **to double-precision.**

sym2poly(poly) **converts the symbolic polynomial** poly **to a vector whose components are its coefficients.**

poly2sym(vector) **returns a symbolic representation of the polynomial whose coefficients are given by the vector.**

poly2sym(vector,'v') **converts a vector into a symbolic polynomial in the variable v.**

digits(d) **sets the precision of symbolic variables to** d **significant decimal digits.**

digits **returns the current precision for symbolic variables.**

vpa(expr) **returns the numerical result of the expression with a number of significant decimal digits of precision determined by** digits.

vpa(expr, n) **or** vpa('expr', n) **returns the numerical result of the expression to** n **significant decimal digits.**

pretty(expr) **displays the symbolic expression using standard mathematical formatting.**

EXERCISE 1-1

Solve the equation $ax^2 + bx + c = 0$ assuming that the variable is x. Also solve it for the variables a, b and c, respectively.

Because MATLAB considers x to be symbolic by default, we can solve the equation directly for x without having to specify it as a symbolic variable using the command solve (note that in MATLAB the equations are introduced within single quotes):

```
>> solve('a*x^2+b*x+c=0')
```

```
ans =

[1/2/a*(-b+(b^2-4*a*c)^(1/2))]
[1/2/a*(-b-(b^2-4*a*c)^(1/2))]
```

However, to solve the equation with respect to the variables *a*, *b* or *c* , it is necessary to first declare them as symbolic variables:

```
>> syms a
>> solve('a*x^2+b*x+c=0',a)
```

ans =

```
-(b*x+c)/x^2
```

```
>> syms b
>> solve('a*x^2+b*x+c=0',b)
```

ans =

```
-(a*x^2+c)/x
```

```
>> syms c
>> solve('a*x^2+b*x+c=0',c)
```

ans =

```
-a*x^2 - b*x
```

EXERCISE 1-2

Find the roots of the polynomial $x^4 - 8 x^2 + 16 = 0$, obtaining the result to default accuracy, to 20 significant figures and to double-precision exact accuracy. Also generate the vector of coefficients associated with the polynomial.

```
>> p = solve('x^4-8*x^2-16=0')
```

p =

```
[  2*(2^(1/2)+1)^(1/2)]
[-2*(2^(1/2)+1)^(1/2)]
[  2*(1-2^(1/2))^(1/2)]
[-2*(1-2^(1/2))^(1/2)]
```

```
>> vpa(p)
```

```
ans =

[    3.1075479480600746146883179061262]
[   -3.1075479480600746146883179061262]
[  1.2871885058111652494708868748364*i]
[ -1.2871885058111652494708868748364*i]
```

```
>> numeric(p)
```

```
ans =

 3.1075
-3.1075
     0 + 1.2872i
     0 - 1.2872i
```

```
>> vpa(p,20)
```

```
ans =

[   3.1075479480600746146]
[  -3.1075479480600746146]
[ 1.2871885058111652495*i]
[-1.2871885058111652495*i]
```

```
>>  syms x
>>  sym2poly(x^4-8*x^2-16)
```

```
ans =

1 0 -8 0 -16
```

EXERCISE 1-3

Find the numerical value, to default precision, of the abscissa of the intersection of the curves y = sin(x) and y = cos(x) in the first quadrant. Find the exact (symbolic) solution. Find the abscissa to a precision of 12 decimal places.

```
>> p = numeric(solve('sin(x) = cos(x)'))
```

```
p =

0.7854
```

```
>> q = sym (p)
```

```
q =

PI/4
```

```
>> digits(12); r=numeric(solve('sin(x)=cos(x)'))
```

```
r =

.785398163398
```

EXERCISE 1-4

Simplify the following expressions as much as possible:

1/2m - 1/3m + 1/4m + 1/5m + 1/6m

1/2 - 1/3 + 1/4 + 1/5 + 1/6

```
>> syms m
>> simplify(1/(2*m) - 1/(3*m) + 1/(4*m) + 1/(5*m) + 1/(6*m))
```

```
ans =

47/60/m
```

```
>> pretty(simplify(1/(2*m) - 1/(3*m) + 1/(4*m) + 1/(5*m) + 1/(6*m)))
```

```
47
--
60
```

```
>> sym(1/2 - 1/3 + 1/4 + 1/5 + 1/6)
```

```
ans =

47/60
```

1-2. Symbolic Vector Variables

A variable that represents a vector of length n can be defined in MATLAB in the following ways:

```
variable = [e1, e2, e3,..., en]
variable = [e1 e2 e3... en]
```

Therefore, to define a vector variable, simply insert brackets around the vector elements, separated by commas or blank spaces.

On the other hand, you can also define *symbolic vector variables*, after previously using the syms command.

```
>> syms t
>> A=sym([sin(t),cos(t)])
```

```
A =

[sin (t), cos (t)]
```

1-3. Symbolic Matrix Variables

To define an array in MATLAB, simply enter in brackets all of its row vectors separated by semicolons. When entering a vector, you can separate its components by spaces or commas, as we've already seen. For example, a 3 × 3 matrix variable can be entered in the following two ways:

```
matrix = [a₁₁ a₁₂ a₁₃;a₂₁ a₂₂ a₂₃;a₃₁ a₃₂ a₃₃]
```

```
matrix = [a₁₁, a₁₂, a₁₃;a₂₁, a₂₂, a₂₃;a₃₁, a₃₂, a₃₃]
```

We would similarly define an M × N variable array. To work with *symbolic matrices,* we simply declare the variables involved to be symbolic with the syms command:

```
>> syms t
>>  A=sym([sin(t),cos(t);tan(t),exp(t)])
```

```
A =

[sin (t), cos (t)]
[tan (t), exp (t)]
```

```
>> b = inv (A)
```

```
b =

[-exp (t) / (-sin (t) * exp (t) + cos (t) * tan (t)), cos (t) / (-sin (t) * exp (t) + cos (t) *
tan (t))]
[tan (t) / (-sin (t) * exp (t) + cos (t) * tan (t)), - sin (t) / (-sin (t) * exp (t) + cos (t) *
tan (t))]
```

Once a matrix variable has been defined, MATLAB provides many ways to insert, extract, renumber, and generally manipulate its elements.

A(m,n) **returns the** (m, n)th **element of the matrix** A **(row** m **and column** n**).**

A(a:b,c:d) **returns the subarray of** A **formed by the** a-th **through** b-th **rows, inclusive, and the** c-th **and** d-th **columns, inclusive.**

A(a:p:b,c:q:d) **returns the subarray of** A **formed by every p-th row between the** a-th **and** b-th **rows and by every q-th column between the** c-th **and** d-th **columns.**

A([a b],[c d]) **returns the subarray of** A **formed by the intersection of rows** c **and** d **and columns** a **and** b.

A([a b c...],[e f g...]) **returns the subarray of** A **formed by the intersection of rows** a,b,c,... **and columns** e,f,g, . . .

A(:,c:d) **returns the subarray of** A **consisting of all the rows of** A **and the** c-th **through** d-th **columns, inclusive.**

A(:,[c d e ...]) **returns the subarray of** A **formed by all rows and columns** c,d,e,...

A(a:b,:) **returns the subarray of** A **formed by all the columns of** A **and the** a-th **through** b-th **rows, inclusive.**

A([a b c...],:) **returns the subarray of** A **formed by all the columns of** A **and rows** a,b,c, . . .

A(a,:) **returns the** a-th **row of the matrix** A.

A(:,b) **returns the** b-th **column of the matrix** A.

A (:) **returns a column vector whose elements are columns of** A **placed in order below one another.**

`A(:,:)` **is equivalent to all rows and columns of the matrix** A.

`[A, B, C,...]` **returns the matrix formed by** A, B, C,...

`SA = [ ]` **deletes the subarray** S **of the matrix** A, **and returns the remaining matrix.**

`diag(v)` **creates a diagonal matrix with the vector** v **in the diagonal.**

`diag(A)` **returns the diagonal of the matrix** A **as a column vector.**

`flipud(A)` **returns the matrix whose rows are placed in reverse order (from top to bottom) to the rows of** A.

`fliplr(A)` **returns the matrix whose columns are placed in reverse order (from left to right) to those of** A.

`rot90(A)` **rotates the matrix** A **90 degrees counterclockwise.**

`reshape(A,m,n)` **returns the** m × n **matrix extracted from the matrix** A, **where consecutive elements of the original matrix fill the new matrix column by column.**

`size(A)` **returns the order (size) of the matrix** A.

`find(condA)` **returns the items in** A **that satisfy the stated condition.**

`length(v)` **returns the length of the vector** v.

`tril(A)` **returns the lower triangular part of the matrix** A.

`triu(A)` **returns the upper triangular part of the matrix** A.

`A'` **returns the transpose of the matrix** A.

`inv(A)` **returns the inverse of the matrix** A.

The most important operations with array variables are summarized below:

`A + B, A - B, A * B` *sum, difference and product of matrices.*

`A\B` **If** *A* **is square,** `A\B = inv (A) * B`. **If** A **is not square,** `A\B` **is the solution, in the sense of least-squares, of the system** `AX = B`.

`B/A` **coincides with** `(A'\B')'`.

`A^n` **coincides with** `A * A * A *... * A` n **times (nth power).**

`P^A` **performs the calculation only if** p **is a scalar**.

1-4. Character Variables

MATLAB is capable of powerful numerical calculation, but it also provides versatility in handling character variables (text variables). A character variable (string) is simply a string of characters, included in single quotes, which MATLAB treats as a vector. For example:

```
>> c = 'string'
```

```
c =

string
```

We have thus defined the variable c as a character variable. Among the MATLAB commands that handle character variables are the following:

abs('string') **returns the vector whose elements are the ASCII values of the characters in the string.**

setstr(numeric_vector) **returns the string of ASCII characters that are equivalent to the elements of the vector.**

str2mat(t1,t2,t3,...) **returns the matrix whose rows are the strings** t1, t2, t3,..., **respectively.**

str2num('string') **converts the string of characters into an exact numerical value using eval.**

num2str(number) **converts the number into its string of equivalent characters with fixed precision.**

int2str(integer) **converts the integer into a string.**

sprintf('format', A) **converts the exact numeric array** A **into a string using the specified format.**

sscanf('string', 'format') **converts the string to a numeric value in the specified format.**

dec2hex(integer) **converts the decimal integer into its equivalent string in hexadecimal.**

hex2dec('string_hex') **converts the hexadecimal string into the equivalent integer.**

hex2num('string_hex') **converts the hexadecimal string into the equivalent IEEE floating-point number.**

lower('string') **converts the string to lowercase.**

upper('string') **converts the string to uppercase.**

strcmp(s1,s2) **compares the strings** s1 **and** s2 **and returns 1 if they are equal, and 0 otherwise.**

strcmp(s1,s2,n) **compares the strings** s1 **and** s2 **and returns 1 if they are equal in their first** n **characters and 0 otherwise.**

strrep(c, 'exp1', 'exp2') **replaces** exp1 **with** exp2 **in the string** c.

findstr(c, 'exp') **returns the position of the expression** exp **in the string** c.

isstr(expression) **or** ischar(expression) **returns 1 if the expression is a string and 0 if it is not.**

strjust(string) **right-justifies the string.**

blanks(n) **generates a string of** n **blank characters.**

deblank(string) **replaces the characters in the string with blanks.**

eval(expression) **executes the expression even if it is a string.**

> disp('string') **displays the string (or array) as written. MATLAB then continues processing.**

> input('string') **displays the string on screen, then MATLAB pauses until the user presses a key to continue.**

Here are some examples:

```
>> eval('4 * atan(1)')
```

```
ans =

3.1416
```

In the following examples you can see how MATLAB numerically evaluates the contents of a string (provided it is in a form recognized by the program):

```
>> hex2dec('3ffe56e')
```

```
ans =

67102062
```

Here, MATLAB has returned a decimal from a string in hexadecimal. The opposite conversion looks like this:

```
>> dec2hex(1345679001)
```

```
ans =

50356E99
```

Here, the program has converted a decimal number to a hexadecimal string.

```
>> sprintf('%f',[1+sqrt(5)/2,pi])
```

```
ans =

2.118034 3.141593
```

With sprintf, the exact numerical components of a vector have been converted to a string (with default precision).

```
>> sscanf('121.00012', '%f')
```

```
ans =

121.0001
```

With `sscanf`, a numeric string was returned in exact numerical format (with default precision).

```
>> num2str (pi)
```

```
ans =

3.142
```

The exact number is now the value of π as a string.

```
>> str2num('15/14')
```

```
ans =

1.0714
```

A string has been converted to an exact numeric value, with default accuracy.

```
>> setstr(32:126)
```

```
ans =

!"#$% &' () * +, -. / 0123456789:; < = >? @ABCDEFGHIJKLMNOPQRSTUVWXYZ [\] ^
_'abcdefghijklmnopqrstuvwxyz {|}~
```

This operation obtained the ASCII characters associated with the whole numbers between 32 and 126.

```
>> abs('{]}><#¡¿?°ª')
```

```
ans =
123 93 125 62 60 35 161 191 63 186 170
```

With the abs command we have obtained the integers corresponding to each ASCII character specified in its argument.

```
>> lower('ABCDefgHIJ')
```

```
ans =

abcdefghij
```

This command translated the text to lowercase.

```
>> upper('abcd eFGHi jKlMn')
```

```
ans =

ABCD EFGHI JKLMN
```

Here we have converted the text to uppercase.

```
>> str2mat ('The world','The country','Daily 16','ABC')
```

```
ans =

The world
The country
Daily 16
ABC
```

The str2mat command has created an array of text whose rows are the strings specified as its arguments.

```
>> disp('This text will appear on the screen')
```

```
This text will appear on the screen
```

This command has displayed as screen text the argument of the command disp.

```
>> c = This is 'a good example';
>> strrep(c, 'good', 'bad')
```

```
ans =

This is a bad example
```

This command has replaced good with bad in the string c. The following command finds the position that the expression is occupies within the string c.

```
>> findstr(c, 'is')
```

```
ans =

3 6
```

1-5. Logic Functions

MATLAB has a group of functions whose output is either true (value 1) or false (value 0). Among them are the following:

exist(A) **tests whether the variable or function A exists (returns 0 if A does not exist, and a number between 1 and 5, depending on the type, if it does exist).**

any(V) **returns 0 if all elements of the vector V are zero, and returns 1 if some element of V is non-null.**

any(A) **returns 0 for each column of the matrix A with all null elements, and returns 1 for each column of the matrix A that has some non-null elements.**

all(V) **returns 1 if all the elements of the vector V are non-null, and returns 0 if some element of V is zero.**

all(A) **returns 1 for each column of the matrix A in which no elements are null, and returns 0 for each column of A that has any null elements.**

find(V) **returns the places (or indices) occupied by the non-zero elements of the vector V.**

isNaN(V) **returns 1 for the elements of V that are indeterminate, and returns 0 for those that are not.**

isinf(V) **returns 1 for the elements of V that are infinite, and returns 0 for those that are not.**

isfinite(V) **returns 1 for the elements of V that are finite, and returns 0 for those that are not.**

isempty(A) **returns 1 if A is an empty array, and returns 0 otherwise (an empty array is one that has one of its dimensions equal to 0).**

issparse(A) **returns 1 if A is sparse, and returns 0 otherwise.**

isreal(V) **returns 1 if all the elements of V are real, and 0 otherwise.**

isprime(V) **returns 1 for all elements of V that are prime numbers, and returns 0 for elements of V that are not prime.**

islogical(V) **returns 1 if V is a logical vector and 0 otherwise.**

isnumeric(V) **returns 1 if V is a numeric vector and 0 otherwise.**

ishold **returns 1 if hold is on and 0 otherwise. When hold is on the current plot and (most) axis properties are held so that subsequent graphing commands add to the existing graph.**

isieee **returns 1 if the computer uses IEEE arithmetic and 0 otherwise.**

isstr(S) **returns 1 if S is a string, and 0 otherwise.**

ischart(S) **returns 1 if S is a string, and 0 otherwise.**

isglobal(A) **returns 1 if A is a global variable, and 0 otherwise.**

isletter(S) **returns 1 if** S **is a letter of the alphabet, and 0 otherwise.**

isequal(A,B) **returns 1 if the matrices or vectors** A **and** B **are equal, and 0 otherwise.**

ismember(V,W) **returns 1 for every element of** V **that is in** W**, and 0 for every element of** V **that is not in** W**.**

Here are some examples:

```
>> isinf([pi NaN Inf -Inf])
```

```
ans =

0    0    1    1
```

```
>> any([pi NaN Inf -Inf])
```

```
ans =

1
```

```
>> ismember([1,2,3,5],[8,12,1,3,56,5])
```

```
ans =

1    0    1    1
```

```
>> A = [2,0,1]; B = [4,0,2];
>> isequal(2*A,B)
```

```
ans =

1
```

```
>> V=[-10,5,3,12,0];
>> isprime(V)
```

```
ans =

0    1    1    0    0
```

```
>> isnumeric(V)
```

```
ans =

1
```

```
>> all(V)
```

```
ans =

0
```

```
>> any(V)
```

```
ans =

1
```

```
>> C = [0 2 3;0 1 2 ;0 4 6],D = [0 0 0 0;4 3 1 2;6 0 0 4]
>> any(C),all(C),any(D),all(D)
```

```
ans =

0 1 1
```

```
ans =

0 1 1
```

```
ans =

1 1 1 1
```

```
ans =

0 0 0 0
```

1-6. Elementary Functions That Support Complex Symbolic Matrices as Arguments

- **Trigonometric**

sin(z)	sine function
sinh(z)	hyperbolic sine function
asin(z)	arcsine function
asinh(z)	hyperbolic arcsine function
cos(z)	cosine function
cosh(z)	hyperbolic cosine function
acos(z)	arccosine function
acosh(z)	hyperbolic arccosine function
tan(z)	tangent function
tanh(z)	hyperbolic tangent function
atan(z)	arctangent function

`atan2(z)`	arctangent function in the fourth quadrant
`atanh(z)`	hyperbolic arctangent function
`sec(z)`	secant function
`sech(z)`	hyperbolic secant function
`asec(z)`	arcsecant function
`asech(z)`	hyperbolic arcsecant function
`csc(z)`	cosecant function
`csch(z)`	hyperbolic cosecant function
`acsc(z)`	arccosecant function
`acsch(z)`	hyperbolic arccosecant function
`cot(z)`	cotangent function
`coth(z)`	hyperbolic cotangent function
`acot(z)`	arccotangent function
`acoth(z)`	hyperbolic arccotangent function

- **Exponential**

`exp(z)`	base e exponential function
`log(z)`	Napierian logarithm function
`log10(z)`	decimal logarithm function
`sqrt(z)`	square root function

- **Complex**

`abs(z)`	modulus or absolute value
`angle(z)`	argument
`conj(z)`	complex conjugate
`imag(z)`	imaginary part
`real(z)`	real part

- **Numerical**

`fix(Z)`	removes the decimal part
`floor(Z)`	rounds decimals to the nearest lower integer
`ceil(Z)`	rounds decimals to the nearest greater integer
`round(Z)`	rounds Z to the nearest integer, rounding values mid way between two integers to the integer with the largest magnitude.
`rem(Z1, Z2)`	remainder of the division of $Z1$ by $Z2$
`sign(Z)`	sign function

- **Matrix**

`expm(Z)`	matrix exponential function by default
`expm1(Z)`	matrix exponential function in M-file
`expm2(Z)`	matrix exponential function via Taylor series
`expm3(Z)`	matrix exponential function via eigenvalues
`logm(Z)`	matrix logarithm
`sqrtm(Z)`	matrix square root
`funm(Z,'function')`	applies the function to the array Z

1-7. Symbolic Functions of Several Variables

Functions of one or several variables are defined using the command maple as follows:

maple('f: = x - > f (x)') or maple f: = x - > f (x) **defines the function** f(x).

maple ('f:=(x,y,z...)- > f(x,y,z...)') **defines the function** f(x,y,z,..).

maple ('f:=(x,y,z...)- > (f1 (x,y...), f2(x,y..),...)') **defines the vector function** (f1(x,y,..), f2(x,y,..),...).

To find the value of the function $(x, y, z) - > f(x,y,z...)$ at the point $(a, b, c,...)$, use the expression maple('f(a,b,c,...)').

We can find the value of the vector function $f:=(x,y,..)->(f1(x,y,..), f2(x,y,..),...)$ at the point $(a,b,...)$ by using the expression maple('f(a,b,..)').

The function $f(x,y) = 2x + y$ is defined in the following way:

```
>> maple ('f:=(x,y) - > 2 * x + y ');
```

$f(2,3)$ and $f(a,b)$ are calculated as follows:

```
>> maple('f(2,3)')
```

---

ans =

7

```
>> maple('f(a,b)')
```

---

ans =

2 * a + b

EXERCISE 1-5

Given the function h, defined as h(x,y) = (cos(x^2-y^2), sin(x^2-y^2)); calculate h(1,2), h(-Pi,Pi) and h(cos(a^2), cos(1 -a^2)). Because we have a vector function of two variables, we use the maple command:

```
>> maple ('h:=(x,y) - > (cos(x^2-y^2), sin(x^2-y^2))');
>> maple ('A = h(1,2), B = h(-pi,pi), C = h (cos(a^2), cos(1-a^2))')
```

---

ans =

A = (cos(3),-sin(3)), B = (1,0),
C = (cos(cos(a^2)^2-cos(-1+a^2)^2), sin(cos(a^2)^2-cos(-1+a^2)^2))

1-8. Functions of Single Variables

Functions of a single variable are a special case of vector functions, but they can also be defined in MATLAB via: f = 'function'. To find the value of the function f at a point, you use the command subs, whose syntax is as follows:

> subs(f, a) **applies the function** f **at the point** a

> subs(f, a, b) **substitutes each occurrence of a by b in the expression f.**

Let's see how to define the function $f(x) = x ^ 2$:

```
>> f ='x ^ 2'
```

```
f =

x ^ 2
```

Now we calculate the values $f(4)$, $f(a+1)$ and $f(3x+x^2)$:

```
>> syms a x
>>  A=subs(f,4),B=subs(f,a+1),C=subs(f,3*x+x^2)
```

```
A =

16

B =

(a+1) ^ 2

C =

(3 * x + x ^ 2) ^ 2
```

It should also be borne in mind that if we use the maple command, the special constants π, e, i, and ∞ are defined as maple('Pi'), maple('exp (1)'), maple('i') and maple('infinity'), respectively.

EXERCISE 1-6

Define the functions f (x) = x^2, g (x) = $x^{1/2}$ and h (x) = x + sin (x). Calculate f (2), g (4) and h (a-b^2).

```
>> f ='x^2'; g = 'x^(1/2)'; h = 'x+sin(x)';

>> syms a b
>> a = subs(f,2), b = subs(g,4), c = subs(h,'a-b^2')
```

```
A =

4

b =

4 ^(1/2)

c =

a - b^2 + sin(a-b^2)
```

We could also have done the following:

```
>> maple('f:=x->x^2: g:=x->sqrt(x):h:=x->x+sin(x)');
>> maple('f(2),g(4),h(a-b^2)')
```

```
ans =

4, 2, a - b^2 + sin(a-b^2)
```

■ ■ ■

CHAPTER 2

Algebraic Expressions and Operations: Factoring Algebraic Fractions

MATLAB handles all calculations involving simple, rational, and complex algebraic expressions with mastery. It quickly and efficiently performs the operations of simplification, factorization, grouping, and expansion of algebraic expressions, no matter how complicated, including trigonometric expressions and expressions involving complex variables. All of this is possible provided the symbolic math Toolbox is available. The following is a list of commands which implement the algebraic transformations most commonly used in work with MATLAB.

2-1. Expansion of Algebraic Expressions

The following commands enable MATLAB to expand or develop algebraic expressions:

expand(expr) **expands an algebraic expression, presenting the result as a sum of products and powers. It applies multiple angle rules for trigonometric expressions and formally applies the properties of exponential and logarithmic functions. It also decomposes quotients of polynomials by expanding the numerator, presenting the original expression as a sum of algebraic quotients.**

maple('expand(expr)') **completely expands the algebraic expression, transforming products and powers into sums of terms, applying multiple angle rules for trigonometric functions and expansion rules for exponential functions. It then simplifies the end result.**

maple('Expand(expr)') **performs the inert expansion of** expr **(that is, it goes through the steps of expansion without evaluation).**

maple('expand(expr) mod n') **performs the expansion of** expr **modulo** n.

maple('Expand(expr) mod n') **gives the inert expansion of** expr **modulo** n.

maple('expand(expr, sub1,...,subn)') **expands** expr **without expanding its subexpressions** sub1,..., subn.

maple('expand(rational)') **expands the numerator of the given rational algebraic expression.**

`maple('expand(equation)')` **expands both sides of the equation.**

`maple('expand([expr1,...,exprn])')` **creates a list of expanded expressions.**

`maple('expand({expr1,...,exprn})')` **creates a set of expanded expressions.**

`maple('expandoff(command)')` **suppresses the expansion of expressions involving the specified command in future calculations.**

`maple('expandoff(com1,...,comn)')` **suppresses the expansion of expressions involving the specified commands in future calculations.**

`maple('expand(expandoff ())')` **suppresses the expansion of expressions for all commands in future calculations.**

`maple('expandon(command)')` **enables the expansion of expressions involving the specified command in future calculations. First, it checks whether the command has been previously affected by** expandoff, **and if so, it eliminates its effect.**

`maple('expandon(com1,...,comn)')` **enables the expansion of expressions involving the specified commands in future calculations.**

`maple('expand(expandon ())')` **enables the expansion of expressions for all commands in future calculations.**

`maple('frontend(command, [expr1,..., exprn])')` **paralyzes the expansion of the given expressions before submitting to the specified command or procedure.**

`maple('frontend(command, [expr1,..., exprn], [arg1,..., argm])')` **paralyzes the expansion of the given expressions** expr1,...,exprn **before submitting to the specified command or procedure, but does not freeze** arg1,...,argm.

Now let's look at several examples of algebraic manipulations using the commands we've just seen:

```
>> syms x y z t a b
>> pretty(expand((x+1)*(x+2)))
```

$$x^2 + 3x + 2$$

```
>> pretty(expand((x+1)/(x+2)))
```

$$\frac{x}{x+2} + \frac{1}{x+2}$$

```
>> pretty (expand (sin (x + y)))
```

$$\sin(x)\cos(y) + \cos(x)\sin(y)$$

```
>> pretty(expand(cos(2*x)))
```

$$2 \cos(x)^2 - 1$$

```
>> pretty(expand(exp(a+log(b))))
```

$$\exp(a) \ b$$

```
>> pretty(expand(log(x/(1-x)^2)))
```

$$\log(x) - 2 \log(1 - x)$$

```
>> pretty(expand((x+1)*(y+z)))
```

$$x \ y + x \ z + y + z$$

```
>> pretty(expand(BesselJ(2,t)))
```

$$2 \ \frac{\text{besselJ}(1, \ t)}{t} - \text{besselJ}(0, \ t)$$

```
>> maple('expandoff(exp):expand(exp(a+b))')
```

```
ans =

exp(a+b)
```

```
>> maple('expandon(exp):expand(exp(c+d))')
```

```
ans =

exp(c)*exp(d)
```

EXERCISE 2-1

Find the greatest common divisor of the following algebraic expressions a and b:

$a = \sin^2(x) + 2\sin(x) + 1$, $b = \sin(x) + 1$

First, we try to solve the problem directly.

```
>> syms a b x
>> maple ('a: = sin (x) ^ 2 + 2 * sin (x) + 1, b: = sin(x) + 1:gcd(a,b)')
```

```
Error, (in gcd) arguments must be polynomials over the rationals.
```

To avoid this error, use the command *frontend* as follows:

```
>> maple('frontend(gcd,[a,b])')
```

```
ans =

sin (x) + 1
```

EXERCISE 2-2

Expand the polynomial $(x+2)^2(x-2)$ as much as possible modulo 3. Also expand the polynomial $(x +\alpha)^2(x -\alpha)$ where α = RootOf $(x^2- 2)$. At the same time, expand the polynomial $(x +\beta)^2(x -\beta)$ modulo 2 where β = RootOf (x^2+x+1).

```
>> pretty(sym(maple('expand( (x+2)^2*(x-2) ) mod 3')))
```

```
          3     2
         x  + 2 x  + 2 x + 1
```

```
>> pretty(sym(maple('alias(a=RootOf(x^2-2)):evala(Expand( (x+a)^2*(x-a) ))')))
```

```
          3     2
         x  + a x  - 2 x - 2 a
```

```
>> pretty(sym(maple('alias(b=RootOf(x^2+x+1)):evala(Expand( (x+b)^2*(x-b) ) mod 2)')))
```

```
          3         2
         x  + x + b x  + b x + 1
```

The command alias is used to define abbreviations for objects, which helps to reduce the complexity of the output.

2-2. Factoring Expressions over Fields and their Algebraic Extensions

The following commands enable Maple to factorize algebraic expressions, whether univariate, multivariate, over the field of real numbers or over the field of their coefficients or algebraic extensions thereof. The command syntax is as follows:

`factor(expr)` **writes an algebraic expression as a product of factors (the reverse of** *expand*)**. Factoring is performed by default over the field or ring defined by the coefficients of the expression. For algebraic fractions, the numerator and denominator are individually factored and common factors are cancelled.**

`maple('factor(expression)')` **factorizes a non-polynomial or polynomial algebraic expression over the field or ring defined by its coefficients.**

`maple('factor(expr,a)')` **factorizes the polynomial algebraic expression over the field defined by its coefficients and the extension element a (where a is usually a simple or compound radical or an algebraic number defined by a RootOf expression).**

`maple('factor(expression,radical)')` **factorizes the polynomial expression over the field extension Q(radical) of Q. For example, Q($\sqrt{2}$) or Q(RootOf(x^2-3)).**

`maple('factor(expr,[rad1,..., radn])` or `factor(expr, {rad1,..., radn})')` **factorizes the polynomial expression over the field extension Q(rad1,..., radn) of Q. For example, Q ($\sqrt{2}$,$\sqrt{3}$).**

`maple('factor(rational)')` **factorizes the numerator and denominator of the given rational expression, normalizing it.**

`maple('factor(equation)')` **factorizes both sides of an equation.**

`maple('factors(expression)')` **returns the factors and their multiplicities for the given polynomial algebraic expression, over the field defined by their coefficients.**

`maple('factors(expr,radical)')` **returns factors and their multiplicities for the given polynomial expression over the field extension Q(radical) of Q. For example,Q($\sqrt{2}$) or Q(RootOf(x^2-3)).**

`maple('factors(expr,[rad1,..., radn])` or `factors(expr, {rad1,..., radn})')` **gives the factors and their multiplicities for the given polynomial expression over the field Q(rad1,..., radn); for example, Q($\sqrt{2}$, $\sqrt{3}$).**

`maple('factor(expr) mod n')` **performs the factorization of the given non-polynomial or polynomial expression over the field determined by its coefficients modulo** *n***.**

`maple('Factor(expression)')` **gives in inert form the factorization of the given polynomial or non-polynomial expression over the field defined by its coefficients.**

`maple('Factors(expression)')` **represents in inert form the factors of the given polynomial expression.**

`maple('Factor(expr) mod n')` **performs the inert factorization of the given expression, whether non-polynomial or polynomial, over the field defined by its coefficients modulo** *n***.**

`maple('Factors(expression)')` **represents in inert form the factors of the given polynomial expression modulo** *n***.**

maple('AFactor(expression)') **performs the inert absolute factorization of the given expression.**

maple('AFactors(expression)') **represents in inert form the factors of the absolute factorization of the given polynomial expression.**

maple('Berlekamp(expr,var)') **represents the inert form of the Berlekamp factorization of varying degrees for the multivariate expression** *expr* **with respect to the variable** *var*.

maple('Berlekamp(expr, var) mod n') **represents the inert form of the Berlekamp factorization of varying degrees modulo n for the multivariate expression expr with respect to var.**

maple('readlib(split):split(expr, variable)') **performs the complete factorization of the given polynomial expression in the specified variable.**

maple('grading(Inert_command(expr1,..., exprn))') **evaluates the specified function or inert command over the field defined by the coefficients of the expressions. Applies to inert commands such as Factor, Factors, AFactor, AFactors, Expand, and so on.**

maple('grading(Inert_command(expr1,..., exprn, n))') **evaluates the specified function or inert command over Z modulo** *n*.

maple('value(expr_inert)') **evaluates the given expression containing inert commands or functions of the type Diff, Int, Product, Sum or Limit.**

Here are some examples:

```
>> syms x y
>> pretty(factor(6*x^2+18*x-24))
```

$$6 (x + 4) (x - 1)$$

In the following example we simplify the numerator and denominator of an algebraic fraction, cancelling common factors:

```
>> pretty (factor ((x^3-y^3) /(x^4-y^4)))
```

$$\frac{x^2 + y\,x + y^2}{(x + y)\,(x^2 + y^2)}$$

The following examples show factorizations of expressions over field extensions defined by the coefficients of the expression and the element(s) given in the second argument:

```
>> pretty(sym(maple('factor(x^3+5, 5^(1/3))')))
```

$$(x^2 - 5^{1/3}\,x + 5^{2/3}) (x + 5^{1/3})$$

```
>> pretty(sym(maple('factor(x^3+5, {5^(1/3),(-3)^(1/2)})')))
```

```
          1/3       1/2  1/3         1/3       1/2  1/3         1/3
   1/4 (2 x - 5    - (-3)    5   ) (2 x - 5    + (-3)    5   ) (x + 5   )
```

```
>> pretty(sym(maple('factor(y^4-2,sqrt(2))')))
```

```
       2    1/2     2    1/2
      (y  + 2   ) (y  - 2   )
```

```
>> pretty (sym (maple ('factor (y^ 4-2, RootOf(x^2-2))')))
```

```
       2              2       2              2
      (y  + RootOf(_Z  - 2)) (y  - RootOf(_Z  - 2))
```

The following example highlights the difference between factoring a polynomial expression over the field defined by its coefficients and the extension of this field by *(- 3) ^(1/2)*:

```
>> pretty (factor(x^3+y^3))
```

```
                  2         2
         (x + y) (x  - x y + y  )
```

```
>> pretty(sym(maple('factor(x^3+y^3,(-3)^(1/2))')))
```

```
                1/2                1/2
   1/4 (2 x - y - (-3)    y) (2 x - y + (-3)    y) (x + y)
```

```
>> pretty (sym (maple ('factor(x^3+5,complex)')))
```

```
 (x + 1.7099759466766969893531088725439). (x - .85498797333834849467655443627193
+ 1.4808826096823642385229974586353 +i)
(x -.85498797333834849467655443627193 - 1.4808826096823642385229974586353 i)
```

In the following examples we perform factorizations using *factors*. This command returns the factors together with their multiplicities.

```
>> maple('readlib(factors)');
>> pretty(sym(maple('factors( 3*x^2+6*x+3 )')))
```

```
             [3, [[x + 1, 2]]]
```

```
>> pretty(sym(maple('Digits:=10:factors( x^4-4.0 )')))
```

$$[1.,[[x+1.414213562, 1], [x-1.414213562, 1], [x^2 +1.999999999, 1]]]$$

```
>> pretty(sym(maple(factors( x^4-4.0,complex)')))
```

$$[1., [[x + 1.414213562, 1], [x + 1.414213562\ i, 1], [x - 1.414213562\ i, 1],$$
$$[x - 1.414213562, 1]]]$$

The following are examples of the inert and complete factorization commands Factor, Factors, AFactor, AFactors, split and Berlekamp.

```
>> pretty(sym(maple('Factor(x^2+3*x+3) mod 7')))
```

$$(x + 6)\ (x + 4)$$

```
>> pretty(sym(maple('alias(sqrt2=RootOf(x^2-2)):evala(Factor(x^2-2,sqrt2))')))
```

$$(x + sqrt2)\ (x - sqrt2)$$

```
>> pretty(sym(maple('evala(Factor(x^2-2*y^2,sqrt2))')))
```

$$(x - sqrt2\ y)\ (x + sqrt2\ y)$$

```
>> pretty(sym(maple('expand((x^3+y^5+2)*(x*y^2+3)) mod 7')))
```

$$x^4 y^2 + 3\ x^3 + y^7 x + 3\ y^5 + 2\ x y^2 + 6$$

```
>> pretty (sym (maple ('Factor ('') mod 7')))
```

$$(x^3 + y^5 + 2)\ (x y^2 + 3)$$

```
>> pretty(sym(maple('Factors(2*x^2+6*x+6) mod 7')))
```

$$[2, [[x + 4, 1], [x + 6, 1]]]$$

```
>> pretty(sym(maple('Factors(x^5+1) mod 2')))
```

$$[1, [[x + 1, 1], [x^4 + x^3 + x^2 + x + 1, 1]]]$$

```
>> pretty(sym(maple('evala(Factors(2*x^2-1,sqrt2))')))
```

$$[2, [[x + 1/2 \text{ sqrt2}, 1], [x - 1/2 \text{ sqrt2}, 1]]]$$

```
>> pretty(sym(maple('alias(sqrtx=RootOf(y^2-x,y)):evala(Factors(x*y^2-1,sqrtx))')))
```

$$\left[x, \left[\left[y + \frac{\text{sqrtx}}{x}, 1\right], \left[-\frac{\text{sqrtx}}{x} + y, 1\right]\right]\right]$$

```
>> pretty (sym (maple ('grading (AFactor(x^2-2*y^2))')))
```

$$(x \text{ sqrt2 } y) (x + \text{sqrt2 } y)$$

```
>> pretty (sym (maple ('grading (AFactors(x^2-2*y^2))')))
```

$$[1, [[x - \text{sqrt2 } y, 1], [x + \text{sqrt2 } y, 1]]]$$

The following are examples of complete and Berlekamp factorizations.

```
>> pretty(sym(maple('readlib(split):split(x^2+x+1,x)')))
```

$$(x - \text{RootOf}(\_Z^2 + \_Z + 1)) (x + 1 + \text{RootOf}(\_Z^2 + \_Z + 1))$$

```
>> pretty(sym(maple('split(x^2+y*x+1+y^2, x, b)')))
```

$$(x - \text{RootOf}(\_Z^2 + y \_Z + 1 + y^2))(x + y + \text{RootOf}(\_Z^2 + y \_Z + 1 + y^2))$$

```
>> pretty(sym(maple('b')))
```

$$\{\text{RootOf}(\_Z^2 + y \_Z + 1 + y^2)\}$$

```
>> pretty(sym(maple('p:= 10^10-33:Berlekamp(x^4+2,x) mod p')))
```

$$\{x^2 + 6972444635 \ x + 9284865757, \ x^2 + 3027555332 \ x + 9284865757\}$$

EXERCISE 2-3

Factorize the polynomial $x^3 + 5$ in the algebraic extension defined by $5^{1/3}$ and the algebraic extension defined by $\{5^{1/3}, \sqrt{-3}\}$. Also perform the complete factorization.

```
>> pretty(sym(maple('factor(x ^ 3 + 5, 5 ^(1/3))')))
```

$$
\begin{array}{c}
2 \quad 1/3 \quad\quad 2/3 \quad\quad 1/3 \\
(x\ -\ 5\quad x + 5\quad)\ (x + 5\quad)
\end{array}
$$

```
>> pretty(sym(maple('factor(x^3+5, {5^(1/3),(-3)^(1/2)})')))
```

$$
\begin{array}{c}
1/3 \quad\quad 1/2\ 1/3 \quad\quad\quad 1/3 \quad\quad 1/2\ 1/3 \quad\quad 1/3 \\
1/4\ (2\ x - 5\quad + i\ 3\quad 5\quad)\ (2\ x - 5\quad - i\ 3\quad 5\quad)\ (x + 5\quad)
\end{array}
$$

```
>> pretty(sym(maple('readlib(split):split(x^3+5,x)')))
```

$$
\begin{array}{c}
2 \quad\quad\quad 3 \quad\quad\quad 3 \quad\quad\quad 2 \\
(x - RootOf(\_Z\ + RootOf(\_Z\ + 5)\ \_Z + RootOf(\_Z\ + 5)\ )) \\
3 \quad\quad\quad 2 \quad\quad\quad 3 \quad\quad\quad 3 \quad\quad\quad 2 \\
(x + RootOf(\_Z\ + 5) + RootOf(\_Z\ + RootOf(\_Z\ + 5)\ \_Z + RootOf(\_Z\ + 5)\ )) \\
\\
3 \\
(x - RootOf(\_Z\ + 5))
\end{array}
$$

EXERCISE 2-4

Find the factors and their multiplicities for the polynomial $x^4 - 4$ over the real numbers, complex numbers, the algebraic extension defined by $\sqrt{2}$, the algebraic extension defined by $\{\sqrt{2}, i\}$, the algebraic extension defined by $\alpha = RootOf(x^2-2)$, the algebraic extension defined by $\beta = RootOf(x^2+2)$, and the algebraic extension defined by $\{\alpha, \beta\}$.

```
>> pretty(sym(maple('readlib(factors):factors( x^4-4 )')))
```

$$
\begin{array}{c}
2 \quad\quad\quad 2 \\
[1, [[x\ - 2, 1], [x\ + 2, 1]]]
\end{array}
$$

```
>> pretty(sym(maple('readlib(factors):factors( x^4-4, complex)')))
```

```
[1, [[x + 1.414213562 i, 1], [x + 1.414213562, 1],
    [x - 1.414213562 i, 1], [x - 1.414213562, 1]]]
```

```
>> pretty(sym(maple('readlib(factors):factors( x^4-4, sqrt(2) )')))
```

$$[1, [[x - 2^{1/2}, 1], [x + 2^{1/2}, 1], [x^2 + 2, 1]]]$$

```
>> pretty(sym(maple('readlib(factors):factors( x^4-4, {sqrt(2), i } )')))
```

$$[1, [[x - i\,2^{1/2}, 1], [x + i\,2^{1/2}, 1], [x - 2^{1/2}, 1], [x + 2^{1/2}, 1]]]$$

```
>> pretty(sym(maple('readlib(factors):alias(a=RootOf(x^2-2)):
alias(b=RootOf(x^2+2)):factors( x^4-4, a )')))
```

$$[1, [[x - a, 1], [x + a, 1], [x^2 + 2, 1]]]$$

```
>> pretty(sym(maple('readlib(factors):factors( x^4-4, b )')))
```

$$[1, [[x + b, 1], [x - b, 1], [x^2 - 2, 1]]]$$

```
>> pretty(sym(maple('readlib(factors):factors( x^4-4, {a,b} )')))
```

$$[1, [[x + b, 1], [x - a, 1], [x + a, 1], [x - b, 1]]]$$

EXERCISE 2-5

Let α = RootOf($x^2 + x + 1$) and β = RootOf($y^2 - x$, y). Factorize modulo 2 the univariate polynomial $x^3 + 1$ over the algebraic extension defined by α . Factorize modulo 5 the bivariate polynomial $x^2 + 2xy + y^2 + 1 + x + y$ over the algebraic extension defined by α . Factorize modulo 5 the following bivariate polynomial: $x^2y + xy^2 + 2\alpha xy + \alpha^2 + 4x\alpha x + y +\alpha$. Find the factors and their multiplicities modulo 5 for the bivariate polynomial $x^2y + xy^2 + 2\alpha xy +\alpha^2 + 4 x\alpha x + y +\alpha$. Find the factors and their multiplicities modulo 2 for the univariate polynomial $x^5 + 1$ over the algebraic extension defined by α . Factorize the bivariate polynomial $xy^2 - 1$ over the algebraic extension defined by β .

```
>> pretty(sym(maple('alias(a=RootOf(x^2+x+1)):Factor(x^3+1,a) mod 2')))
```

$$(x + a + 1) (x + 1) (x + a)$$

```
>> pretty (sym (maple ('Factor(x^2+2*x*y+y^2+1+x+y,a) mod 5')))
```

$$(y + x + 4)\ (y + x + a + 1)$$

```
>> pretty (sym (maple ('Factor(x^2*y+x*y^2+2*a*x*y+a*x^2+4*a*x+y+a) mod 5')))
```

$$(x\ y + x + 1)\ (y + x + a)$$

```
>> pretty (sym (maple ('Factors(x^2*y+x*y^2+2*a*x*y+a*x^2+4*a*x+y+a) mod 5')))
```

$$[1, [[x\ y + x + 1, 1], [y + x + a, 1]]]$$

```
>> pretty (sym (maple ('Factors(x^5+1,a) mod 2')))
```

$$[1, [[x + 1, 1], [x^2 + (a + 1)\ x + 1, 1], [x^2 + x + 1, 1]]]$$

```
>> pretty (sym (maple ('alias (b = RootOf(y^2-x,y)):evala(Factor(x*y^2-1,b))')))))))
```

$$x\ (y - b/x)\ (b/x + y)$$

EXERCISE 2-6

Let p = $x^6 + x^5 + x^4 + x^3 + 2x^2 + 2x + 1$. Find the Berlekamp factorization of p modulo 2. Also factorize the bivariate algebraic expression $x^4y^2 + 3x^3 + y^7x + 3y^5 + 2xy^2 + 6$ over the field defined by its coefficients.

```
>> pretty(sym(maple('p:=x^6+x^5+x^4+x^3+2*x^2+2*x+1:Berlekamp(p,x) mod 2')))
```

$$\{x^4 + x + 1, x^2 + x + 1\}$$

```
>> pretty(sym(maple('factor(x^4*y^2+3*x^3+y^7*x+3*y^5+2*x*y^2+6)')))
```

$$(x\ y^2 + 3)\ (x^3 + y^5 + 2)$$

2-3. Simplifying Algebraic Expressions

The following commands enable MATLAB to simplify algebraic expressions:

simplify(expr) **simplifies an algebraic expression as much as possible. It sums algebraic fractions, but does not completely simplify them.**

simplify(expr, rule1, rule2,..., rulen) **simplifies the expression taking into account the rules specified. The possible values of the rules are Ei, GAMMA, atsign, hypergeom, ln, polar, power, radical, sqrt and trig, which allow simplification of expressions containing the exponential integral, gamma functions, functional operators, hypergeometric functions, logarithms, polar functions, powers, radicals, square roots and trigonometric functions, respectively.**

simplify(expr,assume=property) **simplifies the expression taking into account the specified mathematical property.**

simplify(expr,symbolic) **simplifies the expression so that all radical subexpressions are positive.**

R = simple('expr') **returns the most simplified form R of the algebraic expression. This is the most efficient command to completely simplify an algebraic fraction.**

[R, HOW] = simple('expr') **returns the most simplified form *R* of the given algebraic expression together with a list HOW describing the path followed to reach the simplification (i.e. the commands used).**

maple ('simplify(expression,option1,...,optionn)') **simplifies the given algebraic expression using the specified options. Valid options are atsign, Ei, exp, GAMMA, Hypergeom, ln, polar, power, radical, RootOf, sqrt, trig, symbolic, &*, piecewise and assume.**

maple('simplify(expression,atsign) **or** simplify(expression, '@')') **simplifies expressions containing functional operators, such as the composition of functions and inverse functions. It is particularly useful when simplifying *inversefunction (function (x)) = x*.**

maple('simplify(expression,polar)') **simplifies complex expressions by passing them to polar form and applying the rules of complex operations. If necessary, the complex expression must first be simplified to its polar form with convert(expression,polar) before applying the simplification.**

maple('simplify(expression,power)') **simplifies algebraic expressions containing potential, exponential, and logarithmic functions, applying typical rules of simplification, such as *(a ∧ b) ∧ c = a ∧(b*c), ln(x*y) = ln (x) + ln (y)* and *exp (a * ln (x) + 1) =(x∧a) * exp (1)*.**

maple('simplify(expr,exp)') **simplifies algebraic expressions that contain base e exponential functions, by applying typical rules of simplification such as e^x*e^y = e∧ (x + y) , *(e ∧ x) ∧ a = e ∧(x*a)* and *e ∧ (x+ln (y)*n) =(e∧x) * (y ∧ n)*.**

maple('simplify(expr,radical)') **simplifies algebraic expressions containing radicals or fractional powers, applying typical rules of simplification.**

maple('simplify(expr,radical,symbolic)') **simplifies algebraic expressions containing radicals or fractional powers, applying typical rules of simpllification and assuming that all the radicals are positive.**

`maple('simplify(expr,RootOf)')` **simplifies algebraic expressions containing terms of type RootOf.**

`maple('simplify(expr,sqrt)')` **simplifies algebraic expressions containing square roots or fractional powers of denominator 2, applying typical rules of simplification.**

`maple('simplify(expr,ln)')` **simplifies algebraic expressions containing logarithms, applying typical rules such as** $ln(a^\wedge r) = r * ln(a)$, $ln(a*b) = ln(a) + ln(b)$**, ...**

`maple('simplify(expr,trig)')` **simplifies trigonometric algebraic expressions, applying the typical trigonometric rules such as** $sin(x)^\wedge 2 + cos(x)^\wedge 2 = 1$**,** $cosh(x)^\wedge 2 - sinh(x)^\wedge 2 = 1$**,** $\tan(x) = sin(x)/cos(x)$ **and** $1 + tan(x)^\wedge 2 = 1/cos(x)^\wedge 2$**.**

`maple('simplify(expr,Ei)')` **simplifies algebraic expressions that include functions of the type Ei, Si and Ci, using the existing relationships between them. Sometimes, it is convenient to apply** *convert(expr, Ei)* **before applying this type of simplification.**

`maple('simplify(expr,GAMMA)')` **simplifies algebraic expressions involving** *GAMMA*-**like functions using the existing relationships between the same. Sometimes, it is convenient to apply** *convert(expr, GAMMA)* **before applying this type of simplification**

`maple('simplify(expression,hypergeom)')` **simplifies algebraic expressions involving functions of the type** *hypergeom* **using existing relations between the same. Sometimes, it is convenient to apply convert(expr, hypergeom) before applying this type of simplification.**

`maple('simplify(expression,piecewise)')` **simplifies algebraic expressions involving piecewise-defined functions.**

`maple('simplify(expr,' &* ')')` **simplifies algebraic expressions that include the &* operator.**

`maple('simplify(expr,{equ1,...,equn})')` **or** `maple ('simplify(expr,[equ1,..., equn])')` **simplifies the given algebraic expression subject to the specified equations.**

`maple('simplify(expression,inequality _variable)')` **simplifies the given algebraic expression assuming the specified inequality in some given variable. For example, simplify(expression, a> 0).**

`maple('simplify(expression,variable=type)')` **simplifies the given algebraic expression assuming that all the variables are of the type specified (for example,** *assume = real assume = positive,* **and so on). In general, the type can be any option of the command type.**

`maple('simplify(expression,assume(variable,property))')` **simplifies the given algebraic expression, assuming the property specified for the specified variable (for example,** *integer, rational,* **and so on.). In general, the property can be any option of the command type.**

`maple('simplify(expr,assume(variable, AndProp(prop1,...,propn)))')` **simplifies the given algebraic expression by assuming all the given properties prop1,..., propn for the specified variable.**

`maple('simplify(expr,assume(variable, OrProp(prop1,...,propn)))')` **simplifies the given algebraic expression by assuming some of the properties prop1,..., propn for the specified variable.**

maple('simplify(expression,assume(variable, RealRange(a,b)))') **simplifies the given algebraic expression by assuming that the variable varies in the real closed interval** *[a, b].*

maple('simplify(expr,assume(variable, RealRange(Open(a),Open(b))))') **simplifies the given algebraic expression by assuming that the variable varies in the interval** *(a, b).*

maple('simplify(expr, assume(variable, RealRange(Open(a),b)))') **simplifies the given algebraic expression by assuming that the variable varies in the interval** *(a, b].*

maple('simplify(expr,assume(variable, RealRange(a,Open(b))))') **simplifies the given algebraic expression by assuming that the variable varies in the interval** *[a,b).*

We give several examples which involve the command **simplify**:

```
>> syms x y b c
>> simplify (sin (x) ^ 2 + cos (x) ^ 2)
```

ans =

1

```
>> simplify(exp(a+log(b*exp(c))))
```

ans =

b*exp(a+c)

```
>> pretty(sym(maple('simplify((x^a)^b+4^(1/2), power)')))
```

$$x^{(a\ b)} + 2$$

```
>> pretty (sym (maple ('simplify (sin (x) ^ 4 + 2 * cos (x) ^ 2 - 2 * sin (x) ^ 2 - cos(2*x), trig)')))
```

$$\cos(x)^4$$

```
>> pretty (sym (maple ('simplify(-1/3*x^5*y+x^4*y^2+1/3*x*y^3+1, {x^3=x*y, y^2=x+1})')))
```

$$1 + y^5 + y^4 - y^2 + y^3 - 2y$$

```
>> pretty (sym (maple ('simplify (((x-1) ^ 2) ^(3/2) * sqrt(a^2), assume(x-1>0))')))
```

$$(x^\sim - 1)^3\ \mathrm{csgn}(a)\ a$$

The tilde (~) that appears at the top-right of the variable x indicates that a condition x has been assumed.

```
>> pretty(sym(maple('simplify(exp(5*ln(x)+1), power)')))
```

$$x^5 \, exp(1)$$

```
>> pretty (sym (maple ('simplify (cos (x) ^ 5 + sin (x) ^ 4 + 2 * cos (x) ^ 2 - 2 * sin (x) ^ 2 - cos(2*x))')))
```

$$cos(x)^5 + cos(x)^4$$

```
>> pretty (sym (maple ('simplify(-1/3*x^5*y + x^4*y^2 + 1/3*x*y^3 + 1,{x ^ 3 = x * y, y ^ 2 = x + 1})')))
```

$$1 + y^5 + y^4 - y^2 + y - 2 y^3$$

```
>> pretty(sym(maple('simplify((x+1)^(4/3)-x*(x+1)^(1/3),radical)')))
```

$$(x + 1)^{1/3}$$

```
>> pretty(sym(maple('simplify(Ei(1,i*x)+Ei(1,-i*x),Ei)')))
```

$$-2 \, cosint(x)$$

```
>> pretty(sym(maple('simplify(n!/((2*n)^2)!, GAMMA)')))
```

$$\frac{gamma(n + 1)}{gamma(4 \, n^2 + 1)}$$

We now give some examples of how the simple command works:

```
>> pretty (sym (simple (cos (3 * acos (x)))))
```

$$4 \, x^3 - 3 \, x$$

```
>> [R, HOW] = simple (cos (3 * acos (x)))
```

R =

4 * x ^ 3-3 * x

HOW =

expand

In the latter case, the command that led to the final simplification was expand:

```
>> pretty (simple (cos (x) + (-sin (x) ^ 2) ^(1/2)))
```

$$\cos(x) + i \sin(x)$$

```
>> pretty(simple((x^2-y^2) /(x-y) ^ 3))
```

$$\frac{x + y}{(x - y)^2}$$

EXERCISE 2-7

Given the functions $g(x) = \sqrt{x^2}$ and $e(x) = (-8ab3)^{1/3}$, simplify them as much as possible. Perform the simplification of $g(x)$ for a real argument and a positive argument. Also simplify $e(x)$ for positive radical and then negative b.

```
>> pretty(sym(maple('simplify(sqrt(x^2))')))
```

$$\text{csgn}(x)\ x$$

```
>> pretty(sym(maple('simplify(sqrt(x^2),assume=real)')))
```

$$\text{signum}(x)\ x$$

```
>> pretty(sym(maple('simplify(sqrt(x^2),assume=positive)')))
```

$$x$$

```
>> pretty(sym(maple('simplify((-8*b^3*a)^(1/3))')))
```

$$2 \ (-b^3 \ a)^{1/3}$$

```
>> pretty(sym(maple('simplify((-8*b^3*a)^(1/3),radical,symbolic)')))
```

$$2 \ b \ (-a)^{1/3}$$

```
>> pretty(sym(maple('simplify((-8*b^3*a)^(1/3),assume(b<0),radical)')))
```

$$-2 \ b^\sim \ a^{1/3}$$

EXERCISE 2-8

Directly simplify the expression $((x-1)^2)^{3/2} \ (a^2)^{1/2}$. Then simplify it assuming the condition that $x > 1$. Finally, perform a simplification assuming in addition that $a > 0$.

```
>> pretty(sym(maple('simplify(((x-1) ^ 2) ^(3/2) *(a^2) ^(1/2))')))
```

$$csgn(x - 1) \ (x - 1)^3 \ csgn(a) \ a$$

```
>> pretty(sym(maple('simplify(((x-1)^2)^(3/2)*(a^2)^(1/2),assume(x>1))')))
```

$$(x^\sim - 1)^3 \ csgn(a) \ a$$

```
>> pretty(sym(maple('simplify(((x-1)^2)^(3/2)*(a^2)^(1/2), assume(x>1,a>0))')))
```

$$(x^\sim - 1)^3 \ a^\sim$$

The last expression also can be simplified without assignments, assuming positive radicals with the option symbolic.

```
>> pretty(sym(maple('simplify(((x-1)^2)^(3/2)*(a^2)^(1/2),symbolic)')))
```

$$(x - 1)^3 \ a$$

2-4. Combining Algebraic Expressions

MATLAB allows you to combine terms composed of functions of certain types within an algebraic expression, in order to simplify the expression as much as possible after grouping. Among the commands that enable you to do this are the following (always preceded by the command maple):

combine(expression) **combines terms that contain functions in the given algebraic expression; they may be exponential, logarithmic, trigonometric, sums (Sum), products (Prod), limits (Limit), integrals (Int), derivatives (Diff), and so on. Once the combination or grouping of terms is done according to the different types of functions, there is an overall simplification. Combine can be considered the reverse of expand; for example, expand transforms sin (a + b) into sin (a) * cos (b) + cos (a) * (b) and combine does the opposite.**

combine(expression,option1,...,optionn) **combines terms in the given expression using the specified options. The valid options are atsign, Psi, exp, artan conjugate, polylog, ln, product, power, plus range, RootOf, sqrt, trig, signum, radical, abs and piecewise.**

combine(expression,atsign) **or** combine(expression, '@') **combines expressions that contain functional operators, such as the composition of functions and inverse functions. It is particularly useful when simplifying inversefunction(function (x)) = x.**

combine(expression,product) **combines expressions that contain products.**

combine(expression,plus) **combines expressions that contain sums.**

combine(expression,artan) **combines expressions that contain arctangent functions.**

combine(expression,conjugate) **combines expressions by grouping terms with their conjugates.**

combine(expression,power) **combines terms of expressions containing exponential functions, potentially by applying rules such as $(x \wedge y) * (x \wedge z) = x \wedge (y+z)$, $(x \wedge y) \wedge z = x \wedge (y*z)$, $\sqrt{-a} = i * \sqrt{a}$.**

combine(expression,radical) **combines terms of expressions that contain radicals or fractional powers, applying the typical rules for working with radicals.**

combine(expression,radical,symbolic) **combines terms of expressions that contain radicals or fractional powers, applying the typical rules for working with radicals and assuming that all the radicals are positive.**

combine(expression,abs) **combines terms of expressions that contain absolute values (moduli).**

combine(expression,signum) **combines terms of expressions that contain the function signum.**

combine(expression,ln) **combines terms of expressions that contain logarithms, applying the typical rules of working with logarithms, such as $r * \ln (a) = \ln(a^r)$, $\ln (a) + \ln (b) = \ln(a*b)$, and so on.**

combine(expression,trig) **combines terms of trigonometric expressions, eliminating products and powers of sines and cosines, hyperbolic sines and hyperbolic cosines, using multiple angle trigonometric rules such as sin (a) * cos (b) = sin ((a + b) / 2) + sin ((a-b)/2) or sinh (a) * sinh (b) = cosh ((a + b) / 2)-cosh ((a-b)/2).**

combine(expression,Psi) **combines terms of expressions that include functions of the type Psi, applying rules such as** $\Psi^{(n)}(z+1) = \Psi^{(n)}(z) + (-1)^n\, n!\, z^{(-n-1)}$.

combine(expression,range) **combines terms of expressions that include ranges.**

combine(expression,polylog) **combines terms of expressions that include polylogarithmic functions, using the existing relationships between them.**

combine(expression,exp) **combines expressions that contain base e exponential functions, applying the typical rules for them such as** $(e \wedge x)*(e^y) = e \wedge (x+y)$, $(e \wedge x) \wedge a = e \wedge(x*a)$ **and** $e \wedge (x+\ln(y)*n) = (e^x) * y \wedge n$.

combine(expression,piecewise) **combines terms of expressions involving piecewise-defined functions.**

combine(expression, ln, type) **combines terms of expressions that include logarithmic functions, only simplifying expressions whose coefficients are of the given type.**

Here are some examples:

```
>> pretty(sym(maple('combine(4 * sin (x) ^ 3, trig)')))
```

$$-\sin(3\ x) + \sin(x)\ 3$$

```
>> pretty(sym(maple('combine(exp(x) ^ 2 * exp(y), exp)')))
```

$$\exp(2\ x + y)$$

```
>> pretty(sym(maple('assume(y>0,z>0):combine(2*ln(y)-ln(z),ln)')))
```

$$\ln\left(\frac{y\tilde{}^{\,2}}{z\tilde{}}\right)$$

```
>> pretty(sym(maple('combine((x^a)^2,power)')))
```

$$x^{(2\ a)}$$

```
>> pretty(sym(maple('combine(Psi(-x)+Psi(x),Psi)')))
```

$$2\ \mathrm{Psi}(x) + \mathrm{Pi}\ \cot(\mathrm{Pi}\ x) + 1/x$$

```
>> pretty(sym(maple('combine([2*sin(x)*cos(x),2*cos(x)^2-1],trig)')))
```

$$[\sin(2\ x),\ \cos(2\ x)]$$

```
>> pretty(sym(maple('combine(Int(x,x=a..b)-Int(x^2,x=a..b))')))
```

$$\int_a^b x - x^2 dx$$

```
>> pretty(sym(maple('combine(Limit(x,x=a)*Limit(x^2,x=a)+c)')))
```

$$\lim_{x \to a} x^3 + c$$

```
>> pretty(sym(maple('combine(conjugate(x) ^ 3 + 3 * conjugate(y) * conjugate(z), conjugate)')))
```

```
            3
           x  + 3 y z
```

```
>> pretty(sym(maple('combine(x^3*x^(m-3),power)')))
```

```
            m
           x
```

```
>> pretty(sym(maple('combine((3^n)^m*3^n,power)')))
```

```
          n m  n
        (3 )  3
```

```
>> pretty(sym(maple('assume(m,integer):combine((3^n)^m*3^n,power)')))
```

```
        (n m~ + n)
       3
```

```
>> pretty(sym(maple('combine(exp(x)^7*exp(y),power)')))
```

```
       exp(7 x + y)
```

```
>> pretty(sym(maple('combine(piecewise(x > 0, cos(x) ^ 2 + sin(x) ^ 2, exp(x) ^ 2 * exp(y)))')))
```

```
      | exp(2 x + y)      x <= 0
     {
      |     1             0 < x
```

```
>> pretty(sym(maple('combine(piecewise(x<1, exp(x)*exp(-2*x), x>3, 4*sin(x)^3))')))
```

```
        |      exp(-x)              x < 1
        |
       {          0                x <= 3
        |
        |   3 sin(x) - sin(3 x)     3 < x
```

```
>> pretty(sym(maple('combine(b*ln(y)+3*ln(y)-ln(1-y)+ln(1+y)/2, ln,anything,symbolic)')))
```

$$\ln\left(\frac{y^b \; y^3 \; (1 + y)^{1/2}}{1 - y}\right)$$

EXERCISE 2-9

Simplify as much as possible the trigonometric-exponential expression exp (sin (a) * cos (b)) * exp (cos (a) * (b), as well as the polylogarithmic expression polylog(a, x) + polylog(a,-x). Simplify the polylogarithmic expression defined by polylog(4,x) + polylog(4,1/x) assuming first that x > 1, and secondly that x is between - 1 and 1.

```
>> maple combine (exp (sin (a) * cos (b)) * exp (cos (a) * (b)), [trig, exp])
```

$$\exp(\sin(a + b))$$

```
>> maple combine(polylog(a,x)+polylog(a,-x),polylog)
```

$$2^{(1 - a)} \; \text{polylog}(a, \; x^2)$$

```
>> pretty(sym(maple('polylog(4,x) + polylog(4,1/x)')))
```

$$\text{polylog}(4, \; x) + \text{polylog}(4, \; 1/x)$$

```
>> pretty(sym(maple('assume(x > 1):combine(polylog(4,x) + polylog(4,1/x), polylog)')))
```

$$- \tfrac{1}{12} \ln(-x\tilde{\ })^2 \; \mathrm{Pi}^2 \; - \tfrac{7}{360} \mathrm{Pi}^4 \; - \tfrac{1}{24} \ln(-x\tilde{\ })^4$$

```
>> pretty(sym(maple('assume(x, RealRange(-1,1)):combine(polylog(4,x) + polylog(4,1/x),polylog)')))
```

```
          1   2   2        4            1   4
 - 1/12 ln(- ----)  Pi  - 7/360 Pi  - 1/24 ln(- ----)
           x~                                x~
```

EXERCISE 2-10

Simplify the following expressions as much as possible:

$$\sqrt{2}\sqrt{6}+\sqrt{2}\sqrt{x+1}\,,\ \sqrt{4-\sqrt{3}}\sqrt{4+\sqrt{3}}\,,\ \sqrt{x}\sqrt{y}+\sqrt{2}\sqrt{(x+1)^3}\sqrt{y}$$

```
>> pretty(sym(maple('combine(sqrt(2)*sqrt(6) + sqrt(2)*sqrt(x+1),radical)')))
```

```
             1/2           1/2
          2 3    + (2 x + 2)
```

```
>> pretty(sym(maple('combine(sqrt(4-sqrt(3))*sqrt(4+sqrt(3)),radical)')))
```

```
                    1/2
                  13
```

```
>> pretty(sym(maple('combine(sqrt(x)*sqrt(y) + sqrt(2)*sqrt(x+1)^3*sqrt(y), radical)')))
```

```
      1/2 1/2            1/2          1/2
     x   y    + (x + 1) y    (2 x + 2)
```

EXERCISE 2-11

Combine terms as much as possible in the following expression:

a * ln(x) + 3 * ln(x) - ln(1-x) + ln(1+x)/2

Simplify assuming that is real and x > 0. Additionally, try to simplify assuming that x is real and that it varies between 0 and 1.

```
>> pretty(sym(maple('combine(a*ln(x)+3*ln(x)-ln(1-x)+ln(1+x)/2,ln)')))
```

```
        a ln(x) + 3 ln(x) - ln(1 - x) + 1/2 ln(1 + x)
```

```
>> pretty(sym(maple('assume(a,real):assume(x>0):combine(a*ln(x)+3*ln(x)
-ln(1-x)+ln(1+x)/2,ln)')))
```

$$a\sim \ln(x\sim) - \ln(1 - x\sim) + \ln(x\sim^{3}\ (x\sim + 1)^{1/2}\ )$$

```
>> pretty(sym(maple('assume(a,real):assume(x,RealRange(0,1)): combine(a*ln(x)+3*ln(x)
-ln(1-x)+ln(1+x)/2,ln)')))
```

$$a\sim \ln(x\sim) + \ln\left(\frac{x\sim^{3}\ (x\sim + 1)^{1/2}}{1 - x\sim}\right)$$

The additional assumption does not improve the result.

EXERCISE 2-12

Expand and simplify the following trigonometric expressions as much as possible:

(a) sin[3 x] cos[5 x]

(b) cot[a]^2 + (sec[a])^2 - (csc[a])^2

(c) sin[a] / (1 + cot[a]^2) - sin[a]^3

```
>> pretty(sym(maple('combine(sin(3*x)*cos(5*x),trig)')))
```

$$1/2\ \sin(x\ 8) - 1/2\ \sin(2\ x)$$

```
>> pretty(sym(maple('simplify((cot(a))^2+(sec(a))^2-(csc(a))^2, trig)')))
```

$$-\frac{\cos(a)^2 - 1}{\cos(a)^2}$$

```
>> pretty(sym(maple('simplify(sin(a)/(1 + cot(a) ^ 2)-sin(a) ^ 3, trig)')))
```

$$0$$

EXERCISE 2-13

Simplify the following trigonometric expressions as much as possible:

(a) sin[3 Pi/2 + a] cot[3 Pi/2] / cot[3 Pi/2 + a] + tan[3 Pi/2] cot[Pi/2 + a] / sin[3 Pi/2 + a] cot[-a]

(b) (a² - b²) cot[Pi-a] / tan[Pi/2] - (a² + b²) tan[Pi/2-a] / cot[Pi-a]

(c) (cot[a] + tan[a]) / (cot[a]-tan[a]) - sec[2a]

(d) sin[a-b] cos[c] + sin[b- c] cos[a] + sin[c-a] cos[b]

```
>> pretty(sym(maple('simplify(sin(3*Pi/2+a)*cot(3*Pi/2-a)/cot(3*Pi/2+a)+
(tan(3*Pi/2-a) * cot(Pi/2+a) /sin(3*Pi/2+a) * cot(-a), trig)')))
```

$$\frac{\cos(a)\ \sin(a) - 1}{\sin(a)}$$

```
>> pretty(sym(maple('combine(sin(3*Pi/2+a)*cot(3*Pi/2-a)/cot(3*Pi/2+a)+
(tan(3*Pi/2-a) * cot(Pi/2+a) /sin(3*Pi/2+a) * cot(-a), trig)')))
```

$$\frac{1}{2}\ \frac{\cos(2\ a) + 1 - 2\ \cot(a)\ \tan(a)^2}{\cos(a)}$$

```
>> pretty(sym(maple('simplify((a^2-b^2)*cot(Pi-a)/tan(Pi/2-a)-
(a^2+b^2)*tan(Pi/2-a)/cot(Pi-a),trig)')))
```

$$2\ b^2$$

```
>> pretty(sym(maple('combine((a^2-b^2)*cot(Pi-a)/tan(Pi/2-a)-
(a^2+b^2)*tan(Pi/2-a)/cot(Pi-a),trig)')))
```

$$2\ b^2$$

```
>> pretty(sym(maple('simplify((cot(a)+tan(a))/(cot(a)-tan(a))-sec(2*a), trig)')))
```

$$0$$

45

```
>> pretty (sym (maple ('combine (sin(a-b) * cos(c) + sin(b-c) * cos(a) +
sin(c-a) * cos(b), trig)')))
```

0

In general, you will get the most efficient simplification of trigonometric expressions using the commands combine and simplify, with the option trig.

2-5. Grouping of Similar Terms in Algebraic Expressions

MATLAB allows you to group terms within algebraic expressions according to specified variables. This helps to simplify the expression and possibly to optimize performance. Among the commands that enable the grouping of similar terms in algebraic expressions, we have the following:

maple('collect(expr,x)') **gathers the polynomial algebraic expression in ordinate powers of the variable *x*. If the variable is not specified, it takes by default the main symbolic variable.**

maple('collect(expr,[x,y])') **gathers the polynomial algebraic expression in ordinate powers of the variables *x* and *y*.**

maple('collect(expr,f(x))') **gathers the algebraic expression in ordinate powers of a function f(x) contained in the expression.**

maple('collect(expr,var)') **organises the algebraic expression, taking as the main variable the variable *var*. It gathers terms with respect to the variable.**

maple('collect(expr,[var1,..,varn])') or maple('collect(expr,{var1,...,var n})') **organizes the algebraic expression and gathers terms for the given variables.**

maple('collect(expr,expr1)') **organizes the algebraic expression *expr* by grouping in terms of *expr1*, where *expr1* is typically a *sin(x)* or *exp(2*x)* function.**

maple('collect(expr,[var1,...,varn],distributed)') **organizes the algebraic expression grouping terms by the given variables and presenting the result as polynomial expanded as a sum of terms. Each term of the sum is a product of powers of the specified variables, the coefficient of the term being a constant or any expression in terms of unspecified variables (which are considered constants in this case).**

maple('collect(expr,[var1,...,varn],recursive)') **organizes the algebraic expression by grouping terms with respect to the variables given in a hierarchical manner; that is, it first groups terms with respect to the variable var1, then uses the resulting expression to group terms with respect to the variable var2, and so on.**

maple('collect(expr,[var1,...,varn],option,command)') **organizes the algebraic expression grouping terms with respect to the variables given according to the specified option (distributed or recursive). Organizing occurs once the specified command has been applied to each coefficient of the expression. Any command can be used, but it is usually one that works with algebraic expressions (factor, expand, and so on).**

Let's see some examples of the command *collect*:

```
>> syms x y z p a
>> pretty(collect( (x+1)*(x+2) ))
```

$$x^2 + 3x + 2$$

```
>> pretty (collect (y * (sin (x) + 1) + sin (x), sin (x)))
```

$$(y + 1) \sin(x) + y$$

```
>> pretty(collect(x^3*y+x^2*y^3+x+3, y))
```

$$x^3 y + x^2 y^3 + x + 3$$

```
' p = x * y+ z * x * y+ y* x ^ 2-z * y* x ^ 2 + x + z * x;
>> pretty(collect(p, [x,y]))
```

$$x y + z x y + y x^2 - z y x^2 + x + z x$$

```
>> f = a*log(x)-log(x)*x-x;

>> pretty(collect(f,log(x)))
```

$$(a - x) \ln(x) - x$$

```
>> g = int(x^2*(exp(x)+exp(-x)),x);
>> pretty(collect(g,exp(x)))
```

$$(2 + x^2 - 2 x) \exp(x) + \frac{-2 x^2 - 2 - x}{\exp(x)}$$

```
>> pretty (sym (maple ('collect(x*y+a*x*y+y*x^2-a*y*x^2+x+a*x, [x,y], recursive)')))
```

$$(1 - a) y x^2 + ((1 + a) y + 1 + a) x$$

```
>> pretty (sym (maple ('collect(x*y+a*x*y+y*x^2-a*y*x^2+x+a*x, [y,x], recursive)')))
```

$$((1 - a) x^2 + (1 + a) x) y + (1 + a) x$$

```
>> pretty (sym (maple ('collect(x*y+a*x*y+y*x^2-a*y*x^2+x+a*x, [x,y], distributed)')))
```

$$(1 + a) x + (1 + a) x y + (1 - a) y x^2$$

EXERCISE 2-14

Given the function $f(x) = a^3x - x + a^3 + a$, group terms in the variable x, and then factorize the coefficients. Group terms in x for the function $p(x) = y/x + 2z/x + x^{1/3} - y^{1/3}x$.

```
>> syms a x y z
>> pretty(collect(a^3*x-x+a^3+a, x))
```

$$(a^3 - 1) x + a^3 + a$$

```
>> pretty(sym(maple('collect(a^3*x-x+a^3+a, x,factor)')))
```

$$(a - 1) (a^2 + a + 1) x + a (a^2 + 1)$$

```
>> pretty (collect (y/x+2 * z/x + x ^(1/3) - y* ^(1/3) x, x))
```

$$(1 - y) x^{1/3} + \frac{y + 2 z}{x}$$

EXERCISE 2-15

Given the following differential expression:

$$\left(\frac{\partial^2}{\partial x^2}y(x)\right)\sin(x)-\left(\frac{\partial}{\partial x}y(x)\right)\sin\left(y(x)\right)+\sin\left(\frac{\partial}{\partial x}y(x)\right)+\sin\left(y(x)\right)\left(\frac{\partial^2}{\partial x^2}y(x)\right)$$

Group terms in differentials. Subsequently, group terms into sines.

```
>> pretty (sym (maple ('DF: = diff (y (x), x, x) * sin (x) - diff (y (x), x) * sin (y(x)) +
sin (x) * diff (y (x), x) + sin (y (x)) * diff (y (x), x, x)')));
>> pretty(sym(maple('collect(DF,diff)')))
```

```
                                                         / 2      \
                          /d      \                      |d       |
    (-sin(y (x)) + sin(x)) | - y (x) | +(sin(x) + sin(y(x))) |- y (x) |
                          \dx     /                      | 2      |
                                                         \dx      /
```

```
>> pretty(sym(maple('collect(DF,sin)')))
```

```
 /            / 2    \\            // 2    \            \
 | /d     \  |d     ||            ||d     |  /d     \|
 |-|-- y(x)| + |--- y(x)||  sin(y(x)) + ||--- y(x)| + |-- y(x)||  sin(x)
 | \dx    /  | 2     ||            || 2    |  \dx    /|
 \           \dx    //            \\dx    /            /
```

2-6. Sorting Terms in Algebraic Expressions

MATLAB also allows the sorting of terms within algebraic expressions in terms of specified variables. This helps to generate the best possible expression for optimal performance. Among the commands that enable the management of terms in algebraic expressions are the following:

maple('sort(expression)') **sorts the terms of the multivariate algebraic polynomial expression according to the degrees of all terms of the expression (in descending order). The degree of a term equals the sum of the exponents of its variables.**

maple('sort(expr,plex)') **performs the ordering of the algebraic expression for all the indeterminates using pure lexicographic order (the dictionary order) for each component of the algebraic expression.**

maple('sort(expr,tdeg)') **performs the ordering of the algebraic expression with respect to all the indeterminates using the total degree for each term component of the algebraic expression. For example, the total degree of $x^5y^2z^3$ is 10. (This is the default option.)**

maple('sort(expr,[var1,...,varn],option)') or maple('sort(expr,{var1,...,varn}, option)') **performs the ordering of the multivariate polynomial algebraic expression with respect to the indeterminates var1,..., varn, according to the specified option (plex or tdeg).**

maple('sort(list)') **or** maple('sort(list,lexorder)') **or** maple('sort(list,string)') **sorts the elements of a list using lexicographical order.**

maple('sort([var1,...,varn])') **or** maple('sort(list,'<')') **or** maple('sort(list,numeric)') **sorts numeric values specified in the list in descending numerical order.**

maple('sort(list,address)') **sorts the elements of the list according to their internal addresses assigned by MATLAB.**

Here are some examples:

```
>> pretty(sym(maple('sort([3,2,1])')))
```

$$[1, 2, 3]$$

```
>> pretty(sym(maple('sort(1+x+x^2)')))
```

$$x^2 + x + 1$$

```
>> pretty(sym(maple('sort([c,a,d],lexorder)')))
```

$$[a, c, d]$$

```
>> pretty(sym(maple('sort(y^3+y^2*x^2+x^3,[x,y])')))
```

$$x^2 y^2 + x^3 + y^3$$

```
>> pretty(sym(maple('sort(y^3+y^2*x^2+x^3,[x,y],plex)')))
```

$$x^3 + x^2 y^2 + y^3$$

```
>> pretty(sym(maple('sort((y+x)/(y-x),x)')))
```

$$\frac{x + y}{-x + y}$$

```
>> pretty(sym(maple('sort(x+x^3+w^5+y^2+z^4,[w,x,y,z])')))
```

$$w^5 + z^4 + x^3 + y^2 + x$$

```
>> pretty(sym(maple('sort(x+x^3+w^5+y^2+z^4,[w,x,y,z],plex)')))
```

$$w^5 + x^3 + x + y^2 + z^4$$

```
>> pretty(sym(maple('sort(x+x^3+w^5+y^2+z^4,[w,x,y,z],tdeg)')))
```

$$w^5 + z^4 + x^3 + y^2 + x$$

```
>> pretty(sym(maple('sort(x*y^5+x^3*y*z+w^5*y^3+y^2*z^4+z^4,[w,x,y,z],plex)')))
```

$$w^5 y^3 + x^3 y z + x y^5 + y^2 z^4 + z^4$$

```
>> pretty(sym(maple('sort(x*y^5+x^3*y*z+w^5*y^3+y^2*z^4+z^4,[w,x,y,z],tdeg)')))
```

$$w^5 y^3 + x y^5 + y^2 z^4 + x^3 y z + z^4$$

2-7. Algebraic Fractions

MATLAB also enables you to work fluidly with algebraic fractions. Among the commands that can be used we have the following (all of which must be preceded by the command maple):

normal(exprational) **simplifies the given algebraic fraction.**

normal(expr,expanded) **fully expands the numerator and denominator of the rational algebraic expression after it has been simplified.**

normal([exprat1,...,expratn]) or normal({exprat1,...,expartn}) **normalizes the set or list of rational algebraic expressions.**

Normal(expratn) **returns the inert normalization of a rational algebraic expression.**

normal(expr) mod n **finds the normalization of the given rational algebraic expression modulo *n*.**

numer(exprational) **returns the numerator of the rational algebraic expression after normalizataion.**

denom(exprational) **returns the denominator of the rational algebraic expression after normalization.**

`radnormal(exprational)` **normalizes a rational algebraic expression that contain radical numbers by eliminating all possible radical levels. It is also valid for non-rational algebraic expressions.**

`radnormal(exprational,rationalized)` **normalizes a rational algebraic expression that contains radicals, rationalizing the denominator.**

`readsimp(exprational)` **normalizes a rational algebraic expression that contains radicals. It is also valid for non-rational algebraic expressions.**

`readsimp(exprational,name)` **normalizes the algebraic expression by rationalizing the denominator and assigns the specified name to the simplified expression.**

`expand(exprational)` **expands the numerator of a rational algebraic expression.**

`factor(exprational)` **factors the numerator and denominator of the rational algebraic expression and normalizes it.**

`convert(expr,confrac)` **converts the algebraic expression into an approximate continued fraction. Returns a list with the partial quotients of the continued fraction.**

`convert(expr,confrac,variable)` **converts the polynomial expression to its approximation by the rational polynomial continued fraction in the variable var.**

`convert(numeric expression,confrac,n)` **converts the numeric expression to its continued fraction expansion to at least n partial quotients.**

`convert(expression,parfrac,variable)` **converts the rational expression to simple fractions in the given variable. (Breaks up an algebraic fraction into partial fractions.)**

`convert(expression,parfrac,variable,true)` **applies the command factor to the denominator of the algebraic fraction prior to decomposing it into simple fractions.**

`convert(expression,fullparfrac,variable)` **fully decomposes a rational expression in the variable given into simple fractions (using RootOf expressions if necessary).**

Here are some examples:

```
>> pretty(sym(maple('normal((x^2-y^2) /(x-y) ^ 3)')))
```

$$
\frac{x + y}{(x\ y)^2}
$$

```
>> pretty(sym(maple('normal((f (x) ^ 2-1) / (f (x) - 1))')))
```

$$
f(x) + 1
$$

```
>> pretty(sym(maple('normal({2/x + y/3 = 0})')))
```

$$
\left\{ \frac{1}{3}\ \frac{6 + y\ x}{x} = 0 \right\}
$$

```
>> pretty(sym(maple('normal( 1/x+x/(x+1) )')))
```

$$\frac{x + 1 + x^2}{x\,(x + 1)}$$

```
>> pretty(sym(maple('normal( 1/x+x/(x+1),expanded)')))
```

$$\frac{x + 1 + x^2}{x^2 + x}$$

```
>> pretty(sym(maple('numer( (1+x)/x^(1/2)/y ) ')))
```

$$x + 1$$

```
>> pretty(sym(maple('numer( 2/x + y )')))
```

$$2 + y\,x$$

```
>> pretty(sym(maple('numer( x+1/(x+1/x))')))
```

$$x\,(x + 2)$$

```
>> pretty(sym(maple('denom(x+1/(x+1/x))')))
```

$$x^2 + 1$$

```
>> pretty(sym(maple('Normal( (x^3-2*x^2+2*x+1)/(x^4+1)) mod 5')))
```

$$\frac{x + 3}{x^2 + 3}$$

```
>> pretty(sym(maple('evala(Normal((x^2-2)/(x-RootOf(_Z^2-2))))')))
```

```
                    2
            x + RootOf(_Z-2)
```

```
>> pretty(sym(maple('expand((x+1)/(x+2))')))
```

```
            x        1
          ----- + -----
          x + 2   x + 2
```

```
>> pretty(sym(maple('expand(y^3*(x+1)^3/((x+2)*y^2))')))
```

```
          3        2
         yx       yx        yx      y
        ----- + 3 ----- + 3 ----- + -----
        x + 2     x + 2     x + 2   x + 2
```

```
>> pretty(sym(maple('factor((x^3-y^3)/(x^4-y^4))')))
```

```
            2       2
          x + x y + y
         -----------------
              2   2
          (y + x) (x + y)
```

```
>> pretty(sym(maple('factor(y ^ 3 * (x + 1) ^ 3/((x^2+2*x+1) *(y^2+y)))')))
```

```
                2
          (x + 1) y
          ----------
            y + 1
```

```
>> pretty(sym(maple('radsimp((1 + 2^(1/2))^(-1)/(1 + 2*x + x^2)^(1/2))')))
```

```
                1
          ------------------
              1/2
          (2    + 1) (x + 1)
```

```
>> pretty(sym(maple(' p:= x^5-2*x^4-2*x^3+4*x^2+x-2')))
>> pretty(sym(maple(' f:= 36 / p')))

>> pretty(sym(maple('convert(f,parfrac,x)')))
```

$$\frac{4}{x-2} - \frac{9}{(x-1)^2} - \frac{3}{(x+1)^2} - \frac{4}{x+1}$$

```
>> pretty(sym(maple('convert(f,parfrac,x,sqrfree)')))
```

$$\frac{4}{x-2} - 4\frac{x+2}{x^2-1} - 12\frac{x+2}{(x^2-1)^2}$$

```
>> pretty(sym(maple('f:= 36 / convert(p,sqrfree,x)')))

>> pretty(sym(maple('convert(f,parfrac,x,true)')))
```

$$\frac{4}{x-2} - 4\frac{x+2}{x^2-1} - 12\frac{x+2}{(x^2-1)^2}$$

EXERCISE 2-16

Given the following algebraic fractions:

$$A=\frac{x^2+2x\sqrt2-2x\sqrt3+5-2\sqrt2\sqrt3}{x^2-2x\sqrt3+1}, \ B=\frac{1}{\sqrt2+\sqrt3+\sqrt6}$$

Simplify them all as much as possible and rationalize the denominators.

```
>> maple('A:=((x^2+2*x*2^(1/2)-2*x*3^(1/2)+5-2*2^(1/2)*3^(1/2))/(x^2-2*x*3^(1/2)+1))')
>> pretty(sym(maple(' radnormal(A) ')))
```

$$\frac{-x-2^{1/2}+3^{1/2}}{-x+2^{1/2}+3^{1/2}}$$

```
>> pretty(sym(maple(' readlib(rationalize):rationalize(A) ')))
```

```
      2         1/2      1/2        1/2 1/2   2              1/2
   (- x - 2 x 2 + 2 x 3 - 5 + 2 2    3  ) (x + 1 + 2 x 3 )
 - ----------------------------------------------------------
                          4      2
                         x - 10 x + 1
```

```
>> pretty(sym(maple(' B:= 1/(2^(1/2)+3^(1/2)+6^(1/2)) ')))
>> pretty(sym(maple(' radnormal(B) ')))
```

```
                            1
                  -----------------------
                  1/2     1/2      1/2 1/2
                 2    + 3    + 2    3
```

```
>> pretty(sym(maple(' radnormal(B,rationalized) ')))
```

```
           1/2        1/2 1/2       1/2 12
      5/23 3  - 1/23 2    3  + 7/23 2  - --
                                         23
```

EXERCISE 2-17

Convert the following algebraic fractions to continued fractions:

$$\frac{1}{e^x}, \quad \frac{1+\dfrac{x}{2}+\dfrac{x^2}{12}}{1-\dfrac{x}{2}+\dfrac{x^2}{12}}$$

```
>> pretty(sym(maple(' convert(1/exp(x),confrac,x) ')))
```

```
                         x
      1 + ------------------------
                    x
          -1 + ------------------
                      x
               -2 + --------------
                         x
                    3 + ---------
                        2 1/5 x
```

```
>> pretty(sym(maple(' r:= (1+1/2*x+1/12*x^2) / (1-1/2*x+1/12*x^2) ')))
>> pretty(sym(maple(' convert(r,confrac,x) ')))
```

```
                    12
          1 + ------------
                    12
          x - 6 + ----
                    x
```

EXERCISE 2-18

Break down the following algebraic fractions into simple fractions:

$$\frac{x^5+1}{x^4-x^2}, \ \frac{x}{(x-b)^2}, \ 2\cdot3\cdot\frac{x}{5\cdot4\cdot x^3-2\cdot3\cdot x+1}$$

```
>> pretty(sym(maple(' f:= (x^5+1)/(x^4-x^2) ')))
>> pretty(sym(maple(' convert(f,parfrac,x) ')))
```

```
                1        1
      x + -----   -   ----
              x - 1        2
                          x
```

```
>> pretty(sym(maple(' f:= x/(x-b)^2 ')))
>> pretty(sym(maple('  convert(f,parfrac,x) ')))
```

```
            b          1
        -------- + -----
             2     x - b
        (x - b)
```

```
>> pretty(sym(maple(' f:= (2.3*x)/(5.4*x^3-2.3*x+1) ')))

>> pretty(sym(maple(' convert(f,parfrac,x) ')))
```

```
      .2240312285                  .3421473558 + 1.209768633 x
  - --------------- + .1851851852 --------------------------------
    x +.8091847442                 2
                                   x -.8091847442 x +.2288540244
```

EXERCISE 2-19

Decompose into simple fractions the rational function given by $f(x) = (4 \cdot x^3 - 6 \cdot x^2 - 2) / (x^4 - 2 \cdot x^3 - 2 \cdot x + 4)$ over the field of their coefficients, over the real field, over the complex field, and over the algebraic extension $Q(\sqrt{3})$.

```
>> pretty(sym(maple(' f:= (4*x^3-6*x^2-2)/(x^4-2*x^3-2*x+4) ')))
>> pretty(sym(maple(' convert(f,parfrac,x) ')))
```

```
                                  2
                         1       x
                       ----- + 3 ------
                       x - 2      3
                                 x - 2
```

```
>> pretty(sym(maple(' convert(f,parfrac,x,real) ')))
```

```
     1.000000000       1.000000000         1.259921050 + 2. x
   --------------- +  ----------- + -------------------------------
    x-1.259921050       x - 2.        2
                                     x + 1.259921050 x + 1.587401052
```

```
>> pretty(sym(maple(' convert(f,parfrac,x,complex) ')))
```

```
                  -9                              -9
    1 +.2803082855 10  I             1. -.2803082855 10  I
  ------------------------------ + -------------------------------
  x +.6299605249 + 1.091123636 I   x +.6299605249 - 1.091123636 I
                   -10
    1 +.2631183713 10   I        1.000000000
  + ----------------------- + -----------
       x - 1.259921050           x - 2
```

```
>> pretty(sym(maple(' convert(f,parfrac,x,2^(1/3)) ')))
```

```
            1/3
         2     + 2 x         1          1
       ------------------ + -------- + -----
        2    1/3   2/3        1/3      x - 2
       x + 2 x + 2          x   - 2
```

EXERCISE 2-20

Perform the following algebraic operations, simplifying the results as much as possible:

$$\frac{x}{x+y} - \frac{y}{x-y} + \frac{2xy}{x^2-y^2}, \quad \frac{1+a^2}{b} + \frac{1-b^2}{a} - \frac{a^3-b^2}{ab}$$

To treat operations with algebraic fractions, the best command to use is normal, but you can also use the simple commands factor and simplify:

```
>> pretty (sym (maple ('normal (x / (x + y) - y/(x-y) + 2 * x * y/(x^2-y^2))')))
```

$$1$$

```
>> pretty (sym (maple ('factor (x / (x + y) - y/(x-y) + 2 * x * y/(x^2-y^2))')))
```

$$1$$

```
>> pretty (sym (maple ('simplify (x / (x + y) - y/(x-y) + 2 * x * y/(x^2-y^2))')))
```

$$1$$

```
>> pretty(sym(maple('normal((1+a^2)/b + (1-b^2)/a - (a^3-b^3)/(a*b))')))
```

```
                a + b
                -----
                 a b
```

```
>> pretty(sym(maple('factor((1+a^2)/b + (1-b^2)/a - (a^3-b^3)/(a*b))')))
```

```
                a + b
                -----
                 a b
```

```
>> pretty(sym(maple('simplify((1+a^2)/b + (1-b^2)/a - (a^3-b^3)/(a*b))')))
```

```
                a + b
                -----
                 a b
```

EXERCISE 2-21

Simplify the following algebraic fractions as much as possible:

$$\frac{a^3 - a^2 b + ac^2 - bc^2}{a^3 + ac^2 + a^2 b + bc^2}, \quad \frac{(x^2 - 9)(x^2 - 2x + 1)(x - 3)}{(x^2 - 6x + 9)(x^2 - 1)(x - 1)}$$

Because these are simple algebraic fractions, use the commands *standard*, *factor* or *simplify*.

```
>> pretty(sym(maple('normal((a^3-a^2*b+a*c^2-b*c^2)/(a^3+a*c^2+a^2*b+b*c^2))')))
```

```
                    a - b
                    -----
                    a + b
```

```
>> pretty(sym(maple('factor((a^3-a^2*b+a*c^2-b*c^2)/(a^3+a*c^2+a^2*b+b*c^2))')))
```

```
                    a - b
                    -----
                    a + b
```

```
>> pretty(sym(maple('simplify((a^3-a^2*b+a*c^2-b*c^2)/(a^3+a*c^2+a^2*b+b*c^2))')))
```

```
                    a - b
                    -----
                    a + b
```

```
>> pretty(sym(simple(((x^2-9)*(x^2-2*x+1)*(x-3))/((x^2-6*x+9)*(x^2-1)*(x-1)))))
```

```
                    x + 3
                    -----
                    x + 1
```

EXERCISE 2-22

Perform the following algebraic operations, simplifying the results as much as possible.

a)

$$\left(\frac{3x-1}{x+2} - \frac{5-x}{x-2} - \frac{4x^2}{x^2-4}\right) * (x^2(x+1) - (x+4))) / (4+5x)]$$

b)

$$(x-y)\frac{\left(\dfrac{2x}{4x}\right)^2}{x^2+2xy+y^2}$$

$$\left[\frac{\left(\dfrac{2x}{4x}\right)^2}{x^2+2xy+y^2}\right]$$

$$\left(\frac{1+\dfrac{y}{x}}{1-\dfrac{y}{x}}\right)^4$$

In this type of combined operations, featuring both sums and differences, as well as ratios products and powers of algebraic expressions, the most efficient command is *normal*:

```
>> pretty(sym(maple('normal(((3*x-1)/(x+2)-(5-x)/(x-2)-4*x^2/(x^2-4))*
((x^2*(x^2+1)-(x^4+4))/(4+5*x)))')))
```

$$-2$$

```
>> pretty (sym (maple ('normal (((2 * x /(x-y))/(4*x/(x^2+2*x*y+y^2)))^ 2
/((1+y/x)/(1-y/x))^4)')))
```

$$1/4 \ (x-y)^2$$

2-8. Transforming Algebraic Expressions by Conversion

MATLAB enables the conversion of an algebraic expression dependent on a specific function into another expression that depends on another function related to the first. An expression can be transformed from logarithmic, trigonometric, inverse trigonometric or hyperbolic to exponentials, factorials to gamma functions, and so on. Among the commands that enable you to do this are the following (all of them must be preceded by the maple command):

`convert(expression,exp)` **converts all trigonometric functions of the expression into their corresponding exponential form.**

`convert(expression,ln)` **converts all inverse trigonometric functions of the expression into their corresponding logarithmic form.**

`convert(expression,trig)` **converts all exponential functions of the expression into their corresponding trigonometric or hyperbolic trigonometric form.**

`convert(expression,tan)` **converts the trigonometric functions of the expression so that it depends only on the tangent.**

`convert(expression,sincos)` **converts trigonometric functions of the expressions depending only on sines, cosines, hyperbolic sines, and hyperbolic cosines.**

`convert(expression,expsincos)` **converts the trigonometric functions of the expression in terms of only sines and cosines, and at the same time converts all hyperbolic functions of the expression into its exponential form.**

`convert(expression,expln)` **converts the trigonometric functions of the expression into its exponential form, and at the same time converts inverse trigonometric functions into logarithmic form.**

`convert(expression,GAMMA)` **converts all factorials and binomial and multinomial coefficients of the expression in terms of the GAMMA function.**

`convert(expression,factorial)` **converts all GAMMA functions, binomial and multinomial coefficients of the expression in terms of factorials.**

`convert(expression,binomial)` **converts GAMMA and factorial expressions in terms of the binomial function.**

`convert(expr,piecewise)` **converts an expression containing moduli (abs), sign (signum), or Heaviside functions into a piecewise-defined function.**

`convert(expression,parlist)` **converts an expression containing defined functions into a piecewise function according to the specified list.**

`convert(expr,Heaviside)` **converts an expression containing piecewise functions into an expression in terms of Heaviside functions.**

`convert(expression,surd)` **converts an expression containing roots and standard powers into its equivalent expresssion in terms of the surd function.**

`convert(expression,pair)` **converts an expression containing surd functions into its equivalent expression containing standard powers.**

`convert(expression,erf)` **converts an expression containing erfc functions into its equivalent in terms of the function erf.**

`convert(expression,erfc)` **converts an expression containing the function erf into its equivalent in terms of the function erfc.**

convert(expression,Ei) **converts an expression containing logarithmic, hyperbolic, and trigonometric integrals into an equivalent expression with exponential integrals.**

convert(expression,Airy) **converts an expression containing Bessel functions into its equivalent expression containing Airy functions.**

convert(expression,Bessel) **converts an expression containing Airy functions into an equivalent expression containing Bessel functions.**

convert(expr,'+') **converts an expression in the form of sums (the first level of operators must be sums, for example, a sum of products).**

convert(expr,'.') **converts an expression in the form of products (the first level of operands must be products, for example, a product of sums).**

convert(expression,degree) **converts an expression in radians to degrees.**

convert(expression,radian) **converts an expression in degrees to radians.**

convert(expression,metric) **converts an expression of type** *number * units* **to the metric system (for example,** *34 * feet* **is converted to the decimal metric system).**

convert(expr,metric,US) **converts an expression given in U.S. units to the metric system.**

convert(expr,metric,imp) **converts an expression given in terms of imperial units to the metric system.**

convert(expression,float) **converts all the numeric values of an expression to their floating-point form.**

convert(expr,hypergem) **converts the expression sums (** *sum* **or** *Sum* **) according to terms to the equivalent hypergeometric functions.**

convert(expr,rational) **or** convert(expr,fraction) **converts all floating-point values of an expression to their rational form.**

convert(expr,rational,n) **converts all floating-point values of an expression to its rational form with** *n* **digits of precision.**

convert(expression,rational and exact) **converts all floating-point values of an expression to its rational form with infinite precision.**

convert(expression,mod2) **converts the expression containing the Boolean operators and, or , and not to an expression of the form modulo2 (an expression with only numeric values 0 and 1).**

convert(expression,string) **or** convert(expression,name) **converts the expression to a string.**

convert(exprcompl,polar) **converts the complex to expression to polar form.**

convert(expression,radical) **converts all RootOf expressions to their radical equivalents.**

convert(expression,RootOf) **converts all radical expressions into RootOf notation.**

convert(series,polynom) **converts a Taylor series to a polynomial.**

convert(booleanexpression, 'and') **converts all of the binary operators in a Boolean expression (and, or, & and, or, & nand, $nor, & xor, & diff and & implies) into their equivalent in terms of the operator and.**

convert(booleanexpression,'or') **or** convert(expression,disjcyc) **converts all of the binary operators in the Boolean expression (and, or, & and, or, & nand, $nor, & xor, & diff e & implies) into their equivalents depending on the operator or. The permutations of the expression are converted to disjoint cycles.**

convert(expression,permlist) **converts the expression's disjoint cycles to their equivalent permutations.**

convert(expression,multiset) **converts the expression into a list of lists. For each element of the expression, it returns a list consisting of the element and its multiplicity (the number of times it is repeated).**

convert([expr1,...,exprn],option) **creates a list with the given expressions converted according to the specified option (trig, exp, ln,...).**

convert({expression1,...,expressionn},option) **creates an array with the given expression converted according to the specified option.**

Here are some examples:

```
>> pretty(sym(maple('convert(exp(x^2)-2 * sinh(x^2),exp)')))
```

$$\frac{1}{\exp(x^2)}$$

```
>> pretty(sym(maple('convert(cot(x),expsincos)')))
```

$$\frac{\cos(x)}{\sin(x)}$$

```
>> pretty(sym(maple('convert(sinh(x),expsincos)')))
```

$$\frac{1}{2}\exp(x) - \frac{1}{2}\frac{1}{\exp(x)}$$

```
>> pretty(sym(maple('convert(cot(x),sincos)')))
```

$$\frac{\cos(x)}{\sin(x)}$$

```
>> pretty(sym(maple('convert(tanh(x),sincos)')))
```

$$\frac{\sinh(x)}{\cosh(x)}$$

```
>> pretty(sym(maple('convert(arctanh(x),ln)')))
```

$$\frac{1}{2} \ln(x + 1) - \frac{1}{2} \ln(1 - x)$$

```
>> pretty(sym(maple('convert(1/2*exp(x) + 1/2*exp(-x),trig)')))
```

$$\cosh(x)$$

```
>> pretty(sym(maple('convert(cos(x)*sin(x), expln)')))
```

$$- \frac{1}{2} I \left(\frac{1}{2} \exp(I\ x) + \frac{1}{2} \frac{1}{\exp(I\ x)}\right) \left(\exp(I\ x) - \frac{1}{\exp(I\ x)}\right)$$

```
>> pretty(sym(maple('convert(binomial(m,3),GAMMA)')))
```

$$\frac{1}{6} \frac{\mathrm{GAMMA}(m + 1)}{\mathrm{GAMMA}(m - 2)}$$

```
>> pretty(sym(maple('convert(binomial(m,3),factorial)')))
```

$$\frac{1}{6} \frac{m!}{(m - 3)!}$$

```
>> pretty(sym(maple('convert(erfc(x),erf)')))
```

$$1 - \mathrm{erf}(x)$$

```
>> pretty(sym(maple('convert(erfc(2,x),erf)')))
```

$$\frac{1}{2} x^2 - \frac{1}{2} x^2\ \mathrm{erf}(x) - \frac{1}{2} \frac{x \exp(-x^2)}{\mathrm{Pi}^{1/2}} + \frac{1}{4} - \frac{1}{4}\ \mathrm{erf}(x)$$

```
>> pretty(sym(maple('convert(",erfc) ')))
```

```
                                           2
                                    x exp(-x )
       2         2
   1/2 x  - 1/2 x  (1 - erfc(x)) - 1/2 ---------- + 1/4 erfc(x)
                                          1/2
                                         Pi
```

```
>> pretty(sym(maple('convert(BesselI(1/3,x),Airy) ')))
```

```
    / 1/3   2/3\ 1/2
    |3     2   |
1/2 |---------|
    |    2/3   |
    \   x      /

      1/2          2/3 1/3 2/3              2/3 1/3 2/3
   (-3    AiryAi(1/2 3   2   x  ) + AiryBi(1/2 3   2   x  ))
```

```
>> pretty(sym(maple('convert(HankelH2(-2/3,z),Bessel)')))
            BesselJ(-2/3, z) - I BesselY(-2/3, z)
>> pretty(sym(maple('convert(sin(BesselK(1/3,z^2)),Airy)')))
```

```
           / 1/3   2/3\1/2
           |3     2   |                  2/3 1/3   2 2/3
    sin(Pi |---------|   AiryAi(1/2 3   2   (z )   ))
           |    2 2/3 |
           \  (z )    /
```

2-9. Subexpressions and Parts of Expressions

MATLAB implements a broad group of commands that allow you to work with subexpressions, either to operate on parts of expressions in general, to perform assignments of parts of expressions, to make substitutions in expressions, or for any other operations on the contents of algebraic expressions. The most important commands for this kind of task are summarized below (all of them must be preceded by the maple command):

indets(expression) **determines all the indeterminate***s* **contained in the expression.**

indets(expression,name) **returns all subexpressions of the expression of the type given by** name.

has(expression,subexpression) **determines whether the given expression contains the specified subexpression.**

has(expr,[subexp1,...,subexpn]) **or** has(expr,{subexp1,...,subexpn}) **determines whether the expression expr contains one of the given subexpressions.**

hasfun(expression,command) **determines whether the expression contains a call to the command or function specified.**

hasfun(expression,function,variable,etc.) **determines whether the expression contains the specified function of the given variable.**

hasfun(expression,[fun1,...,funn]) **or** hasfun(expression,{fun1,...,funn}) **determines whether the expression contains at least one of the specified functions.**

hasfun(expr,function,[var1,...,varn]) **or** hasfun(expr,function,{var1,..., varn}) **determines whether the expression contains at least one of the functions function(vari) i = 1... n.**

hastype(expression,type) **determines whether the expression contains a subexpression of the specified type.**

readlib(freeze): freeze(expr) **replaces the (usually very long) expression by the variables _R0, _R1, etc. This is used to avoid overcomplicating expressions.**

readlib(freeze): thaw(var) **replaces the variable var by the expression that was previously assigned to it by freeze.**

alias(name=expression) **or** macro(name=expression) **assigns to the alias name the given expression. The aim is to work more easily with long expressions and subexpressions.**

alias(name1=expr1,...,namen=exprn) **or** macro(name1=expr1,...,namen=exprn) **assigns all the aliases to the specified expressions.**

alias(name=name) **or** macro(name=name) **removes the alias for name.**

assign({var1=expr1,...,varn=exprn}) **or** assign([var1=expr1,...,varn=exprn]) **assigns the specified expressions to the given variables. This is usually used for long expressions or complicated subexpressions to facilitate further work.**

assign(variable=expression) **or** assign(variable,expression) **assigns the given expression to the aforementioned variable.**

unassign('var1',...,'varn') **removes the assignments for the given variables.**

op(expression) **displays the first level of elements, parts, or operands of the expression.**

op(i,expression) **returns the ith element (part or operat or) of the expression according to the first level of operations.**

op(i..j,expression) **returns the ith through to the jth elements of the expression.**

nops(expression) **returns the number of elements (parts or operators) of the expression according to the first level of operations.**

nops(op(i expression)) **returns the number of elements of the ith element of the expression.**

subsop(i=expresion2,expression1) **replaces the ith element of expression1 according to the first level of operations with expression2.**

op(0,expression) **returns the type of the expression.**

op(-i, expression) **returns the ith element of the expression starting from the end according to the first level of operations.**

applyop(function,expr) **applies the function or specified command to the nth element of the expression according to the first level of operations.**

`select(function,expression)` **applies the Boolean function or command to each term of the expression (sum or product) and selects the terms for which the Boolean function or command returns true.**

`remove(function,expression)` **applies the Boolean function or command to all of the terms of the expression of sums or products and removes those for which the given Boolean function or command is true.**

`map(function,expr)` **applies the function to each operand of expr.**

`map2(function,arg,expr)` **applies the function with specified first argument to each operator of the expression expr.**

`add(expression,variable=a..b)` **sums the sequence obtained by evaluating the expression for the variable ranging over a, a+1,..., b-1, b.**

`mul(expression,variable=a..b)` **returns the product of the sequence obtained by evaluating the expression for the variable ranging over the values a, a+1,..., b-1, b.**

`seq(expression,variable=a..b)` **creates the sequence of expressions obtained by evaluating the specified expression for the variable over the values a, a+1,..., b-1, b.**

`numboccur(expr,subexpr)` **determines how many times the subexpression specified occurs in the given expression.**

`readlib(optimize):` `optimize (expression)` **optimizes the representation of the algebraic expression using common subexpressions.**

`readlib(optimize):` `optimize(expression, name=expression)` **optimizes the specified equation whose right-hand side is an algebraic expression.**

`readlib(optimize):` `optimize(expression,[name1=expr1,...,namen=exprn])` **optimizes the specified equations whose right-hand sides are algebraic expressions.**

`shake(expression)` **creates a range of floating-point numbers that approximates the value of the expression.**

`shake(expression,n)` **creates a range of floating-point numbers that approximates the value of the expression with an accuracy given by n.**

`subs(exprold=exprnew,expression)` **replaces** `exprold` **with** `exprnew` **in the specified expression.**

`subs(expold1=expn1,expold2=expn2,..., expoldn=expnn, expression)` **replaces the specified old expressions in the given expression by the new expressions, sequentially.**

`subs({expold1=expn1,expold2=expn2,...,expoldn=expnn},expression)` **or** `subs ([expold1=expn1,expold2=expn2,...,expoldn=expnn],expression)` **replaces the old expressions with the new expression, simultaneously.**

`subsop(n1=expr1,...,nk=exprk,expr)` **replaces the elements n1, n2,..., nk of the expression by expressions expr1,..., exprk respectively (according to the first level of operations), simultaneously.**

`readlib(trigsubs):` `trigsubs(identity,expression)` **applies the given trigonometric identity to the specified expression.**

`algsubs(exprold=exprnew,expr)` **substitutes exprnew in place of exprant in the given expression.**

`algsubs(exprold=exprnew,expression,exact)` **substitutes exprnew in place of exprant in the given expression only if the exact division of monomials is possible.**

`asubs(exprold=exprnew,expression)` **substitutes exprnew in place of exprold in the given expression in terms of sums.**

`asubs(exprold=exprnew,expression,always)` **substitutes exprnew in place of exprold in the given expression in all its addends.**

`LHS(equation)` **returns the left-hand side of the equation.**

`LHS(inequality)` **returns the left-hand side of the inequality.**

`LHS(range)` **returns the left side of an expression of type range.**

`RHS(equation)` **returns the right-hand side of the equation.**

`RHS(inequality)` **returns the right-hand side of the inequality.**

`RHS(range)` **returns the right side of an expression of type** `range`.

`readlib(isolate): isolate (equation, expression)` **isolates the specified expression in the given equation.**

`readlib(isolate): isolate (expr1, expr2)` **isolates the subexpression expr2 in the equation expr1 = 0.**

`readlib(isolate): isolate (equation, expression, n)` **isolates the specified expression in the given equation by running at least n transformations or passes.**

`setattribute(expression,attri1,...,attrin)` **assigns the attributes attri1,..., attrin for the specified expression. Only strings, lists, sets, floating-point values, and unevaluated function calls can have attributes.**

`setattribute(expression)` **removes all attributes previously assigned to the specified expression.**

`attributes(expression)` **returns all the attributes previously assigned to the specified expression.**

Here are some examples:

```
>> pretty(sym(maple('indets(x*y + z/x)')))
```

$$\{y, z, x\}$$

```
>> pretty(sym(maple('e:= x^(1/2) + exp(x^2) + f(9):')))
>> pretty(sym(maple('indets(e),  indets(e,function)')))
```

$$\{x^{1/2}, x, \exp(x^2)\}, \{\exp(x^2), x(9)\}$$

```
>> pretty(sym(maple('f:= (a+b^3+c)^(4/3)')))
>> pretty(sym(maple('has( f, a ),  has( f, b^3 ),  has( f, b^2 ),  has( f, a+b^3+c )')))
```

---

true, true, false, true

```
>> pretty(sym(maple('f:= Int(g(t),t=a..b)')))
>> pretty(sym(maple('has(f,a),   has(f,g),   has(f,t)')))
```

---

true, true, true

```
>> pretty(sym(maple('e:= sin(x)+exp(y)+1')))
>> pretty (sym (maple (' hasfun(e,exp), hasfun(e,cos), hasfun(e,exp,y), hasfun(e,exp,x),
   hasfun(e,exp,[x,y]), hasfun(e,{sin,cos},x)')))
```

---

true, false, true, false, true, true

```
>> pretty(sym(maple(' f:= x^(1/2)*y ')))

>> pretty(sym(maple('hastype(f,`*`), hastype(f, `+`), hastype(f, name^fraction),
   hastype(f,integer^fraction), hastype(f,radical ), hastype( f,function )')))
```

---

true, false, true, false, true, false

```
>> pretty(sym(maple('readlib(freeze): z:= freeze(x+y)')))
>> pretty(sym(maple(' thaw(z) ')))
```

---

x + y

```
>> pretty(sym(maple('w:= f(g(a,b),h(c,d))')))
>> pretty(sym(maple('op(1,op(2,w)), op([2,1],w), op([-1,-1],w)')))
```

---

c, c, d

```
>> pretty(sym(maple('Int(sin(sqrt(x)),x=0..t)')))
```

$$\int_0^t \sin(\sqrt{x})dx$$

```
>> pretty(sym(maple('subsop( [1,1]=u, " ), subsop( 1=2*u*op(1,"), [2,1]=u, " ),
   applyop( sqrt, [2,2,2], " )')))
```

$$\int_0^t \sin(u)dx, \ \int_0^t 2u\sin(u)du, \ \int_0^{\sqrt{t}} 2u\sin(u)dx$$

```
>> pretty (sym (maple ('readlib (isolate): isolate (4 * x * sin (x) = 3, sin (x)),
   isolate(x^2-3*x-5,x^2)')))
```

$$\sin (x) = 3/4\ x,\ x = 3\ x^2 + 5$$

```
>> pretty(sym(maple(' f:= 2*exp(a*x)*sin(x)*ln(y) ')))
>> pretty(sym(maple('select(has, f, x),    remove(has, f, x)')))
```

$$\exp (w\ x)\ \sin (x),\ 2\ \ln (y)$$

```
>> pretty(sym(maple('attributes(a), setattribute(a,blue), attributes(a)')))
```

$$a,\ blue$$

```
>> pretty(sym(maple('setattribute(a,yellow,green)')))
```

$$A$$

```
>> pretty(sym(maple('attributes(a)')))
```

$$yellow,\ green$$

EXERCISE 2-23

Perform the substitution sin $(x)^2$= 1-cos $(x)^2$ in the following expression: sin $(x)^3$ - cos (x) sin $(x)^2$ + cos $(x)^2$ sin (x) + cos $(x)^3$. Also substitute PV/T = R in the expression P^2 V/T^2 - PR.

```
>> pretty (sym (maple ('f: = sin (x) ^ 3-cos (x) * sin (x) ^ 2 + cos (x) ^ 2 * sin (x) +
   cos (x) ^ 3')))
>> pretty (sym (maple ('algsubs (sin (x) ^ 2 = 1 - cos (x) ^ 2, f)')))
```

$$\sin (x)^3 - \cos (x) + 2 \cos (x)$$

```
>> pretty(sym(maple('algsubs( P*V/T=R, P^2*V/T^2-P*R) ')))
```

$$-P\ R + \frac{R\ P}{T}$$

EXERCISE 2-24

Perform the replacement defined by $x^2 + 3 = k$ in the expressions $(x^2 + 3x + 3)^3 + x$ and $((x^2 + 3x + 3)^3 + x) / (x^2 + 2)^2$.

```
>> pretty(sym(maple('readlib(asubs):')))
>> pretty(sym(maple('asubs( x^2 + 3 =k, (x^2 + 3*x + 3 ) ^ 3 + x )')))
```

$$(3 x + k)^3 + x$$

```
>> pretty(sym(maple('asubs( x^2 + 3 =k, (x^2 + 3*x + 3 ) ^ 3 + x ,always)')))
```

$$(3 x + k)^3 + x - x^2 - 3 + k$$

```
>> pretty(sym(maple('asubs( x^2 + 3 =k, ((x^2 + 3*x + 3 ) ^ 3 + x)/(x^2 +2)^2)')))
```

$$\frac{(3 x + k)^3 + x}{(-1 + k)^2}$$

EXERCISE 2-25

Change the variable $x = r^{1/3}$ in the expression $3x\ln(x^3)$ and also change the variable $\sin(x) = y$ in the expression $\sin(x) / (1 - \sin(x))^{1/2}$.

```
>> pretty(sym(maple('subs(x=r^(1/3), 3*x*log(x^3))')))
```

$$3 r^{1/3} \log(r)$$

```
>> pretty (sym (maple ('subs (y= sin (x), sin (x) / (1 - sin (x)) ^(1/2)')))
```

$$\frac{y}{(1 - y)^{1/2}}$$

CHAPTER 3

■ ■ ■

Polynomial Divisibility, Interpolation, and Algebraic Extensions

3-1. Commands for Handling Polynomial Expressions

This chapter is about working with polynomials and algebraic extensions. We will study the MATLAB commands that enable you to perform polynomial operations, working with roots, Galois extensions, Gröbner bases, polynomial interpolation, and operations modulo an integer. We will also present the commands that Maple implements to the same effect.

MATLAB enables agile work with polynomials, providing several commands for handling polynomial algebraic expressions. These expressions can also be treated as general algebraic expressions, but MATLAB offers particular tools for polynomial algebraic expressions, including case-specific commands. Let's take a look at some of these commands:

> conv(a,b) **returns the vector whose entries are the coefficients of the polynomial defined as the product of the polynomials whose coefficients are given by the vectors** a **and** b.

> [q,r] = deconv(a,b) **gives the vector** q **of coefficients of the polynomial defined as the quotient of polynomials whose coefficients are given by the vectors** a **and** b, **and the vector** r **of coefficients of the remainder polynomial.**

> poly2sym(a) **returns the polynomial whose coefficients are those specified by the vector** a.

> sym2poly(poly) **returns the vector of coefficients of the specified polynomial (the reverse of the previous operation).**

> roots(a) **gives the roots of the polynomial whose coefficients are given by the vector** a.

> poly(v) **gives the polynomial whose roots are the components of the vector** v.

> poly(A) **gives the characteristic polynomial of the matrix** A.

> polyder(a) **gives the vector whose coefficients are those of the first derivative of the polynomial defined by** a.

> polyder(a,b) **gives the vector whose coefficients are those of the first derivative of the product of polynomials defined by** a **and** b.

[q,d] = polyder(a,b) **returns the numerator** q **and denominator** d **of the derivative of the polynomial quotient** a/b **(here all arguments are vectors of coefficients of polynomials).**

polyval(p,S) **evaluates the polynomial** p **at** S.

polyvalm(p,S) **evaluates the polynomial** p **at a matrix** S.

[r,p,k] = residue(a,b) **gives the column vectors** r, p **and** k **such that:**
b(s)/a(s)=r1/(s-p1)+r2/(s-p2)+...+rn/(s-pn) +k(s).

[a,b] = residue(r, p, k) **performs the reverse of the previous operation.**

Now let's look at some examples of the above defined commands:

Let's decompose the fraction $(-x^2 + 2x + 1)/(x^2-1)$ into the sum of its simple fractions:

```
>> [r,p,k]=residue([-1,2,1],[1,0,-1])
```

```
r =

    1.0000
    1.0000

p =

   -1.0000
    1.0000

k =

   -1
```

So the decomposition will be:

(-x ^ 2 + 2 x + 1) /(x^2-1) = 1 /(-1+x) + 1 / (x + 1) - 1

The same result can be obtained in the following way:

```
>> pretty(sym(maple('convert((-x^2+2*x+1)/(x^2-1),parfrac,x)')))
```

```
              1        1
      -1 + ----- + -----
           x - 1   x + 1
```

Next we will evaluate the polynomial $x^4-6*x^3-x^2+10*x-11$ at the point $x=5$ and at the unit matrix of order 4.

```
>> polyval([1,-6,-1,10,-11],5)
```

ans =

   -111

```
>> polyvalm([1,-6,-1,10,-11],ones(4))
```

ans =

```
   -37 - 26 - 26 - 26
   -26 - 37 - 26 - 26
   -26 - 26 - 37 - 26
   -26 - 26 - 26 - 37
```

Now let's find the roots of the polynomial x^3-x:

```
>> roots([1,0,-1,0])
```

ans =

        0
   -1.0000
    1.0000

Now we solve the equation $-x^5+2*x^4+x^3+x^2=0$:

```
>> roots([-1,2,1,1,0,0])
```

ans =
        0
        0
    2.5468
   -0.2734 + 0.5638i
   -0.2734 - 0.5638i

EXERCISE 3-1

Consider the polynomials with coefficients a = [2 - 4, 5, 8, 0, 0, 1] and b = [- 7, 15, 0, 12, 0]. Calculate the coefficients of the product and the quotient of polynomials defined by **a** and **b**, and also calculate the coefficients of the derivatives of the product and quotient of the polynomials defined by **a** and **b**.

```
>> a=[2,-4,5,8,0,0,1]; b=[-7,15,0,12,0];
>> conv(a,b)
```

```
ans =

   -14    58   -95    43    72    60    89    15     0    12     0
```

```
>> [q,r]=deconv(a,b)
```

```
q =

   -0.2857   -0.0408   -0.8017
r =

      0         0         0   23.4548    0.4898    9.6210    1.0000
```

```
>> polyder(a)
```

```
ans =

    12   -20    20    24     0     0
```

```
>> polyder(a,b)
```

```
ans =

  -140-522 - 760 301 432 300 356 45 0 12
```

```
>> [q, d] = polyder(a, b)
```

```
q =

   -28 118 -120 251 -192 180 220 -45 0 -12
d =

    49 -210 225 -168 360 0 144 0 0
```

In the previous calculations, we could instead have transformed the coefficient vectors into the equivalent polynomials with the command poly2sym, obtaining the results in polynomial form. The product polynomial is:

```
>> pretty(poly2sym(conv(a,b)))
```

$$-14 x^{10} + 58 x^9 - 95 x^8 + 43 x^7 + 72 x^6 + 60 x^5 + 89 x^4 + 15 x^3 + 12 x$$

The quotient polynomial is:

```
>> pretty(poly2sym(q))
```

$$-2/7 x^2 - 2/49 x - \frac{275}{343}$$

The first derivative of the polynomial defined by a is:

```
>> pretty(poly2sym(polyder(a)))
```

$$12 x^5 - 20 x^4 + 20 x^3 + 24 x^2$$

The first derivative of the product of polynomials defined by a and b is:

```
>> pretty(poly2sym(polyder(a,b)))
```

$$-140 x^9 + 522 x^8 - 760 x^7 + 301 x^6 + 432 x^5 + 300 x^4 + 356 x^3 + 45 x^2 + 12$$

The first derivative of the polynomial quotient a/b will be q/d where q and d are as follows:

```
>> [q,d]=polyder(a,b);
>> pretty(poly2sym(q))
```

$$-28 x^9 + 118 x^8 - 120 x^7 + 251 x^6 - 192 x^5 + 180 x^4 + 220 x^3 - 45 x^2 - 12$$

```
>> pretty(poly2sym(d))
```

$$49 x^8 - 210 x^7 + 225 x^6 - 168 x^5 + 360 x^4 + 144 x^2$$

EXERCISE 3-2

Find the characteristic polynomial of the matrix whose rows are the vectors [2,-4,5,8], [0,0,0,1], [-7,15,0,12] and [0,-1,-1,0]. Also find the roots of this polynomial and verify that the matrix satisfies the characteristic polynomial equation.

```
>> A=[2,-4,5,8;0,0,0,1;-7,15,0,12;0,-1,-1,0]
```

```
A =
     2    -4     5     8
     0     0     0     1
    -7    15     0    12
     0    -1    -1     0
```

```
>> p=poly(A)
```

```
p =

    1.0000   -2.0000   48.0000   -67.0000    33.0000
```

```
>> pretty(poly2sym(p))
```

```
                    4       3        2
                   x  - 2 x  + 48 x  - 67 x + 33
```

To find the roots of the characteristic polynomial we do the following:

```
>> roots(p)
```

```
ans =

    0.2836 + 6.8115i
    0.2836 - 6.8115i
    0.7164 + 0.4435i
    0.7164 - 0.4435i
```

To verify that the matrix A satisfies the characteristic polynomial, we evaluate the characteristic polynomial at the matrix A and observe that it (almost) returns the null matrix.

```
>> polyvalm(p,A)
```

```
ans =

  1.0E-012 *

    0.4619 - 0.9663   0.0426 - 0.9095
    0.0016 - 0.0071   0.0142   0.0142
    0.1181 - 0.0568   0.6466   0.7390
   -0.0995   0.2132 - 0.0140   0.1634
```

EXERCISE 3-3

Expand the following polynomial expressions:

a) $(5x^3 y^2 z - 4xy^2 z^3)^3$

b) $(x+y)(x^4 + x^2 y^2 + y^4)(x-y)$

```
>> syms x y z
>> pretty(expand(simple(5*x^3*y^2*z-4*x*y^2*z^3)^3))
```

```
           9  6  3        7  6  5        5  6  7       3  6  9
     125 x  y  z  - 300 x  y  z  + 240 x  y  z  - 64 x  y  z
```

```
>> pretty(expand((x+y)*(x^4+x^2*y^2+y^4)*(x-y)))
```

```
                         6    6
                        x  - y
```

Here we see that the first polynomial presents difficulties when we try to expand it using only the command `expand`; we need to use the `simple` command first.

EXERCISE 3-4

Factorize the following polynomial expressions as much as possible.

a) $4x^2 + y^2t^2 + z^4 - 4xyt + 4xz^2 - 2ytz^2$

b) $x^4 - x^2y^2 + 2xy^2 + x^2 - 2x^3 - y^2$

c) $amx + amy - bmx - bmy + bnx - anx - any + bny$

```
>> syms x y z t a b m n
>> pretty(factor(4*x^2+y^2*t^2+z^4-4*x*y*t+4*x*z^2-2*y*t*z^2))
```

$$(2\,x - y\,t + z^2)^2$$

```
>> pretty(factor(x^4- x^2*y^2+2*x*y^2+x^2-2*x^3-y^2))
```

$$(x - 1)^2\ (x - y)\ (x + y)$$

```
>> pretty(factor(a*m*x+a*m*y-b*m*x-b*m*y+b*n*x-a*n*x-a*n*y+b*n*y))
```

$$-\ (x + y)\ (n - m)\ (- b + a)$$

In general, in polynomial expressions, the command expand performs operations and simplifies the result, and the command factor factorizes as much as possible.

3-2. Extracting Parts of a Polynomial

The following commands enable MATLAB to extract various parts of a polynomial (after prior use of the maple command):

coeff(polynomial,var,n) **extracts the coefficient of the polynomial in** var **corresponding to the monomial of power n. Before applying** coeff, **be sure it is suitable to do so, by first applying** collect **to group the terms in the variable.**

coeff(polynomial,expression) **extracts the coefficient corresponding to the specified expression in the given polynomial.**

coeffs(polynomial,variable) **extracts the sequence of all the coefficients of the polynomial in the given variable.**

coeffs(polynomial) **extracts the sequence of all the coefficients of all the variables of the specified multivariable polynomial.**

coeffs(polynomial,{var1,...,varn}) or coeffs(polynomial,[var1,...,varn]) **extracts the sequence of coefficients of the given multivariate polynomials corresponding to the specified set of variables.**

coeffs(poly,var,name) **finds the sequence of polynomial coefficients corresponding to the variable** var **and assigns to it the specified name.**

sign(poly) **returns the sign of the leading coefficient of the given multivariate polynomial. If the polynomial is positive, returns 1, and if it is negative, returns - 1.**

sign(poly,var) **gives the sign of the leading coefficient of the polynomial in the variable** var.

sign(poly,[var1,...,varn]) **gives the sign of the leading coefficient of the polynomial in the variables** var1,..., varn.

lcoeff(polynomial) **finds the leading coefficient of the multivariate polynomial with respect to all variables appearing in the polynomial.**

lcoeff(polynomial,variable) **finds the leading coefficient of the polynomial with respect to the given variable.**

lcoeff(polynomial,{var1,...,varn}) or lcoeff(polynomial,[var1,...,varn]) **finds the leading coefficient of the polynomial for the given variable set.**

tcoeff(polynomial) **finds the trailing coefficient of the polynomial for all its variables.**

tcoeff(polynomial,variable) **finds the trailing coefficient of the polynomial output in the given variable.**

tcoeff(polynomial,{var1,...,varn}) or tcoeff(polynomial,[var1,...,varn]) **finds the trailing coefficient of the polynomial for the given variables.**

ldegree(polynomial,var) **determines the lowest degree of the polynomial in the given variable.**

ldegree(polynomial) **determines the lowest degree of the polynomial with respect to all of its variables.**

ldegree(polynomial,{var1,...,varn}) or ldegrace(polynomial, [var1,...,varn]) **determines the lowest degree of the polynomial with respect to the given set of variables.**

degree(polynomial,variable) **determines the highest degree of the polynomial in the given variable.**

degree(polynomial) **determines the highest degree of the polynomial with respect to all of its variables.**

degree(polynomial,{var1,...,varn}) or dgree(polynomial,[var1,...,varn]) **determines the highest degree of the polynomial for the given variables.**

Here are some examples:

```
>> pretty (sym (maple('p:= 2*x^2 + 3*y^3-5:'))))
>> pretty(sym(maple('coeff(p,x,2), coeff(p,x^2), coeff(p,x,0) ')))
```
$$2, 2, 3\,y^3 - 5$$

```
>> pretty (sym (maple ('q: = 3 * a * (x + 1) ^ 2 + sin (a) * x ^ 2 * y - y ^ 2 * x + x - a:')))
>> pretty(sym(maple('coeff(q,x)')))
```

$$6\,a^2 - y + 1$$

```
>> pretty(sym(maple('q := collect(q,x)')))
```

$$q: = (\sin (a)\,y + 3a)\,x^2 + (6\,a^2 - y + 1)\,x + 2a$$

```
>> pretty(sym(maple('coeff(q,x)')))
```

$$6\,a^2 - y + 1$$

```
>> pretty(sym(maple('s := 3*v^2*w^3*x^4+1')))
```

$$s: = 3\,v^2\,w^3\,x^4 + 1$$

```
>> pretty(sym(maple('lcoeff(s), tcoeff(s), lcoeff(s, [v,w], t), t')))
```

$$3, 1, 3\,x^4, v^2\,w^3$$

```
>> maple('degree(2/x^2+5+7*x^3,x), ldegree(2/x^2+5+7*x^3,x),degree(x*sin(x),x)')
```

$$3, - 2, FAIL$$

```
>> maple('degree(x*sin(x),sin(x)), degree((x+1)/(x+2),x),degree(x*y^3+x^2,[x,y]) ')
```

$$1, FAIL, 2$$

```
>> pretty(sym(maple('degree(x*y^3+x^2,{x,y}), ldegree(x*y^3+x^2,[x,y]) ')))
```

4, 4

```
>> pretty(sym(maple('expr := 3*x^2*y^4 - 2*x*y^5 + x')))
>> pretty(sym(maple('indets(expr), sign(expr), sign(expr, [x,y]), sign(expr, [y,x]),
   sign(expr, [y,x], a), a')))
```

{x, y}, 1, 1, - 1, - 1, x * y ^ 5

3-3. Factorization of Polynomials

This section presents the commands that implement various polynomial factorizations (following prior use of the maple command).

> factor(polynomial) **factorizes a multivariate polynomial over the ring determined by its coefficients (integer, real, rational, and so on).**
>
> factor(polynomial,radical) **factorizes the polynomial over the algebraic extension** Q(radical).
>
> factor(polynomial,RootOf) **factorizes the polynomial over the algebraic extension** Q(RootOf).
>
> factor(polynomial,[radical1,...,radicaln]) **factorizes the polynomial over the algebraic extension** Q(radical1,...,radicaln).
>
> factor(polynomial,[RootOf1,..,RootOfn]) **factorizes the polynomial over the algebraic extension** Q(RootOf1,...,RootOfn).
>
> factor([polynomial1,..., polynomialn] **or** factor({polynomial1,...,polynomial n})) **factorizes the specified polynomials.**
>
> factors(polynomial) **returns a list with the multivariate polynomial factors and their multiplicities.**
>
> factors(polynomial,radical) **returns a list with the multivariate polynomial factors and their multiplicities in the algebraic extension** Q(radical).
>
> factors(polynomial,RootOf) **returns a list with the multivariate polynomial factors and their multiplicities in the algebraic extension** Q(RootOf).
>
> factors(polynomial,[rad1,...,radn]) **or** factors(polynomial,{rad1,...,radn}) **returns a list with the multivariate polynomial factors and their multiplicities in the algebraic extension** Q(radical1,...,radicaln).
>
> factors(poly,[RootOf1,...,RootOfn]) **or** factors(poly,{RootOf1,...,RootOfn}) **returns a list with the multivariate polynomial factors and their multiplicities in the algebraic extension** Q(RootOf1,...,RootOfn).
>
> Factor(polynomial) **performs the inert factorization of the polynomial.**
>
> factor(n) **returns a row vector of prime factors of the positive integer** n.

`ifactor(n,option)` **gives the entire factorization of** n **according to the given option. Possible option values are** sqfof **(which uses the square free factorization method),** pollard **(which uses the Pollard method),** lenstra **(which uses the Lenstra method) and** easy **(which calculates only the easy factorizations).**

`Factor(polynomial)` modn **performs the inert factorization of the polynomial modulo** n.

`grading(Factor(polynomial,expr),option)` **factorizes the polynomial in the algebraic extension defined by** expr **according to the method given in the option (**lenstra, trager, **or** linear**).**

`Factors(polynomial)` **returns inert form factors and their multiplicities for the given polynomial.**

`Factors(polynomial)` modn **gives the factors and their multiplicities for** polynomial modulo n.

`grading(Factors(polynomial,expression),option)` **gives the list of factors and multiplicities of the polynomial in the given algebraic extension defined by the expression according to the specified option (**lenstra, trager, **or** linear**).**

`Afactor(polynomial)` **performs the inert absolute factorization of the polynomial.**

`Afactors(polynomial)` **returns the list of factors of the inert absolute factorization of the polynomial.**

`Berlekamp(poly,variable)` **returns the inert form of the Berlekamp factorization of varying degrees for the polynomial** poly **with respect to the given variable.**

`Berlekamp(poly,var)` modn **as above, but working modulo** n.

`Berlekamp(variable,radical,polynomial)` **returns the inert form of the Berlekamp factorization of varying degrees for the polynomial over the algebraic extension defined by radical.**

`DistDeg(polynomial,var)` **returns the inert form of the factorization of varying degrees of the polynomial given with respect to the variable** var.

`DistDeg(poly,var)` mod n **gives the factorization of varying degrees of the given polynomial with respect to the variable** var **modulo** n.

`readlib(split):split(polynomial,variable)` **performs the complete factorization of the polynomial with respect to the variable given over the ring determined by its coefficients.**

`readlib(splits):splits(polynomial,variable)` **returns the factors and their multiplicities for the complete factorization of the polynomial with respect to the given variable.**

`sqrfree(polynomial)` **returns the square-free factors and their multiplicities of a polynomial with rational coefficients.**

`sqrfree(polynomial,variable)` **returns the square-free factors and their multiplicities of a polynomial with rational coefficients in the specified variable.**

`Sqrfree(polynomial)` **returns the inert square-free factors and their multiplicities of a polynomial with rational coefficients.**

`Sqrfree(polynomial)` modn **returns the inert square-free factors and their multiplicities of a polynomial with rational coefficients modulo** n.

with(lattice): mipolys(n,p) **gives the number of irreducible univariate monic polynomials of degree** n **over** Z (modp).

with(lattice): mipolys(n,p,m) **gives the number of irreducible univariate monic polynomials of degree** n **over the Galois field defined by** p^m.

irreduc(polynomial) **determines whether the multivariate polynomial is irreducible over the ring defined by its coefficients.**

irreduc(polynomial,radical) **determines whether the multivariate polynomial is irreducible over the algebraic extension** Q(radical).

irreduc(polynomial,{rad1,...,radn}) **or** irreduc(polynomial,[rad1,...,radn]) **determines whether the multivariate polynomial is irreducible over the extension** Q(radical1,...,radicaln).

Irreduc(polynomial) **represents the inert form of** irreduc.

Irreduc(polynomial) mod n **determines whether the multivariate polynomial is irreducible over the ring defined by its coefficients modulo** n.

Here are some examples:

```
>> pretty(sym(maple('factor(x^3+5)')))
```

$$x^3 + 5$$

```
>> pretty(sym(maple('factor(x^3+5.0)')))
```

$$(x + 1.709975947). (x^2 - 1.709975947\ x + 2.924017740).$$

```
>> pretty(sym(maple('factor(a^3+a^2+a+1) ')))
```

$$(a + 1)^2 (a + 1)$$

```
>> pretty(sym(maple('factor(a^3+a^2+a+1,complex) ')))
```

$$(a + 1.) (a + 1.)\ I) (a - 1.\ I)$$

```
>> pretty(sym(maple('readlib(factors):factors(a^10-2*a^5+1) ')))
```

$$[1, [[a - 1, 2], [a^4 + a^3 + a^2 + a + 1, 2]]]$$

```
>> pretty(sym(maple('readlib(factors):factors(a^10-2*a^5+1,real) ')))
```

$$[1, [[a^2 + 1.618033989\ a + 1.000000000, 2], [a - 1., 2],]]$$
$$[[[a.6180339888\ a^2 + 1.000000000, 2]]]$$

```
>> pretty(sym(maple('Factors(a^10-2*a^5+1) mod 7')))
```

$$[1, [[a + 6, 2], [a^4 + a^3 + a^2 + a + 1, 2]]]$$

```
>> pretty(sym(maple('Factor(a^10-2*a^5+1) mod 7')))
```

$$(a + 6)^2 (a^4 + a^3 + a^2 + a + 1)^2$$

```
>> pretty(sym(maple('Factor(a^10-2*a^5+1)')))
```

$$\text{Factor}(a^{10} - 2 a^5 + 1)$$

```
>> pretty(sym(maple('evala(")')))
```

$$(a^4 + a^3 + a^2 + a + 1)^2 (a - 1)^2$$

```
>> pretty(sym(maple('readlib(split): split(x^2+x+1,x)')))
```

$$(x - \text{RootOf}(\_Z^2 + \_Z + 1)) (x + 1 + \text{RootOf}(\_Z^2 + \_Z + 1))$$

```
>> pretty(sym(maple('readlib(splits): splits(x^2+x+1,x)')))
```

$$[1,[[x - \text{RootOf}(\_Z^2 + \_Z + 1), 1], [x + 1 + \text{RootOf}(\_Z^2 + \_Z + 1), 1]]]$$

```
>> pretty(sym(maple(' f := x^3*y-x^3-x^2*y^2+x^2*y')))
>> pretty(sym(maple('sqrfree(f,x) ')))
```

$$[y - 1, [[-y + x, 1], [x, 2]]]$$

```
>> pretty(sym(maple('sqrfree(f,y)')))
```

$$[-x^2, [[-x y + x + y^2 - y, 1]]]$$

```
>> pretty(sym(maple('sqrfree(f,[x,y])')))
```

$$[1, [[y - 1, 1], [-y + x, 1], [x, 2]]]$$

```
>> pretty(sym(maple('Sqrfree(4*x^2+4*x+1) mod 7')))
```

$$[4, [[x + 4, 2]]]$$

```
>> pretty(sym(maple('irreduc( x^3+5 )')))
```

true

```
>> pretty(sym(maple('irreduc( x^3+5, 5^(1/3))')))
```

false

```
>> pretty(sym(maple('Irreduc(2*x^2+6*x+6) mod 7,Factor(2*x^2+6*x+6) mod 7')))
```

false,   2*(x+6)*(x+4)

```
>> pretty(sym(maple('Irreduc(x^4+x+1) mod 2,   Factor(x^4+x+1) mod 2')))
```

true,   x^4+x+1

As we have already seen many examples and exercises relating to factorization of univariate and multivariate polynomials, we shall present only a pair of exercises.

EXERCISE 3-5

Factorize the polynomial $a^4 - 9/4$ in the following cases:

(a) over the field defined by its coefficients

(b) over the real field

(c) over the complex field

(d) over the algebraic extension Q($\sqrt{2},\sqrt{3}$)

(e) over the algebraic extension Q($\sqrt{2},\sqrt{3}$, i)

(f) over the algebraic extension Q(RootOf(Z^2+3/2)).

```
>> pretty(sym(maple('factor(a^4-9/4)')))
```

$$1/4 \ (2 \ a^2 - 3) \ (2 \ a^2 + 3)$$

```
>> pretty(sym(maple('factor(a^4-9/4,real)')))
```

$$(a + 1.224744871) \ (a - 1.224744871) \ (a^2 + 1.499999999)$$

```
>> pretty(sym(maple('factor(a^4-9/4,complex)')))
```

$$(a + 1.224744871)(a + 1.224744871 \ I)(a-1.224744871 \ I)(a-1.224744871)$$

```
>> pretty(sym(maple('factor(a^4-9/4,{(3)^(1/2),2^(1/2)})')))
```

$$- 1/8 \ (2 \ a^2 + 3) \ (2 \ a + 3^{1/2} \ 2^{1/2}) \ (-2 \ a + 3^{1/2} \ 2^{1/2})$$

```
>> pretty(sym(maple('factor(a^4-9/4,{(3)^(1/2),2^(1/2),I})')))
```

$$1/16 \ (-2 \ a + I \ 3^{1/2} \ 2^{1/2}) \ (2 \ a + I \ 3^{1/2} \ 2^{1/2}) \ (2 \ a + 3^{1/2} \ 2^{1/2})$$

$$(-2 \ a + 3^{1/2} \ 2^{1/2})$$

```
>> pretty(sym(maple('factor(a^4-9/4,RootOf(Z^2+3/2))')))
```

$$1/2 \ (2 \ a^2 - 3) \ (a + RootOf(2 \ \_Z^2 + 3)) \ (a - RootOf(2 \ \_Z^2 + 3))$$

```
                        EXERCISE 3-6
```

Determine whether the polynomial $x^9 + 1$ is irreducible in the following cases:

(a) over the field defined by its coefficients

(b) over the algebraic extension Q($\sqrt{3}$ i).

Perform its factorization where possible.

```
>> pretty(sym(maple('irreduc(x^9+1)')))
```

$$\text{false}$$

```
>> pretty(sym(maple('factor(x^9+1)')))
```

$$(x + 1)\ (x^2 - x + 1)\ (x^6 - x^3 + 1)$$

```
>> pretty(sym(maple('irreduc(x^9+1,(-3)^(1/2))')))
```

$$\text{false}$$

```
>> pretty(sym(maple('factor(x^9+1,(-3)^(1/2))')))
```

$$1/16\ (-2 x^3 + 1 + I\ 3^{1/2})\ (2 x^3 - 1 + I\ 3^{1/2})\ (-2 x + 1 + I\ 3^{1/2})$$
$$(2 x - 1 + I\ 3^{1/2})\ (x + 1)$$

3-4. Roots of Polynomials

The following group of MATLAB commands, all of which require the prior use of the maple command, may be used to work with roots of polynomials:

> roots(polynomial) **gives univariate polynomial roots by offering a list of lists with the roots and their multiplicities. The calculation is performed over the ring defined by the coefficients.**

> roots(polynomial,radical) **finds the roots of the univariate polynomial over the algebraic extension** Q(radical) **or** Q(RootOf).

> roots(polynomial,[rad1,...,radn]) **or** roots(polynomial,{rad1,...,radn}) **finds the roots of a univariate polynomial over** Q(rad1,...,radn) **or** Q(RootOf1,...,RoofOfn).

Roots(poly) **returns the inert form of the roots of the polynomial** poly.

Roots(poly) modn **gives the roots of the polynomial** poly **modulo** n.

reallib(realroot): realroot(polynomial) **finds intervals in which the real roots of a univariate polynomial with integer coefficients are contained.**

reallib(realroot): realroot(polynomial,n) **finds intervals with a maximum width of** n **in which the real roots of a univariate polynomial with integer coefficients are contained.**

reallib(proot): proot(poly,n) **calculates the** nth **root of the given polynomial with rational coefficients.**

reallib(psqrt): psqrt(poly) **computes the square root of the given polynomial with rational coefficients.**

with(numtheory): cyclotomic(n,variable) **returns the n-th cyclotomic polynomial in the given variable.**

readlib(sturm): sturmseq(polynomial,variable) **gives a list of polynomials representing the Sturm sequence for the given polynomial.**

readlib(sturm): sturm(expression,variable,a,b) **returns the number of real roots of the polynomial in the interval** (a, b] **using the Sturm sequence.**

readlib(lattice): minpoly(r,n) **returns a polynomial of degree less than or equal to** n **with small integer coefficients, such that** r **is one of its roots.**

readlib(lattice): minpoly(r,n,e) **returns a polynomial of degree less than or equal to** n **with small integer coefficients, such that** r **is one of its approximate roots with an accuracy given by** e.

Here are some examples. First, we find the roots and their multiplicities over the field defined by the coefficients of the given polynomials:

```
>> pretty(sym(maple('roots(2*x^3+11*x^2+12*x-9)')))
```

$$[[-3, 2], [1/2, 1]]$$

```
>> pretty(sym(maple('roots(x^3+(-6-b-a)*x^2+(6*a+5+5*b+a*b)*x-5*a-5*a*b,x)')))
```

$$[[5, 1]]$$

Next, we find modular integer roots and their multiplicities.

```
>> pretty(sym(maple('Roots(x^3-x) mod 6')))
```

$$[[0, 1], [1, 1], [2, 1], [3, 1], [4, 1], [5, 1]]$$

```
>> pretty(sym(maple('Roots(x^3-1) mod 2')))
```

$$[[1, 1]]$$

```
>> pretty(sym(maple('alias(a=RootOf(x^2+x+1))'))) ;
>> pretty(sym(maple('Roots(x^3-1,a) mod 2')))
```

$$[[a + 1, 1], [1, 1], [a, 1]]$$

Next we solve a third-degree polynomial with integer coefficients that has 1.2324 as an approximate root:

```
>> pretty(sym(maple('readlib(lattice) : minpoly(1.234,3)')))
```

$$109.\ 61\ \_X + 5\ \_X^2 - 22\ \_X^3$$

Next we generate a Sturm sequence for a given polynomial in order to find the number of roots of the polynomial in the specified ranges:

```
>> pretty(sym(maple('readlib(sturm): sturmseq(expand((x-1)*(x-2)*(x-3)),x)')))
```

$$[x^3 - 6\ x^2 + 11\ x - 6,\ x^2 - 4\ x + 11/3,\ x - 2,\ 1]$$

```
>> pretty(sym(maple('sturm(",x,3/2,4)')))
```

$$2$$

```
>> pretty(sym(maple('sturm("",x,1,2)')))
```

$$1$$

Next we calculate the square and cubic roots of the given polynomials:

```
>> pretty(sym(maple('readlib(psqrt): psqrt(x^2+2*x*y+y^2)')))
```

$$x + y$$

```
>> pretty(sym(maple('readlib(proot): proot(x^3+3*x^2+3*x+1,3)')))
```

$$x + 1$$

EXERCISE 3-7

Find the roots and their multiplicities of the polynomial $x^4 - 4$ in the following cases:

(a) over the field defined by its coefficients

(b) over the algebraic extension $Q(\sqrt{2})$

(c) over the algebraic extension $Q(\sqrt{2}, i)$

(d) over the algebraic extension $Q(RootOf(x^2 - 2))$

(e) over the algebraic extension $Q(RootOf(x^2 - 2), RootOf(x^2 + 2))$

```
>> pretty(sym(maple('roots(x^4-4)')))
```

```
>> pretty(sym(maple('roots(x^4-4,x)')))
>> pretty(sym(maple('roots(x^4-4,sqrt(2))')))
```

$$[[2^{1/2}, 1], [-2^{1/2}, 1]]$$

```
>> pretty(sym(maple('roots(x^4-4, {sqrt(2),I})')))
```

$$[[I\,2^{1/2}, 1], [-I\,2^{1/2}, 1], [2^{1/2}, 1], [-2^{1/2}, 1]]$$

```
>> pretty(sym(maple('alias(a = RootOf(x^2-2))'))) ;
>> pretty(sym(maple('alias(b = RootOf(x^2+2))'))) ;
>> pretty(sym(maple('roots((x^4-4), x, a)')))
```

$$[[a, 1], [-a, 1]]$$

```
>> pretty(sym(maple('roots(x^4-4, {a, b})')))
```

$$[[b, 1], [-b, 1], [, 1], [-a, 1]]$$

EXERCISE 3-8

Find the intervals in which the real roots of the polynomial $x^8 + 5x^7 - 4x^6 - 20x^5 + 4x^4 + 20x^3$ are located, with the following specifications:

(a) intervals with default width

(b) intervals with a width of one unit

(c) intervals with a half-unit width

(d) intervals with a width of one thousandth of a unit

```
>> pretty(sym(maple('readlib(realroot)')));
>> pretty(sym(maple('realroot(x^8+5*x^7-4*x^6-20*x^5+4*x^4+20*x^3)')))
```

$$[[0, 0], [0, 8], [-4, 0], [-8, -4]]$$

We deduce that zero is a root.

```
>> pretty(sym(maple('realroot(x^8+5*x^7-4*x^6-20*x^5+4*x^4+20*x^3,1)')))
```

$$[[0, 0], [1, 2], [-1, -2] [-5, -5]]$$

We deduce that -5 is another root.

```
>> pretty(sym(maple('realroot(x^8+5*x^7-4*x^6-20*x^5+4*x^4+20*x^3,1/2)')))
```

$$[[0, 0], [1, 3/2], [-3/2, -1], [-5, -5]]$$

```
>> pretty(sym(maple('realroot(x^8+5*x^7-4*x^6-20*x^5+4*x^4+20*x^3,1/1000)')))
```

$$\left[[0, 0], \left[\frac{181}{128}, \frac{1449}{1024}\right], \left[\frac{-1449}{1024}, \frac{-181}{128}\right], [-5, -5]\right]$$

93

3-5. Grouping and Ordering Terms

This section presents commands that allow you to group terms into univariate and multivariate polynomials, as well as to manage them according to certain criteria. The syntax of these commands is as follows (after using the maple command):

> collect(polynomial,variable) **organizes the multivariate polynomial, taking the specified variable as the main variable and gathering terms with respect to the same.**

> collect(polynomial,[var1,...,varn]) **or** collect(polynomial,{var1,...,varn}) **gathers terms in the polynomial with respect to the specified variables.**

> sort(polynomial) **sorts the univariate polynomial in decreasing order of powers.**

> sort(polynomial) **or** sort(polynomial, tedeg) **sorts the polynomial according to the degree of its monomial multivariate components (in descending order).**

> sort(polynomial, plex) **sorts the multivariate polynomial in lexicographical order.**

> sort(poly,[var1,...,varn],option) **or** sort(poly,{var1,...,varn},option) **sorts the polynomial with respect to the specified variable according to the given option (plex or tedeg).**

Here are some examples:

```
>> pretty(sym(maple('collect(x*y+a*x*y+y*x^2-a*y*x^2+x+a*x,[x,y],recursive)')))
```
$$(1 - a)\ y\ x^2\ + ((1 + a)\ y + 1 + a)\ x$$

```
>> pretty(sym(maple('collect(x*y+a*x*y+y*x^2-a*y*x^2+x+a*x,[y,x],recursive)')))
```
$$((1 - a)\ x^2\ + (1 + a)\ x)\ y + (1 + a)\ x$$

```
>> pretty(sym(maple('collect(x*y+a*x*y+y*x^2-a*y*x^2+x+a*x,[x,y], distributed)')))
```
$$(1 + a)\ x + (1 + a)\ x\ y + (1 - a)\ y\ x^2$$

```
>> pretty(sym(maple('collect(x^3*y+x^2*y^3+x+3,y)')))
```
$$x^3\ y + x^2\ y^3\ + x + 3$$

```
>> pretty(sym(maple('sort(",y)')))
```
$$x^2\ y^3\ + x^3\ y + x + 3$$

```
>> pretty(sym(maple('sort(y^3+y^2*x^2+x^3,[x,y])')))
```

$$x^2 y^2 + x^3 + y^3$$

```
>> pretty(sym(maple('sort(y^3+y^2*x^2+x^3,[x,y],plex)')))
```

$$x^3 + x^2 y^2 + y^3$$

```
>> pretty(sym(maple('sort(y^3+y^2*x^2+x^3,[x,y],tdeg)')))
```

$$x^2 y^2 + x^3 + y^3$$

3-6. Handling of Polynomials

This section presents a group of commands that allow you to perform certain manipulations on univariate and multivariate polynomials, such as conversions, compositions, working with their operands, and so on. The syntax of these commands (following prior use of the `maple` command) is presented below:

compoly(poly,variable) **determines the possible composition of the polynomial in the specified variable. The result is a list whose first element is the polynomial basis** polyb, **and whose second element is the polynomial equation** eqnc **such that** sub(eqnc,polyb) = poly.

compoly(poly,{var1,...,varn}) **determines the possible composition of the polynomial in the variables** var1,...,varn.

compoly(polynomial) **determines the composition of the multivariate polynomial in all its indeterminates.**

indets(polynomial) **determines all the indeterminates of the given polynomial.**

readlib(student): completesquare(polynomial) **transforms quadratic expressions to completed square form.**

readlib(numaprox): hornerform(polynomial,variable) **converts the polynomial in the given variable into Horner form.**

convert(poly,horner,var) **converts the polynomial in the variable** var **to Horner form.**

convert(polynomial,horner,{var1,...,varn}) **converts the polynomial in the given variables to Horner form without specifying the order.**

convert(polynomial,horner,[var1,...,varn]) **converts the polynomial in the given variables into Horner form in the order specified.**

convert(polynomial,horner) **converts the polynomial in all its variables to Horner form.**

`convert(poly,mathorner,var)`**converts the polynomial in the given variable into matrix Horner form.**

`convert(poly,sqrfree,var)` **converts the polynomial in the given variable into a square-free polynomial by factoring it into its square-free factors.**

`content(polynomial,variable)` **determines the greatest common divisor of the coefficients of the polynomial in the given variable.**

`content(polynomial,[var1,...,varn])` **or** `content(polynomial,{var1,...,varn})` **determines the greatest common divisor of the coefficients of the polynomial with respect to the specified variables.**

`content(polynomial)` **determines the greatest common divisor of the coefficients of the polynomial with respect to all of its variables.**

`Content(polynomial,variable)` **determines the greatest common divisor of the coefficients of the polynomial in the given variable in inert form.**

`Content(poly,var) mod n` **determines the greatest common divisor of the coefficients of the polynomial in the given variable modulo n.**

`primpart(polynomial)` **determines a rational value such that dividing the polynomial by this value yields a primitive polynomial over the integers. If the primitive polynomial is already over the integers, this command is equivalent to** `content`**.**

`with(combinat): fibonacci(n,variable)` **gives the nth Fibonacci polynomial in the given variable.**

`with(combinat): euler(n, var)` **gives the nth Euler polynomial in the variable** `var`**.**

`with(linalg): hermite(M,var)` **determines the Hermite normal form of the matrix** `M` **of univariate polynomials in the given variable.**

`with(linalg): hermite(M,var) mod n` **determines the Hermite normal form of the matrix** `M` **of univariate polynomials in the given variable modulo n.**

`with(linalg): smith(M,var)` **determines the Smith normal form of the matrix** `M` **of univariate polynomials in the given variable.**

`with(linalg): smith(M,var) mod n` **determines the Smith normal form of the matrix M of univariate polynomials in the given variable modulo n.**

`readlib(bernstein): bernstein(n,var->exprvar,variable1)` **finds the degree** `n` **Bernstein polynomial in** `variable1` **that approximates the functional operator** `var - > exprvar` **in the interval [0,1].**

`op(polynomial)` **returns a string with all the operands (monomials) of the polynomial. Any operand can be substituted using** `subsop`**.**

`op(n,rationalfunction)` **gives the first operand (numerator) and the second operand (the inverse of the denominator) of the rational function given as a ratio of two polynomials.**

Here are some examples:

```
>> pretty(sym(maple('compoly( x^2+2*x*y-7*x+y^2-7*y+16 )')))
```

$$16 - 7 y + y^2 , \ y = y + x$$

```
>> pretty(sym(maple('compoly( x^4+4*x^3*y^3+6*x^2*y^6+4*x*y^9+y^12+x+y^3-1, {x,y})')))
```

$$-1 - 3 y + 6 y^2 - 4 y^3 + y^4 , \ y = x + 1 + y^3$$

```
>> pretty(sym(maple('indets( x*y + z/x )')))
```

$$\{z, \ y, \ x\}$$

```
>> pretty(sym(maple('e:=x^(1/2)+exp(x^2)+ f(9): indets(e), indets(e,function)')))
```

$$\{\exp(x^2), \ x^{1/2}, \ x\}, \ \{f(9), \ \exp(x^2)\}$$

```
>> pretty(sym(maple('convert(x^2+3*x+4,horner,x)')))
```

$$4 + (3 + x) \ x$$

```
>> pretty(sym(maple('poly := y^2*x^2 + 2*y^2*x + 2*y*x^2 + 4*y*x + x^2 + 2*x: ')))
>> pretty(sym(maple('convert(poly,horner,x)')))
```

$$(2 y^2 + 4 y + 2 + (y^2 + 2 y + 1) \ x) \ x$$

```
>> pretty(sym(maple('convert(poly,mathorner,x)')))
```

$$2 y^2 + 4 y + 2 + (y^2 + 2 y + 1) \ x \ \&* \ x$$

```
>> pretty(sym(maple('convert(poly,horner,[x,y])')))
```

$$(2 + (4 + 2 y) \ y + (1 + (2 + y) \ y) \ x) \ x$$

```
>> pretty(sym(maple('convert(x^2+4*x+4,sqrfree,x)')))
```

$$(x + 2)^2$$

```
>> pretty(sym(maple('content(3*x*y+6*y^2,x ), content(3*x*y+6*y^2,[x,y])')))
```

$$3\,y, \; 3$$

```
>> pretty(sym(maple('icontent(3*x*y+6*y^2)')))
```

$$3$$

```
>> pretty(sym(maple('op(y^2*x^2 + 2*y^2*x + 2*y*x^2 + 4*y*x + x^2 + 2*x)')))
```

$$y^2\,x^2, \; 2\,y^2\,x, \; 2\,y\,x^2, \; 4\,y\,x, \; x^2, \; 2\,x$$

EXERCISE 3-9

Transform into square-free form with respect to the variable x the polynomial $y^2x^3 + 2y^2x^2 + y^2x + 2yx^3 + 4yx^2 + 2yx$. Also transform the same polynomial into square-free form with respect to the variable y. Finally, find the greatest common divisor of the coefficients of the polynomial with respect to all variables, with respect to the variable x only, and with respect to the variable y only.

```
>> pretty (sym (maple('poly:= y^2*x^3+2*y^2*x^2+y^2*x+2*y*x^3+4*y*x^2+2*y*x:')))
>> pretty(sym(maple('convert(poly,sqrfree,x) ')))
```

$$(y^2 + 2\,y)\,x\,(x + 1)^2$$

```
>> pretty(sym(maple('convert(poly,sqrfree,y)')))
```

$$(x^3 + x^2 + 2\,x)\,(y^2 + 2\,y)$$

```
>> pretty(sym(maple('content(poly)')))
```

$$1$$

```
>> pretty(sym(maple('content(poly,x)')))
```

$$2\,y^2 + y$$

```
>> pretty(sym(maple('content(poly,y)')))
```

$$x^3 + 2\,x^2 + x$$

EXERCISE 3-10

Transform the second degree polynomial $9\,x^2 + 24\,x + 16$ into completed square form. Transform $x^2 - 2xa + a^2 + y^2 - 2yb + b^2 = 23$ into completed square form with respect to the variable x. Transform the same expression into completed square form simultaneously with respect to both variables x and y, and with respect to the variable a.

```
>> pretty(sym(maple('with(student):completesquare(9*x^2 + 24*x + 16)')))
```

$$9\,(x + 4/3)^2$$

```
>> pretty(sym(maple('with(student):completesquare(x^2 - 2*x*a + a^2 +
   y ^ 2-2 * y * b + b ^ 2 = 23, x)')))
```

$$(x - a)^2 + y^2 - 2\,y\,b + b^2 = 23$$

```
>> pretty(sym(maple('with(student):completesquare(x^2 - 2*x*a + a^2 +
   y^2-2*y*b + b^2 = 23, [x,y])')))
```

$$(y - b)^2 + (x - a)^2 = 23$$

```
>> pretty(sym(maple('with(student):completesquare(x^2 - 2*x*a + a^2 +
   y^2-2*y*b + b^2 = 23, a)')))
```

$$(a - x)^2 + y^2 - 2\,y\,b + b^2 = 23$$

EXERCISE 3-11

Find the 10th Fibonacci and Euler polynomials in the variable x. Also find the degree 5 Bernstein polynomial in the variable x that approximates the functional operator y→sin(y) in the interval [0,1].

```
>> pretty(sym(maple('with(combinat):fibonacci(10,x)')))
```

$$x^9 + 8x^{-7} + 21x^5 + 20x^3 + 5x$$

```
>> pretty(sym(maple('with(combinat):euler(10,x)')))
```

$$x^{10} - 5x^9 + 30x^7 - 126x^5 + 255x^3 - 155x$$

```
>> pretty(sym(maple('readlib(bernstein):bernstein(5,y->sin(y),x)')))
```

$$(5x - 20x^2 + 30x^3 - 20x^4 + 5x^5)\sin(1/5)$$

$$+ (10x^2 - 30x^3 + 30x^4 - 10x^5)\sin(2/5)$$

$$+ (10x^3 - 20x^4 + 10x^5)\sin(3/5) + (5x^4 - 5x^5)\sin(4/5) + x^5\sin(1)$$

EXERCISE 3-12

Given the following polynomial matrix:

$$M = \begin{pmatrix} x-1 & x+1 \\ x^2-1 & x^2+1 \end{pmatrix}$$

Find its Hermite normal form in the variable x.

Find its Smith normal form in the variable x.

Find its Hermite normal form in the variable y.

Find its Smith normal form in the variable y.

```
>> maple('p:=x-1;q:=x+1;r:=x^2-1;s:=x^2+1');
>> maple('M:=[[p,q],[r,s]]') ;
>> pretty(sym(maple('with(linalg):hermite(M,x)')))
```

```
                    [x - 1    1]
                    [          ]
                    [  0      x]
```

```
>> pretty(sym(maple('with(linalg):smith(M,x)')))
```

```
                  [1        0   ]
                  [             ]
                  [         2   ]
                  [0     x  - x ]
```

```
>> pretty(sym(maple('with(linalg):hermite(M,y),smith(M,y)')))
```

```
            [1    0] [1    0]
            [     ], [     ]
            [0    1] [0    1]
```

3-7. Divisibility and Operations with Polynomials

MATLAB provides various tools for the analysis of divisibility. It can also perform a wide variety of operations on polynomials. We summarize below the commands it provides for these tasks (each of which requires the prior use of the maple command):

discrim(polynomial,variable) **returns the discriminant of the polynomial with respect to the specified variable.**

Discrim(polynomial,variable) **returns the inert discriminant of the polynomial with respect to the specified variable.**

Discrim(polynomial,variable) modn **returns the inert discriminant of the polynomial with respect to the specified variable modulo n.**

resultant(poly1,poly2,var) **returns the resultant of the given polynomials with respect to the specified variable.**

Resultant(poly1,poly2,var) **returns the inert resultant of the given polynomials with respect to the specified variable.**

Resultant(poly1,poly2,variable) mod n **returns the inert resultant of the given polynomials with respect to the specified variable modulo n.**

divide(poly1,poly2,name) **determines whether** poly1 **is divisible by** poly2, **and if so assigns the specified name to the ratio.**

Divide(poly1,poly2,name) **determines whether** poly1 **is divisible by** poly2, **and if so assigns the specified name to the inert ratio.**

Divide(polynomial1,polynomial2,name) mod n **determines whether** polynomial1 **is divisible by** polynomial2 **modulo** n, **and if so, assigns the specified name to the inert ratio.**

quo(poly1,poly2,var) **returns the quotient polynomial of the ratio** poly1/poly2 **with respect to the variable var.**

quo(poly1,poly2,var,name) **returns the quotient polynomial of the ratio** poly1/poly2 **with respect to the variable** var **and gives the remainder the name** name.

Quo(poly1,poly2,var) **returns the inert quotient polynomial of the ratio** poly1/poly2 **with respect to the variable** var.

Quo(poly1,poly2,var) mod n **returns the quotient polynomial of the ratio** poly1/poly2 **modulo** n **with respect to the variable** var.

rem(poly1,poly2,variable) **returns the remainder of the division of two polynomials in the given variable.**

rem(poly1,poly2,var,name) **returns the remainder of the division of the two polynomials and gives the quotient polynomial the name** name.

Rem(poly1,poly2,variable) **returns the inert remainder of the division of two polynomials with respect to the given variable.**

rem(poly1,poly2,var) mod n **returns the remainder of the division of two polynomials with respect to the given variable modulo** n.

readlib(fixdiv): fixdiv(poly,var) **computes the fixed divisor of the given polynomial, i.e. the largest integer that divides poly(n) for all integers n.**

gcd(poly1,poly2) **returns the greatest common divisor of two polynomials with rational coefficients.**

gcd(poly1,poly2,name1,name2) **returns the greatest common divisor of two polynomials with rational coefficients and assigns** name1 **to** poly1/gcd(poly1,poly2) **and** name2 **to** poly2/gcd(poly1,poly2).

gcdex(poly1,poly2,var,name1,name2) **returns the greatest common divisor of two polynomials in** var **with rational coefficients and assigns** name1 **to** poly1/gcd(poly1,poly2) **and** name2 **to** poly2/gcd(poly1,poly2) **using the extended Euclidean algorithm.**

gcdex(poly1,poly2,poly3,var,name1,name2) **returns the greatest common divisor of two polynomials in** var **with rational coefficients and assigns to** name1 **and** name2 **expressions such as** poly3 = name1 * poly1 + name2 * poly2.

Gcd(poly1,poly2) **returns the inert form of the greatest common divisor of two polynomials with rational coefficients.**

Gcd(poly1,poly2) mod n **returns the greatest common divisor modulo** n **of polynomials with rational coefficients.**

Gcdex(poly1,poly2,var,name1,name2) **returns the inert form of the greatest common divisor of the polynomials in** var **with rational coefficients and assigns** name1 **to** poly1/gcd(poly1,poly2) **and** name2 **to** poly2/gcd(poly1,poly2) **using the extended Euclidean algorithm.**

Gcdex(poly1,poly2,var,name1,name2) mod n **returns the greatest common divisor modulo** n **of polynomials in** var **with rational coefficients and assigns** name1 **to** poly1/gcd(poly1,poly2) **and** name2 poly2/gcd(poly1,poly2) **using the extended Euclidean algorithm.**

lcm(poly1,...,polyn) **returns the least common multiple of the specified polynomials.**

ispoly(expression,n,variable) **determines whether the expression is a polynomial of degree** n **in the specified variable.** n **can be replaced by** 'linear', 'quadratic', 'cubic' **or** 'quartic' **for** n = 1, 2, 3, 4, **respectively.**

ispoly(expression,n,name0,...,namen) **determines whether the expression is a polynomial of degree** n **in the specified variable and assigns the coefficient of degree** i **to** namei **for** i = 1... n.

norm(polynomial,n,variable) **calculates the** nth **norm of the polynomial, whose value is** $S\,(abs\,(c))^n$**, where** c = coeffs(polynomial,variable)$^{1/n}$.

norm(polynomial,n) **calculates the** nth **norm of the polynomial with respect to** indets(polynomial).

norm (poly,infinity,variable) **computes the infinity norm of the polynomial in the given variable (the coefficient of the polynomial with greatest absolute value).**

maxnorm(polynomial) **calculates the infinity norm of the fully expanded polynomial.**

readlib(maxorder): maxorder(RootOfexpression) **returns a basis for the field extension determined by the** RootOf **expression.**

readlib (maxorder): maxorder({RootOfexpression1,..., RootOfexpressionn}) **returns a basis for the field extension determined by the given set of** RootOf **expressions.**

minpoly(algebraicnum,n) **computes a polynomial of degree** n **or less with small integer coefficients; the given algebraic number is one of its roots.**

readlib(lattice): minpoly(algebraicnum,n,expression) **computes a polynomial of degree** n **or less with small integer coefficients such that the given algebraic number is one of its roots, up to an accuracy given by** expression.

Nextprime(polynomial,var) **the inert command that finds the irreducible polynomial in the variable** var, **which is the next highest with respect to the given polynomial.**

Nextprime(poly,var,ext) **the inert command that finds the irreducible polynomial in the variable** var, **over the algebraic extension defined by** expr, **which is the next highest with respect to the given polynomial.**

Nextprime(poly,var) mod n **the inert command that finds the irreducible polynomial in the variable** var, **modulo** n, **which is the next highest with respect to the given polynomial.**

Prevprime(polynomial,var) **the inert command that finds the irreducible polynomial in the variable** var **which is the next lowest with respect to the given polynomial.**

Prevprime(poly,var,ext) **the inert command that finds the irreducible polynomial in the variable** var **which is the next lowest with respect to the given polynomial over the algebraic extension defined by** expr.

Prevprime(poly,var) mod n **the inert command that finds the irreducible polynomial, modulo** n, **in the variable** var **which is the next lowest with respect to the given polynomial over the algebraic extension defined by** expr.

modpol(expr,poly,var,p) **evaluates the rational expression** expr **over Q in the variable** var **with respect to the quotient space** Zp[var]/poly(var), *where* p **is prime and** poly **is a polynomial in** var **over Q.**

Power(polynomial,n) **returns the nth inert power of the polynomial.**

Power(polynomial,n) mod m **returns the nth inert power of the polynomial modulo** m.

Powmod(poly1,n,poly2,var) **gives the inert remainder** Rem((poly1)n, poly2) **with respect to** var.

Powmod(poly1,n,poly2,var) mod n **gives the inert remainder** ((poly1)n, poly2)**with respect to** var **modulo** n.

prem(poly1,poly2,var) **returns the pseudo-remainder of the quotient of polynomials** poly1/poly2 **with respect to the variable** var.

prem(poly1,poly2,var,namen,nameq) **returns the value** rem **that satisfies the condition** namen * poly1 = poly2 * nameq + rem.

Prem(poly1, poly2,var) **gives the inert pseudo-remainder of the quotient of polynomials** poly1/poly2 **with respect to the variable** var.

Prem(poly1,poly2,var) mod n **gives the pseudo-remainder modulo** n **of the quotient of polynomials** poly1/poly2 **with respect to the variable** var.

sprem(poly1,poly2,var) **returns the sparse pseudo-remainder of the quotient of polynomials** poly1/poly2 **with respect to the variable** var.

sprem(poly1,poly2,var,namen,nameq) **returns the value** sprem **that fulfills the condition** namen* poly1 = poly2 * nameq + sprem.

Sprem(poly1,poly2,var) **gives the inert sparse pseudo-remainder of the quotient of polynomials** poly1/poly2 **with respect to the variable** var.

Sprem(poly1,poly2,var) mod n **gives the inert sparse pseudo-remainder of the quotient, modulo** n, **of polynomials** poly1/poly2 **with respect to the variable** var.

chrem([poly1,...,polyn],[m1,...,mn]) **finds the polynomial** p **such that** p mod mj = polyj j = 1... n.

primpart(polynomial,variable) **gives the primitive part of the polynomial in the given variable. The primitive part is the polynomial divided by the greatest common divisor of its coefficients.**

primpart(polynomial) **gives the primitive part of the polynomial with respect to all of its variables.**

primpart(polynomial,{var1,...,varn}) **or** primpart(polynomial,[var1,...,varn]) **gives the primitive part of the polynomial with respect to the specified variables.**

Primpart(polynomial,variable) **gives the primitive part of the polynomial in the variable given in inert form.**

Primpart(polynomial,variable) mod n **gives the primitive part of the polynomial in the given variable in inert form, modulo** n.

Primitive(polynomial) **determines whether the univariate polynomial is primitive.**

Primitive(polynomial) mod n **determines whether the univariate polynomial is primitive modulo** n.

Primfield({expr1,...,exprn}) **gives the inert form of the algebraic extension given by the** RootOf **expressions** expr1,...,exprn.

Primfield({expr1,...,expren}) mod n **gives the inert form, modulo** n, **of the algebraic extension given by the** RootOf **expressions** expr1,...,exprn.

Primfield(expr1,expr2) **gives the primitive element of the extension defined by the first set of** RootOf **expressions over the extension defined by the second set of** RootOf **expressions.**

randpoly(variable) **creates a univariate random polynomial of degree 6 in the specified variable.**

randpoly({variable1,...,variablen}) **or** randpoly([variable1,...,variablen]) **creates a multivariate random polynomial in the variables specified.**

randpoly(variable,coeffs=rand(a..b)) **creates a polynomial whose coefficients are random numbers between** a **and** b.

randpoly(variable,expons=rand(n)) **creates a polynomial whose exponents are random numbers between 0 and** n-1.

randpoly(variable,terms=n) **creates a random polynomial of** n **terms.**

randpoly(variable,dense) **creates a dense random polynomial.**

randpoly(variable,degree=n) **creates a dense random polynomial of degree** n. **In case of conflict,** degree **takes precedence over** terms.

Randpoly(n,variable) **creates an inert random polynomial of degree** n **in the given variable.**

Randpoly(n,variable) mod m **creates an inert random polynomial of degree** n **in the given variable, modulo** m.

Randprime(n,variable) **creates an inert random irreducible and monic polynomial of degree** n.

Randprime(n,variable) mod p **creates an irreducible and monic random polynomial of degree** n **modulo** *p* **(prime).**

Randprime(n,variable,expr) **creates a random irreducible monic polynomial of degree** *n* **over the algebraic extension defined by** expr.

readlib(ratrecon): ratrecon(poly1,poly2,variable,n1,n2,name1,name2) **assigns** name1 **and** name2 **such that** name1/name2 = poly1 mod poly2. **If the allocation can be made, the command returns true, and if it can't, it returns false. The limits of the assigned values are such that** degree(name1)≤*n1* **and** degree(name2) ≤*n2*.

readlib(iratrecon): iratrecon(m1,m2,n1,n2,name1,name2) **assigns** name1 **and** name2 **such that** name1/name2 = m1 mod m2 **with** abs(name1)<n1, abs(name2)<n2.

Ratrecon(poly1,poly2,variable,n1,n2,name1,name2) **assigns in inert form** name1 **and** name2 **such that** name1/name2 = poly1 mod poly2.

Ratrecon(poly1,poly2,variable,n1,n2,name1,name2) mod n **assigns, modulo** n, name1 **and** name2 **such that** name1/name2 = poly1 mod poly2.

readlib(recipoly):recipoly(polynomial,variable) **determines whether the polynomial is self-reciprocal.**

readlib(recipoly): recipoly(poly,var,name) **assigns the specified name to the polynomial** p **of degree** degree(poly,var)/2 **that meets the condition** var ^ (degree(poly,var)/2) * p(var+1/var) = poly.

readlib(translate): translate(polynomial,variable,number) **translates the polynomial into the polynomial in the new variable given by** variable+number.

ztrans(expr,var1,var2) **finds the z-transform of** expr(var1) **with respect to** var2.

readlib(ztrans): invztrans(expression,var1,var2) **returns the inverse z-transform of the expression given in the old variable** var1, **with the result being an expression based on the new variable** var2.

Eval(poly,var=exp) **evaluates in inert form the polynomial with the given variable replaced by** expr.

Eval(poly,var=exp) mod n **evaluates the polynomial with the given variable replaced by** expr **modulo** n.

Eval(polynomial,{varible1=expr1,...,variablen=exprn}) **evaluates in inert form the polynomial with the given variables replaced by** expr1,...,exprn.

grading(Fnc(expr1,...,exprn)) **evaluates the inert command or function** Fnc, **whose parameters are the given expressions, over the minimal algebraic closure of the field defined by their coefficients. This applies to inert commands such as** Factor, Factors, Afactor, Afactors, Norm, Content, Gcd, Gcdex, Prem, Primfield, Quo, Rem, Resultant, Sprem, Sqrfree, independence, **and so on.**

readlib(evalgf):evalgf(Fnc(expr1,...,exprn),n) **evaluates the inert command or function** Fnc, **whose parameters are the specified expressions, over the minimal algebraic extension of the finite field** Zn.

Here are some examples. First, we find the discriminant of the polynomial $ax^2 + bx$:

```
>> pretty(sym(maple('p := a*x^2 + b*x + c: discrim(p,x)')))
```

$$-4\, c + b^2$$

Now we calculate the resultant of several polynomials:

```
>> pretty(sym(maple('resultant(a*x+b,c*x+d,x),    resultant((x+a)^5,(x+b)^5,x)')))
```

$$-c\, b + d\, a, \quad (-a + b)^{25}$$

```
>> pretty(sym(maple('Resultant(2*x+1, 3*x+4, x) mod 7')))
```

$$5$$

```
>> pretty(sym(maple('r := x + RootOf(_Z^2-2): s := RootOf(_Z^2-2)*x + 1:
   evala(Resultant(r,s,x))')))
```

$$-1$$

Next we check divisibility among polynomials, and in the positive case, find the ratios:

```
>> pretty(sym(maple('divide(x^3-y^3, x-y, q),q')))
```

$$\text{true,} \quad x^2 + x\,y + y^2$$

```
>> pretty(sym(maple('Divide(x^3+x^2+2*x+3,x+2,q) mod 5,q')))
```

$$\text{true,} \quad x^2 + 4\,x + 4$$

Next we find quotients and remainders of division between polynomials:

```
>> pretty(sym(maple('rem(x^3+x+1, x^2+x+1, x, q), q')))
```
$$x + 2, \ x - 1$$

```
>> pretty(sym(maple('quo(x^3+x+1, x^2+x+1, x) ')))
```
$$x - 1$$

```
>> pretty(sym(maple('a := x^4+5*x^3+6: b := x^2+2*x+7: r := Rem(a,b,x,q) mod 13, q')))
>> maple r
```

ans =

5*x+6, x^2+3*x

EXERCISE 3-13

Find the greatest common divisor and least common multiple of the polynomials $x^2 - y^2$ and $x^3 - y^3$, and also the polynomials $x+2$ and $x+3$ modulo 7. Find the greatest common divisor for each of the sets of polynomials $\{x^3 - 1, x^2 - 1\}$ and $\{x^2 + x + 1, x^2 - x + 1\}$, identifying the elements of Euclid's algorithm. Also find the greatest common divisor modulo 11 of the polynomials $x^2 + 3x + 2$ and $x^2 + 4x + 3$, identifying the elements of Euclid's algorithm.

```
>> pretty(sym(maple('gcd(x^2-y^2,x^3-y^3),lcm(x^2-y^2,x^3-y^3)')))
```

$$-y + x, \quad x^4 - x^3 y + y^3 x - y^4$$

```
>> pretty(sym(maple('gcd(x+2,x+3) mod 7, lcm(x+2,x+3) mod 7')))
```

$$1, \quad x^2 + 5x + 6$$

```
>> pretty(sym(maple('gcdex(x^3-1,x^2-1,x,s,t),s,t')))
```

$$x - 1, \quad 1, \quad -x$$

```
>> pretty(sym(maple('gcdex(x^2+x+1,x^2-x+1,x,u,v),u,v')))
```

$$1, \quad 1/2 - 1/2 x, \quad 1/2 + 1/2 x$$

```
>> pretty(sym(maple('Gcd(x^2+3*x+2,x^2+4*x+3,f,g) mod 11, f, g')))
```

$$1 + x, \quad x + 2, \quad x + 3$$

EXERCISE 3-14

Find the 1, 2 and infinity norms of the polynomial x-3y. Also find the third and fourth powers of the polynomial x + 1 modulo 2.

```
>> pretty(sym(maple('norm(x-3*y,1),norm(x-3*y,2),norm(x-3*y,infinity)')))
```

$$4, \quad 10^{1/2}, \quad 3$$

```
>> pretty(sym(maple('Power(x+1,3) mod 2, Power(x+1,4) mod 2')))
```

$$x^3 + x^2 + x + 1, \quad x^4 + 1$$

EXERCISE 3-15

Find the polynomials r, m and q in the variable x such that

$m(x^4 + 1) = q(cx^4 + 1) + r$.

There are two solutions to the problem; one via the pseudo-remainder between the polynomial $x^4 + 1$ and $cx^2 + 1$, and the other via the sparse pseudo-remainder between those polynomials.

```
>> pretty(sym(maple('a := x^4+1: b := c*x^2+1: r := prem(a,b,x,m,q)')))
>> pretty(sym(maple('r,m,q')))
```

$$c^2(c^2 + 1), \quad c^3, \quad x^2c^2 - c$$

```
>> maple('restart') ;
>> pretty(sym(maple('a := x^4+1: b := c*x^2+1: r := sprem(a,b,x,m,q)')))
>> pretty(sym(maple('r,m,q')))
```

$$c^2 + 1, \quad c^2, \quad cx^2 - 1$$

EXERCISE 3-16

Find the primitive part of the polynomial $4xy + 6y^2$ and $x/a-1/2$ in the variable x. Also find the primitive part of the polynomial $x(y+4) + y^2 + 4$ in the variable x modulo 5.

```
>> maple ('restart')
>> pretty(sym(maple('primpart(-4*x*y + 6*y^2, x), primpart(x/a - 1/2,x)')))
```

$$3, - 2 x, 2 x - a$$

```
>> pretty(sym(maple('Primpart(x * (y+4) + y ^ 2 + 4 x) mod 5')))
```

$$x + y + 1$$

EXERCISE 3-17

Perform the following tasks concerning random polynomials:

Create a random polynomial in x of 6 terms.

Create a random 20 term polynomial in the variables x and y.

Create a random polynomial in x, cos(x) and sin(x).

Create a polynomial with random coefficients between 1 and 100.

Create a polynomial with random exponents between -5 and 5.

```
>> pretty(sym(maple('randpoly(x)')))
```

$$-85 x^5 - 55 x^4 - 37 x^3 - 35 x^2 + 97 x + 50$$

```
>> pretty(sym(maple('randpoly([x, y], terms = 20)')))
```

$$56 + 49 x + 63 y + 57 x y - 59 x^2 y + 45 x^5 - 8 x^4 - 93 x^3 + 92 x^2$$
$$+ 43 y^3 - 62 x y^2 + 77 x^3 y + 66 x^2 y^2 + 54 x y^3 - 5 x^4 y$$
$$+ 99 x^3 y^2 - 61 x^2 y^3 - 50 x y^4 - 12 y^4 - 18 y^5$$

```
>> pretty(sym(maple('randpoly([x, sin(x), cos(x)])')))
```

$$-47\ x\ -\ 61\ x\ \cos(x)\ +\ 41\ x\ \sin(x)\ \cos(x)\ -\ 58\ x\ \cos(x)^2$$

$$-\ 90\ \sin(x)\ \cos(x)^3\ +\ 53\ \sin(x)^3\ \cos(x)^2$$

```
>> pretty(sym(maple('randpoly(x,coeffs=rand(1..100))')))
```

$$82\ x^5\ +\ 71\ x^4\ +\ 98\ x^3\ +\ 64\ x^2\ +\ 77\ x\ +\ 39$$

```
>> pretty(sym(maple('randpoly(z,expons = rand(-5..5))')))
```

$$\frac{82}{Z^5}\ +\ \frac{23}{z}\ +\ 104\ z^5\ +\ 88\ z$$

EXERCISE 3-18

Change the variable x of the polynomial x^2 to the variable x + 1. Make the change of variable $x = r^{1/3}$ in the expression $3x\ln(x^3)$ and also the change of variable sin(x) = y in the expression $\sin(x) / (1-\sin(x))^{1/2}$.

The first change of variable is a simple translation of a polynomial variable, so it will be done via the command translate, but the other two changes involve general algebraic expressions, so we will use the command subs as described in the previous chapter.

```
>> pretty(sym(maple('readlib(translate):translate(x^2,x,1)')))
```

$$1\ +\ 2\ x\ +\ x^2$$

```
>> pretty(sym(maple('subs(x=r^(1/3), 3*x*log(x^3))')))
```

$$3\ r^{1/3}\ \log(r)$$

```
>> pretty (sym (maple ('subs (y = sin (x),sin (x) / (1 - sin (x)) ^(1/2))')))
```

$$\frac{y}{(1 - y)^{1/2}}$$

EXERCISE 3-19

Find the reciprocal polynomial of the polynomial $x^4 + x^3 + x + 1$. Also calculate the resultant of the polynomial and its reciprocal.

```
>> pretty(sym(maple('readlib(recipoly):recipoly(x^4+x^3+x+1,x,'p'),p')))
```

$$true, \quad -2 + x + x^2$$

```
>> pretty(sym(maple('resultant(x^4+x^3+x+1,x^2+x-2,x)')))
```

$$28$$

3-8. Interpolation and Polynomial Fitting

MATLAB provides several commands for polynomial interpolation and fitting that we will study next:

polyfit(x,y,n) **gives the vector of coefficients of the polynomial** p(x) **of degree** n **in** x **which best fits the data** (xi,yi) **in the least-squares sense (**p(xi) = yi**).**

Yi = interp1(X,Y,Xi,'method') **gives the vector** Yi **such that** (Xi,Yi) **is the total set of points found by interpolation between the given points** (X, Y)**. The option** method **can take the values** linear, spline, **or** cubic, **depending on whether the interpolation is linear (the default option), staggered, or cubic (for** xi **uniformly separated). One-dimensional interpolation.**

Zi = interp2(X,Y,Z,Xi,Yi,'method') **gives the vector** Zi **such that** (Xi,Yi,Zi) **is the total set of points found by interpolation between the given points** (X,Y,Z)**. The option** method **can take the value** linear **or** cubic, **depending on whether the interpolation is linear (the default) or cubic (for** xi **uniformly separated). Two-dimensional interpolation.**

`Zi = griddata(X,Y,Z,Xi,Yi)` **gives the vector** `Zi` **that determines the interpolation points** (`Xi,Yi, Zi`) **between the given points** (X, Y, Z). **A method of inverse distance is used to interpolate.**

`Y = interpft(X,n)` **gives the vector** Y **containing the values of the periodic function** X **sampled at** n **equally spaced points. The original vector** x **is transformed to the domain of Fourier transform frequencies using the Fast Fourier transform (FFT) algorithm. It satisfies** n≥length(X).

`maple('interp([exprx1,...,exprxn+1],[expry1,...,expryn+1],var)')` **returns a polynomial in the specified variable of degree at least** n **that represents the interpolated polynomial for points from** [exprx1,expry1] **to** [exprxn+1,expryn+1]. **The coordinates of the points must all be different.**

`maple('Interp([exprx1,...,exprxn+1], [expry1,...,expryn+1], variable)')` **returns in inert mode a polynomial in the specified variable of degree at least** n **that represents the interpolated polynomial for points from** [exprx1, expry1] **to** [exprxn+1,expryn+1]. **The coordinates of the points must all be different.**

`maple('Interp([exprx1,...,exprxn+1], [expry1,...,expryn+1], variable) mod m')` **returns a polynomial modulo** m **in the specified variable of degree at least** n **that represents the interpolated polynomial for points from** [exprx1, expry1] **to** [exprxn+1,expryn+1]. **The coordinates of the points must all be different.**

`maple('readlib(thiele): thiele([exprx1,...,exprxn],[expry1,...,expryn],variable)')` **finds an expression in the given variable that represents the entire function resulting in Thiele interpolation points** (exprxi,expryi) i = 1... n.

EXERCISE 3-20

Calculate the interpolated degree 2 polynomial passing through the points (- 1,4), (0,2) and (1,6) which is the best fit in the least-squares sense.

```
>> x=[-1,0,1];y=[4,2,6];p=poly2sym(polyfit(x,y,2))
```

```
p =

3 * x ^ 2 + x + 2
```

EXERCISE 3-21

Represent 200 points of cubic interpolation between the points (x,y) given by the values that the exponential function e ^ x takes at 20 equally spaced x values between 0 and 2. Also represent the difference between the function e ^ x and its approximation by interpolation. Use cubic interpolation.

First, we define the 20 given points *(x, y)*, for x values equally spaced between 0 and 2:

```
>> x = 0:0.1:2;
>> y = exp(x);
```

Now we find 200 points *(xi, yi)* using cubic interpolation, equally spaced between 0 and 2, and plot them on a graph, together with the 20 initial points *(x, y)* (indicated by asterisks). See Figure 3-1:

```
>> xi = 0:0.01:2;
>> yi = interp1(x,y,xi,'cubic');
>> plot(x,y,'*',xi,yi)
```

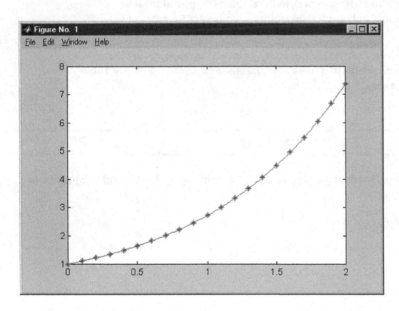

Figure 3-1.

We now graphically represent the difference between the exact function $y = e$ ^ x and the function obtained by the above interpolation. In the case of zero error, the graph would be a horizontal line coinciding with the x axis. See Figure 3-2.

```
>> zi=(exp(xi));
>> di=yi-zi;
>> plot(xi,di)
```

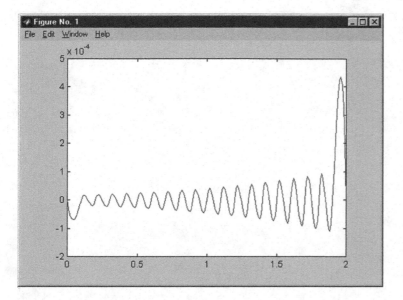

Figure 3-2.

<hr>

EXERCISE 3-22

Find 25 interpolation points of the parametric function X = cos(t), Y = sin(t), Z = tan(t) for values of t between 0 and π/6, based on the set of points defined for values of t = iπ/6 with 0 ≤ i ≤ 6.

First, we define the 25 given points *(x, y, z)*, equally spaced between 0 and π/6.

```
>> t = 0: pi/150: pi/6;
>> x = cos (t); y = sin (t); z = tan (t);
```

Now we find the 25 points of interpolation *(xi, yi, zi)*, for values of the parameter *t* equally spaced between 0 and π/6.

```
>> xi = cos (t); yi = sin (t);
>> zi = griddata(x,y,z,xi,yi);
>> points = [xi, yi, zi']
```

```
points =

    1.0000 0       0.0000
    0.9998 0.0209 0.0161
    0.9991 0.0419 0.0367
    0.9980 0.0628 0.0598
    0.9965 0.0837 0.0836
    0.9945 0.1045 0.1057
    0.9921 0.1253 0.1269
    0.9893 0.1461 0.1480
    0.9860 0.1668 0.1692
    0.9823 0.1874 0.1907
    0.9781 0.2079 0.2124
    0.9736 0.2284 0.2344
    0.9686 0.2487 0.2567
    0.9632 0.2689 0.2792
    0.9573 0.2890 0.3019
    0.9511 0.3090 0.3249
    0.9444 0.3289 0.3483
    0.9373 0.3486 0.3719
    0.9298 0.3681 0.3959
    0.9219 0.3875 0.4203
    0.9135 0.4067 0.4452
    0.9048 0.4258 0.4706
    0.8957 0.4446 0.4969
    0.8862 0.4633 0.5236
    0.8763 0.4818 0.5505
    0.8660 0.5000 0.5774
```

EXERCISE 3-23

Find 30 interpolation points (xi, yi) for the periodic function y = sin(x) for values of x that are equally spaced, interpolating them between values of (x, y) given by y = sin(x) for 20 x values evenly spaced in the interval (0,2π), and using the interpolation method based on the fast Fourier transform (FFT).

First, we define the 20 x values equally spaced between 0 and 2π:

```
>> x =(0:pi/10:2*pi);
```

Now we find the 30 interpolation points *(x, y)*.

```
>> y = interpft(sin(x), 30);
>> points = [y', (asin(y))']
```

```
points =

    0.0000  0.0000
    0.1878  0.1890
    0.4499  0.4667
    0.6070  0.6522
    0.7614  0.8654
    0.9042  1.1295
    0.9618  1.2935
    0.9963  1.4848
    0.9913  1.4388
    0.9106  1.1448
    0.8090  0.9425
    0.6678  0.7312
    0.4744  0.4943
    0.2813  0.2852
    0.0672  0.0673
   -0.1640 - 0.1647
   -0.3636 - 0.3722
   -0.5597 - 0.5940
   -0.7367 - 0.8282
   -0.8538 - 1.0233
   -0.9511 - 1.2566
   -1.0035 - 1.5708 - 0. 0837i
   -0.9818 - 1.3799
   -0.9446 - 1.2365
   -0.8526 - 1.0210
   -0.6902 - 0.7617
   -0.5484 - 0.5805
   -0.3478 - 0.3553
   -0.0807 - 0.0808
    0.0086   0.0086
```

EXERCISE 3-24

Find the degree 3 polynomial that best fits the set of points (i, i^2) for $1 \leq i \leq 7$, in the least-squares sense. Find the value of the polynomial at $x = 10$ and graphically represent the fitted curve.

```
>> x=(1:7);y=[1,4,9,16,25,36,49];p=poly2sym(polyfit(x,y,2))
```

```
p =

4503599627370495/4503599627370496 * x ^ 2 +
310800181380337/79228162514264337593543950336 * x-
3598276744230861/316912650057057350374175801344
```

Now we calculate the numerical value of the polynomial p at $x = 10$.

```
>> numeric(subs(p,10))
```

```
ans =

   100
```

We can also approximate the coefficients of the polynomial p to 5 digits.

```
>> vpa(p,5)
```

```
ans =

1.00000 * x ^ 2 + 3 9228e-15 * x-1. 1354e-14
```

Figure 3-3 shows the graph of the fitted curve.

```
>> ezplot(p,[-5,5])
```

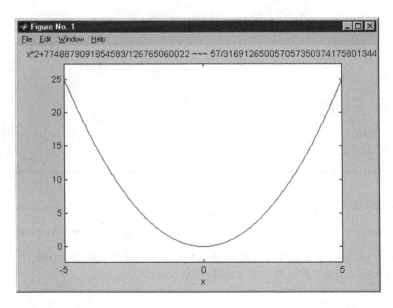

Figure 3-3.

EXERCISE 3-25

Find the interpolated degree 2 polynomial passing through the points (-1,4), (0,2) and (1,6). Find the interpolated polynomial modulo 3 and, finally, perform Thiele interpolation for this case.

```
>> interp([-1,0,1],[4,2,6],x);
```

$$3 x^2 + x + 2$$

```
>> Interp([-1,0,1],[4,2,6],x) mod 3;
```

$$x + 2$$

```
>> readlib(thiele):thiele([-1,0,1],[4,2,6],x);
```

$$4 + \frac{x + 1}{- 1/2 + 3/2\, x}$$

3-9. Galois Extensions

The Maple program has commands which enable you to work with the Galois theory of finite fields and their extensions. The syntax of these commands is as follows:

maple('galois(polynomial)') **returns the Galois group of the given rational univariate irreducible polynomial of degree less than or equal to 8. It returns a list of three expressions: the first is the name of the Galois group and includes a plus sign (+) as the first character if the group is even and (-) if it is odd; the second is an integer representing the order of the group, and the third is a set of strings representing the group generators.**

maple('readlib(GF):GF(p,n,polynomial)') **returns a module of procedures and constants for working in the finite Galois field with p^n elements defined by the field extension GF(p)[x]/polynomial. The polynomial is irreducible of degree n modulo p (prime p). Once this has been done one can make use of the operator T to implement various operations in the Galois field.**

T[input] and T[output] convert between an integer in the range 1.. p^n and its corresponding polynomial in the Galois field. Alternatively T[ConvertIn] and T[ConvertOut] convert an element of the Galois field to a Maple sum of products. T['+'], T['-'], T['*'], T['^'], T['inverse'] and T['/'] execute the specified operations in the Galois field. T[random] returns a random element of the Galois field. T[0] and T[1] represent the additive and multiplicative inverse, respectively. T[trace], T[norm] and T[order] compute the trace, norm and order for elements of the Galois field. T[PrimitiveElement] returns a primitive element of the Galois field. T[isPrimitiveElement] determines whether an element is primitive. T[extension] returns the polynomial extension used for the Galois field.

EXERCISE 3-26

Find the Galois group for each of the univariate polynomials $x^4 + x + 1$, $t^5 - 5t + 12$, $x^5 + 2$ and $x^7 + 4x^5 - 3x^2 + 5$.

First, we check if the polynomials are irreducible; if so, we will calculate the Galois groups.

```
>> pretty(sym(maple('irreduc(x^4+x+1),irreduc(t^5-5*t+12),irreduc(x^5+2),
   irreduc(x^7+4*x^5- 3*x^2+5)')))
```

                    true, true, true, true

```
>> pretty(sym(maple('galois(x^4+x+1)')))
```

                S4, 24, {(1 2 3 4), (1 2)}

```
>> pretty(sym(maple('galois(t^5-5*t+12)')))
```

            +D5, 10, {(1 2 3 4 5), (2 5)(3 4)}

```
>> pretty(sym(maple('galois(x^5+2)')))
```

            F20, 20, {(1 2 3 4 5), (2 3 5 4)}

```
>> pretty(sym(maple('galois(x^7+4*x^5-3*x^2+5)')))
```

            S7, 5040, {(1 2 3 4 5 6 7), (1 2)}

EXERCISE 3-27

Consider the polynomial q = $\alpha^4 + \alpha + 1$. Verify that it is irreducible over the integers and over the integers modulo 2. Consider the finite Galois field GF(2^4) and the Galois extension GF(2)[x]/(q). Perform the operations 3 + 4, 3 * 4 and 34 in this field. Convert the integer 12∈ [0,2^4- 1] to the corresponding element in the finite Galois field GF(2^4), and then do the reverse conversion. Convert the polynomial α to a Maple sum of products 'a' in the finite Galois field GF(2^4). Calculate α^2 and α^4 and check if a is a primitive element in GF(2^4). Find the corresponding value of x =a^8 in the interval [0,2^4- 1] and its polynomial form in the Galois extension.

```
>> pretty(sym(maple('irreduc(alpha^4+alpha+1)')))
```

true

```
>> pretty(sym(maple('Irreduc(alpha^4+alpha+1) mod 2')))
```

true

```
>> pretty(sym(maple('readlib(GF):')))
>> pretty(sym(maple('G16 := GF(2,4,alpha^4+alpha+1):')))
>> pretty(sym(maple('G16[`+`](3,4),   G16[`*`](3,4),   G16[`^`](3,4)')))
```

5,   4,   3

```
>> pretty(sym(maple('G16[input](12)')))
```

1000100000000

```
>> pretty(sym(maple('G16[output](")')))
```

12

```
>> pretty(sym(maple('a := G16[ConvertIn](alpha)')))
>> pretty(sym(maple('a')))
```

10000

```
>> pretty(sym(maple('G16[`*`](a,a),   G16[`^`](a,4)')))
```

100000000,   10001

```
>> pretty(sym(maple('G16[isPrimitiveElement](a)')))
```

---

                              true

```
>> pretty(sym(maple('x := G16[`^`](a,8)')))
>> pretty(sym(maple('x')))
```

                          100000001

```
>> pretty(sym(maple('G16[output](x)')))
```

                              5

```
>> pretty(sym(maple('G16[ConvertOut](x)')))
```

                              2
                          Alpha + 1

EXERCISE 3-28

Consider the polynomial q = $b^5 + 7b^4 + b^2 + b+1$. Check that it is irreducible over the integers and over the integers modulo three. Consider the finite Galois field GF(3^5) and the Galois extension GF(3)[x]/(q). Calculate the product (b^5+ 1)(b^3+ b^2+ 1) in the Galois extension and calculate its inverse.

First, we check that the polynomial is irreducible over the integers and over the integers modulo 3.

```
>> pretty(sym(maple('irreduc(b^5+7*b^4+b^2+b+1),irreduc(b^5+7*b^4+ b^2+b+1) mod 3')))
```

---

                          true, true

Then we transform the given polynomial to its corresponding value in the Galois field *GF(3^5)* and find the stated product in this field.

```
>> pretty(sym(maple('readlib(GF):')))
>> pretty(sym(maple('G243 := GF(3,5,b^5+7*b^4+b^2+b+1):')))
>> pretty(sym(maple('a1:=G243[ConvertIn](b^5+1)')))
>> pretty(sym(maple('a1')))
```

                      20000000200020000

```
>> pretty(sym(maple('a2:=G243[ConvertIn](b^3+b^2+1)')))
>> pretty(sym(maple('a2')))
```

                        1000100000001

```
>> pretty(sym(maple('prod1:=G243[`*`](a1,a2)')))
>> pretty(sym(maple('prod1')))
```

                    20000000100000001

Finally, we convert the value to its corresponding value in the extension *GF(3)[x]/(q)*.

```
>> pretty(sym(maple('prod2:=G243[ConvertOut](prod1)')))
>> pretty(sym(maple('prod2')))
```

$$2 b^4 + b^2 + 1$$

To find the inverse of the product, we first convert it to the corresponding element in the Galois field *GF(3⁵)*. After finding the inverse we find the corresponding element in the extension *GF(3)[x]/(q)*.

```
>> pretty(sym(maple('inv1:=G243[inverse](prod1)')))
>> pretty(sym(maple('inv1')))
```

                    20000000200010001

```
>> pretty(sym(maple('G243[`*`](prod1,inv1)')))
```

                        1

```
>> pretty(sym(maple('inv2:=G243[ConvertOut](inv1)')))
>> pretty(sym(maple('inv2')))
```

$$2 b^4 + 2 b^2 + b + 1$$

3-10. Gröbner Bases

Gröbner bases are used in the solution and analysis of solutions of systems of polynomial equations. The related MATLAB commands are as follows:

maple('with(groebner)') **loads into memory the MATLAB package that contains commands for working with Gröbner bases.**

maple('finduni(variable,[polynomial1,...,polynomin],[var1,...,varn])') **finds the univariate polynomial in the given variable of least degree in the ideal generated by the specified set of polynomials for the given variables.**

maple('finduni(variable,[variable],[poly1,...,polym])') **constructs the Gröbner basis for the given polynomials in all of their variables.**

maple('finite([polynomial1,...,polynomialm],[variable1,...,variablen])') **determines whether the specified set of polynomials has a finite number of solutions for the set of specified variables. If the answer is** True, **one can apply the command** finduni.

maple('finite([poly1,..,polyn])') **determines whether the specified set of polynomials has a finite number of solutions with regard to all its variables.**

maple('solvable([poly1,...,polym],[var1,...,varn])') **determines whether the given system of polynomials is solvable (algebraically consistent) with respect to the given set of variables.**

maple('solvable([poly1,...,polym])') **determines whether the given system of polynomials is solvable with respect to all of its variables.**

maple('solvable([poly1,...,polym,],[var1,...,varn],tdeg)') **determines whether the given system of polynomials is solvable with respect to the set of variables using total degree.**

maple('gsolve([poly1,..., polym])') **or** maple('gsolve({poly1,...,polym})')) **gives a reduced Gröbner basis for the given set of polynomials with respect to all of the variables. Returns a list of lists where each list is a small subsystem of polynomials identical to the original system roots. It can be applied to each reduced basis** solve. **Essentially,** gsolve **prepares the algebraic system for solution.**

maple('gsolve([poly1,...,polym],{polyr1,...,polyrn})') **prevents the roots of the second set of polynomials from being considered in the computation of Gröbner bases.**

maple('gsolve([poly1,...,polyn],[var1,...,varn],{polyr1,...,polyrn})') **specifies that the presentation of the specified variables will be used in the computation of Gröbner bases.**

maple('gbasis([poly1,...,polym],[var1,...,varn])') **returns a minimal reduced Gröbner basis for the specified polynomials in the given variables. The result is a list of polynomials.**

maple('gbasis([poly1,...,polym],[var1,...,varn],plex)') **gives a Gröbner basis in which the polynomial terms are sorted lexicographically.**

maple('gbasis([poly1,...,polym],[var1,...,varn],tdeg)') **gives a Gröbner basis in which the polynomial terms are arranged by total degree.**

maple('normalf(polynomial,[poly1,...,polym],[var1,...,varn])') **gives the full reduced form of the given polynomial with respect to the Gröbner basis represented by the given polynomials in the specified variables. You can use the** plex **option to sort the results into lexicographic order.**

maple('leadmon(polynomial,[var1,...,varn])') **returns the leading monomial of the given polynomial with respect to the specified variables. It produces a list of two elements. The first element is the coefficient of the monomial and the second is the rest of the monomial. You can use the** Plex **option to sort the results into lexicographic order.**

maple('spoly(poly1,poly2,[var1,...,varn])') **returns the s-polynomial of** poly1 **and** poly2 **with respect to the given variables.**

EXERCISE 3-29

Consider the following system of three polynomials: $x^2 - 2xz + 5$, $xy^2 + yz^3$, $3y^2 - 8z^3$. Test whether the system is solvable with respect to its three variables and has a finite number of solutions. Find a Gröbner basis for such a system and from that try to solve it. Also find a minimal reduced Gröbner basis in lexicographical order and total order.

First, we try to solve the system directly, but we find that this is not possible; only an approximate solution can be found.

```
>> pretty(sym(maple('solve({x^2-2*x*z+5=0,x*y^2+y*z^3=0,3*y^2-8*z^3=0})')))
```

```
                2
{x = RootOf(_Z + 5), y = 0, z = 0}, {}
                     2        5        4
    x = - 3/4 %1 - 9/20% 1 + 12/5% 1,

                2        2      3
    y = 2/5 %1 (- 16% 1 + 3% 1 + 5), z = 2 %1}

                   3        5        6
%1: = RootOf(30 _Z + 25-48 _Z + 9 _Z)
```

```
>> pretty(sym(maple('allvalues({x^22*x*z+5=0,x*y^2+y*z^3=0,3*y^28*z^3=0})')))
```

```
         2                   2   3       2   3
    { x - 2 z x + 5 = 0, x y + y z = 0, 3 y - 8 z = 0}
```

Now we confirm that the system is solvable with a finite number of solutions.

```
>> pretty(sym(maple('with(grobner):F:=[x^2-2*x*z+5,x*y^2+y*z^3,3*y^2-8*z^3]: ')))
>> pretty(sym(maple('solvable(F);  finite(F)')))
```

$$\text{true, true}$$

Then we find a Gröbner basis for the system with the command gsolve, and subsequently try to solve it with the command solve.

```
>> pretty(sym(maple('gsolve(F)')))
```

$$[[y, z, x^2 + 5], [80\, y^5 - 3\, z^4 + 32\, z^2 - 40\, z^2,$$

$$-96\, z^4 + 640\, x^5 + 9\, z^2 + 120\, z^3, 240\, z^3 + 1600 - 96\, z^5 + 9\, z^6]]$$

A solution of the system could be obtained with solve in the following way:

```
>> pretty(sym(maple('solve({y=0, z=0, x^2 + 5=0})')))
```

$$\{x = \text{RootOf}(\_Z^2 + 5), y = 0, z = 0\}$$

```
>> pretty(sym(maple('allvalues(")')))
```

$$\{y = 0, x = I\, 5^{1/2}, z = 0\}, \{y = 0, x = -I\, 5^{1/2}, z = 0\}$$

The rest of the solutions can be found as follows:

```
>> pretty(sym(maple('solve({80*y-3*z^5+32*z^4-40*z^2=0, 96 * z ^ 4 + 640 * x + 9 * z ^ 5 +
   120 * z ^ 2 = 0, 240 * z ^ 3 + 1600-96 * z ^ 5 + 9 * z ^ 6 = 0}) ')))
```

$$\{y = 2/5\, \%1^2\, (-16\, \%1^2 + 3\, \%1^3 + 5), z = 2\, \%1,$$

$$x = -\, 3/20\, \%1^2\, (-16\, \%1^2 + 3\, \%1^3 + 5)\}$$

$$\%1 := \text{RootOf}(30\, \_Z^3 + 25 - 48\, \_Z^5 + 9\, \_Z^6)$$

```
>> pretty(sym(maple('allvalues(")')))
```

```
{x = -.9186354143 + 1.100517108 I, y = 2.449694438 - 2.934712287 I,

   z = -1.576863306 - .7885511972 I},

  {x = -.9186354143 - 1.100517108 I, y = 2.449694438 + 2.934712287 I,

   z = -1.576863306 + .7885511972 I},

  {x = .2580043290 + 1.169756595 I, y = -.6880115440 - 3.119350920 I,

   z = .5785194088 - 1.453171854 I},

  {x = .2580043290 - 1.169756595 I, y = -.6880115440 + 3.119350920 I,

   z = .5785194088 + 1.453171854 I},

  {x = 2.058161202, y = -5.488429872, z = 2.243757078},

  {z = 10.41959738, x = 20.59643412, y = -54.92382432}
```

Then we find a minimal reduced Gröbner basis, first in lexicographical order and then in order of total degree.

```
>> pretty(sym(maple('gbasis(F,[y,x,z],plex)')))
```

```
     2       3        3      8      7      5   2
[3 y  - 8 z , 80 y z  - 3 z  + 32 z  - 40 z , x  - 2 x z + 5,

        7     8       5        3
   -96 z  + 9 z  + 120 z  + 640 z  x,

        6         3      8      9
   240 z  + 1600 z  - 96 z  + 9 z  ]
```

```
>> pretty(sym(maple('gbasis(F,[x,y,z],tdeg) ')))
```

```
  2                    2      3       2      3      4        3       2
[x  - 2 x z + 5, -3 y  + 8 z , 8 x y  + 3 y , 9 y  + 48 z y  + 320 y  ]
```

3-11. The mod Operator: Modular Operations with Polynomials

The operator mod evaluates an expression modulo m for a non-zero natural number m. MATLAB uses two representations for an integer modulo m. The positive mod m representation is an integer between 0 and m-1. The symmetric mod m representation is an integer between -floor((abs(m)-1)/2) and floor(abs(m)/2). The first operand of the mod operator generally tends to be an expression that will be evaluated by MATLAB over the ring of integers modulo n. For polynomials, MATLAB reduces the coefficients modulo m. When the first operand is a power, MATLAB uses the inert representation of the power, for example, i & ^ j mod m is calculated as i^j mod m. Among the commands that use the mod operator with polynomials are, in addition to those we've already seen, the following (all require the prior use of the maple command):

'mod'(expr,m) **is equivalent to** expr mod m (expr **can be a polynomial).**

modp1(Fnc(expr1,...,exprn),m) (m **is a positive integer) uses efficient arithmetic methods to calculate the inert command or function** Fnc **modulo** m. **The** n **given expressions are univariate polynomials expressed in** modp1 **format. To express any standard polynomial in the form** modp1 **modulo** m **it is necessary to use the command** modp1(convertIn). **Here** modp1 **refers to univariate polynomials with the operator** mod **in its positive representation.**

modp1(Add(polyp11,...,polyp1n),m) **adds polynomials in the form** modp1.

modp1(Coeff(polyp1,n),m) **returns the coefficient of** x^n **of the polynomial, in the form** modp1.

modp1(Degree(polyp1),m) **returns the degree of the polynomial, in the form** modp1.

modp1(Det(M),m) **returns the determinant of the matrix** M **whose elements are polynomials, in the form** modp1.

modp1(Gausselimin(M),m) **applies Gauss elimination to the matrix** M **whose elements are polynomials, in the form** modp1.

modp1(Gaussjord(M),m) **returns the reduced Gauss-Jordan form for the matrix** M **whose elements are polynomials, in the form** modp1.

modp1(Lcoeff(polyp1),m) **returns the leading coefficient of the polynomial** polyp1 **in the form** modp1.

modp1(Lcm(polyp1,polyp2),m) **finds the least common multiple of the polynomials** polyp1 **and** polyp2, **in the form** modp1.

modp1(Subtract(polyp1,polyp2),m) **finds the difference** polyp1-polyp2 **of the given polynomials , in the form** modp1.

modp1(Multiply(polyp1,poly2),m) **finds the product** polyp1*polyp2 **of the polynomials in the form** modp1.

modp1(Ldegree(polyp1),m) **returns the smallest degree of the polynomial** polyp1 **in** modp1 **form.**

modp1(Power(polyp1,n),m) **returns the** n **th power of the polynomial** polyp1 **in the form** modp1. **With** modp1 **you can also use inert commands such as** Tcoeff, Chrem, Diff, divided, Embedded, Eval, Factors, Gcd, Gcdex, Interp, Irreduc, Powmod, Prem, Quo, Rem, spot, Root, Smith, Sgrfr, Vnormal, **and so on.**

`modp1(ConvertIn(polynomial,variable),m)` **converts the given univariate polynomial with integer coefficients in the given variable to the format** `modp1` **modulo** `m`. **This operation takes precedence over any of the operating commands** `modp1`. **Any polynomial that is an argument of any operational function** `modp1` **should be previously transformed with** `modp1(ConvertIn)`.

`modp1(ConvertOut(polynomial1,variable),m)` **converts the specified polynomial in the form** `modp1` **to standard format.**

`modp1(ConvertOut(poly1),m)` **gives the list of coefficients of the polynomial converted to standard format.**

`modp1(Constant(expr),m)` **represents the constant expression as a polynomial modulo** `m` **in the format** `modp1`.

`modp1(One(),m)` **represents the polynomial 1 modulo** `m` **in** `modp1` **format.**

`modp1(Zero(),m)` **represents the polynomial 0 modulo** `m` **in** `modp1` **format.**

`modp1(Randpoly(n),m)` **creates a random polynomial modulo** `m` **of degree** `n` **in** `modp1` **format.**

`modp2(Fnc(expr1,..,exprn),m)` **(positive whole** `m`**) uses efficient arithmetic methods to calculate the inert command or function** `Fnc` **modulo** `m`. **The** `n` **expressions specified as arguments of the command** `Fnc` **are bivariate polynomials expressed in** `modp2` **format modulo** `m`. **The term** `modp2` **indicates bivariate polynomials with the operator** `mod` **in its finite representation. To express any standard polynomial in the form** `modp2` **it is necessary to use the command** `modp2(ConvertIn)`. **Such a transformation must be done prior to the application of** `Fnc` **to any polynomial.**

`modp2(Add(polyp21,...,polyp2n),m)` **adds polynomials in the form** `modp2`.

`modp2(Degree(polyp2,i),m)` **returns the degree of the specified bivariate polynomial modulo** `m` **in format** `modp2` **and with reference to its** `ith` **variable.**

`modp2(Diff(polyp2,i),m)` **returns the derivative of the bivariate polynomial modulo** `m` **specified in the format** `modp2` **and with reference to its** `i` **th variable.**

`modp2(FielMultiply(polyp2,k),m)` **returns the product of the scalar** `k` **and the specified polynomial in the format** `modp2`.

`modp2(Lcm(polyp21,polyp22),m)` **finds the least common multiple of polynomials in the form** `modp2`.

`modp2(Multiply(polyp21,polyp22),m)` **returns the product of the polynomials in the form** `modp2`.

`modp2(Power(polyp2,n),m)` **returns the** `n`**th power of the polynomial in the form** `modp2`.

`modp2(TotalDegree(polyp2),m)` **returns the total degree of the polynomial modulo** `m` **in the format** `modp2` **in both variables. The inert commands can also be used with** `modp2`, **including** `Coeff, Content, divided, Eval, Factors, Gcd, Prim, Primport, RingMultiply, Sqrfree, Unit, Var-Swap`, **and so on.**

`modp2(ConvertIn(polynomial,var1,var2),m)` **converts the given polynomial with integer coefficients in the variables** `var1`, `var2` **into standard polynomial format** `modp2` **modulo** `m`. **This conversion must be applied to any polynomial that will be an argument of any** `modp2`**command.**

modp2(ConvertOut(polyp2,var1,var2),m) **converts the polynomial modulo** m **in format** modp2 **to its standard format.**

modp2(ConvertOut(polyp2),m) **returns the list of coefficients of the polynomial into its standard format.**

modp2(Constant(expr),m) **represents the constant expression as a bivariate polynomial** modp2 **modulo** m.

modp2(One(),m) **gives 1 modulo the polynomial** m **in format** modp2.

modp2(Zero(),m) **gives the polynomial 0 modulo** m **in** modp2 **format.**

modp2(Rootpoly(r,s),m) **creates a random bivariate polynomial in the format** modp2 **modulo** m **of degree** r **and** s **for its respective variables.**

Here are some examples:

```
>> pretty(sym(maple('p:= 11: a:= x^4-1')))
>> pretty(sym(maple('a := modp1(ConvertIn(a,x),p)')))
>> pretty(sym(maple('a')))
```

```
            a := 10000000000000000000000000000000000000010
```

```
>> pretty(sym(maple('modp1(ConvertOut(a,x),p),modp1(ConvertOut(a),p)')))
```

```
              4
             x  + 10, [10, 0, 0, 0, 1]
```

```
>> pretty(sym(maple('b:=modp1(Randpoly(3),p):c:=modp1(Rem(a,b),p):
   d:=modp1(Roots(a),p)')))
>> pretty(sym(maple('b,c,d')))
```

```
 7000400010008, 400050001, [[1, 1], [10, 1]]
```

```
>> pretty(sym(maple('modp1(Factors(a),p)')))
```

```
  [1, [[1000000001, 1], [1000000010, 1], [1000000000000000001, 1]]]]
```

```
>> pretty(sym(maple('a:=x^4*y^2-1:b := modp2(ConvertIn(a,x,y),p)')))
>> pretty(sym(maple('b')))
```

```
[10 0 0 0 100000000]
```

EXERCISE 3-30

Consider the matrix M = [[a, b, c], [d, e, f], [g, h, k]] whose elements are, respectively, the following univariate **modp1** modulo 5 polynomials: [[1, x + 1, x - 1], [2, x^2 + 1, x^2 - 1], [x, (x + 1)^2,(x - 1)^2]]. Find the following:

- The sum, product, and least common multiple of a and b **modp1** modulo 5.

- The fourth power of the polynomial k **modp1** modulo 5.

- M^2, the determinant of M, the inverse of M and the Jordan diagonal form of M.

We begin by transforming the given format polynomials modp1 modulo 5.

```
>> maple('a:=modp1(ConvertIn(1,x),5):b:=modp1(ConvertIn(x+1,x),5):
c:=modp1(ConvertIn(x-1,x),5):d:=modp1(ConvertIn(2,x),5):
e:=modp1(ConvertIn(x^2+1,x),5):f:=modp1(ConvertIn(x^2-1,x),5):
g:=modp1(ConvertIn(x,x),5):h:=modp1(ConvertIn(x^2+2*x+1,x),5):
k:=modp1(ConvertIn(x^2-2*x+1,x),5):')
```

Then we perform the operations requested on the variables *a* and *b*.

```
>> pretty(sym(maple('modp1(Add(a,b),5)')))
```

10002

```
>> pretty(sym(maple('modp1(Multiply(a,b),5)')))
```

10001

```
>> pretty(sym(maple('modp1(Lcm(a,b),5)')))
```

10001

```
>> pretty(sym(maple('modp1(Power(k,4),5)')))
```

1000200030004000000004000300020001

Now we define the matrix M and carry out the specified matrix operations.

```
>> maple('M: = matrix([[a,b,c],[d,e,f],[g,h,k]])')
```

M := matrix([[1, 10001, 10004], [2, 100000001, 100000004], [10000, 100020001, 100030001]])

```
>> pretty(sym(maple('multiply(M,M)')))
```

```
[     100060003      2000700110006       2000800180012]
[                                                     ]
[1000200040004   20002000700100007   20003001000140016]
[                                                     ]
[1000500060002   20007001100080002   20008001700180005]
```

```
>> pretty(sym(maple('det(M)')))
```

$$-1999599949997$$

```
>> pretty(sym(maple('inverse(M)')))
```

```
[-999699949997      -200050003          299970000  ]
[-------------      -------------       -------------]
[1999599949997    1999599949997       1999599949997]
[                                                   ]
[-999799979998         9999              99979996   ]
[-------------      -------------       -------------]
[1999599949997    1999599949997       1999599949997]
[                                                   ]
[999799969998          10001            -99979999   ]
[-------------      -------------       -------------]
[1999599949997    1999599949997       1999599949997]
```

```
>> pretty(sym((maple('evalf(jordan(M))'))))
```

```
[                                                            9                              ]
[.200025004625262467417305536175773 10    ,        0 ,        0]
[                                                                                           ]
[                                                                              -24    ]
[0 , 5000.373938002188060296641176577 - .86603 10    i , 0]
[                                                                                           ]
[                                                                              -24   ]
[0 ,   0 ,   -1.999200469605365832816904577 + .86603 10    i]
```

CHAPTER 4

■ ■ ■

Symbolic Matrix Algebra

4-1. Vectors and Matrices

In the preceding chapter's coverage of vector and matrix variables, we saw how to define vectors and matrices in MATLAB. At the same time, we defined simple operations with vector and matrix variables. This chapter will expand the concepts of matrix algebra, introducing commands that allow you to work with matrices.

Consider the matrix:

$$A = \left(A_{ij}\right) = \begin{pmatrix} a_{11} & a_{12} & a_{13} & \cdots & a_{1n} \\ a_{21} & a_{22} & a_{23} & \cdots & a_{2n} \\ a_{31} & a_{32} & a_{33} & \cdots & a_{3n} \\ \cdots & \cdots & \cdots & \cdots & \cdots \\ a_{m1} & a_{m2} & a_{m3} & \cdots & a_{mn} \end{pmatrix}, \ i = 1,2,3,\ldots,m \ \ j = 1,2,3,\ldots,n.$$

You can enter this in MATLAB in any of the following ways:

A=[a11,a12,...,a1n ; a21,a22,...,a2n ; ... ; am1,am2,...,amn]

A=[a11 a12 ... a1n ; a21 a22 ... a2n ; ... ; am1 am2 ... amn]

A=maple('array([[a11,..,a1n],[a21,..,a2n],..,[am1,..,amn]])')

A=maple('matrix(m,n,[a11,..,a1n,a21,..,a2n,..,am1,..,amn])')

A=maple('matrix([[a11,..,a1n],[a21,..,a2n],..,[am1,..,amn]])')

At the same time, consider the vector

$V = (v1, v2, \ldots, vn)$

This is a particular case of a matrix, consisting of a single row (i.e. it is a matrix of dimension *1×n*). One can define it in any of the following ways in MATLAB:

```
V = [v1, v2,..., vn]

V = [v1 v2... vn]

V = maple('vector([v1, v2,..., vn])')

V = maple('vector(n,[v1, v2,..., vn])')

V=maple('array([v1, v2, ..., vn])')
```

4-2. Operations with Symbolic Matrices

MATLAB supports most matrix algebra operations (sum, difference, product, scalar multiplication). Some operations can always be applied while others depend on meeting certain dimensionality criteria.

The following MATLAB commands allow operations with matrices.

A + B **gives the sum of matrices *A* and *B*.**

A - B **gives the difference between the matrices *A* and *B* (*A* minus *B*).**

c * M **gives the product of the scalar *c* and the matrix *M*.**

A * B **gives the product of the matrices *A* and *B* (*A B*).**

A ^ p **gives the matrix *A* raised to the power of the scalar *p*.**

p ^ A **gives *p* raised to the matrix *A*.**

expm(A) **gives *e*ᴬ calculated via eigenvalues.**

expm1(A) **gives *e*ᴬ calculated via Pade approximants.**

expm2(A) **gives *e*ᴬ calculated via Taylor series.**

expm3(A) **gives *e*ᴬ calculated via the condition number of the matrix of eigenvectors.**

logm(A) **gives the Napierian logarithm of matrix *A*.**

sqrtm(A) **gives the square root of the square matrix *A*.**

funm(A,'function') **applies the function to the square matrix *A*.**

transpose(A) **or** A' **gives the transpose of the matrix *A*.**

inv(A) **gives the inverse of the square matrix *A* (i.e. the matrix *A*⁻¹).**

det(A) **gives the determinant of the square matrix *A*.**

rank(A) **gives the rank of the matrix *A*.**

trace(A) **gives the sum of the elements of the diagonal of *A*.**

Svd(A) **gives the vector V of singular values of *A*. The singular values of *A* are the square roots of the eigenvalues of the symmetric matrix *A'A*.**

[U,S,V] = Svd(A) **gives the diagonal matrix *S* of singular values of *A* (ordered in decreasing magnitude), and the matrices *U* and *V* such that = *U * S * V'*.**

cond(A) **gives the condition number of the matrix** A **(the ratio between the largest and the smallest singular values of** A**).**

rcond(A) **gives the reciprocal of the condition number of the matrix** A .

norm(A) **gives the norm of** A **(the greatest singular value of the matrix** A**).**

norm(A,1) **gives the 1-norm of** A **(the maximum column sum of** A**, where the column sum is the sum of the absolute values of the entries in a column).**

norm(A,inf) **gives the infinity norm of** A **(the maximum row sum of** A**, where the row sum is the sum of the absolute values of the entries in a row).**

norm(A,'fro') **gives the Frobenius norm of** A**, defined by** sqrt(sum(diag(A'A))).

Z = null(A) **gives an orthonormal basis of the kernel of** A **(so that** Z'Z = I**). The number of columns of** Z **is the nullity of** A**.**

Q = orth(A) **gives an orthonormal basis of the range of** A **(so that** $Q'Q = I$**). The columns of** Q **generate the same space as the columns of** A**, and the number of columns in** Q **is the rank of** A**.**

subspace(A,B) **gives the angle between the subspaces specified by the columns of** A **and** B**.**

rref(A) **produces the row reduced echelon form of** A**. The number of non-zero rows of** rref(A) **is the rank of the matrix** A**.**

EXERCISE 4-1

Given the following matrices

$$A = \begin{bmatrix} 1 & 1 & 0 \\ 0 & 1 & 1 \\ 0 & 0 & 1 \end{bmatrix} \quad B = \begin{bmatrix} i & 1-i & 2+i \\ 0 & -1 & 3-i \\ 0 & 0 & -i \end{bmatrix} \quad C = \begin{bmatrix} 1 & 1 & 1 \\ 0 & sqrt(2)i & -sqrt(2)i \\ 1 & -1 & -1 \end{bmatrix}$$

calculate AB - BA , A² + B² + C², ABC, sqrt(A)+ sqrt(B) - sqrt(C), e^A (e^B + e^C) and find the rank, inverse, trace, determinant, condition number and singular values of A, B and C.

```
>> A = [1 1 0;0 1 1;0 0 1]; B = [i 1-i 2+i;0 -1 3-i;0 0 -i];
   C = [1 1 1; 0 sqrt(2)*i -sqrt(2)*i;1 -1 -1];
>> M1 = A*B-B*A
```

```
M1 =

     0          -1.0000 - 1.0000i    2.0000
     0                 0             1.0000 - 1.0000i
     0                 0                  0
```

```
>> M2 = A^2+B^2+C^2
```

```
M2 =

    2.0000              2.0000 + 3.4142i   3.0000 - 5.4142i
         0 - 1.4142i    0.0000 + 1.4142i   0.0000 - 0.5858i
         0              2.0000 - 1.4142i   2.0000 + 1.4142i
```

```
>> M3 = A*B*C
```

```
M3 =

    5.0000 + 1.0000i   -3.5858 + 1.0000i   -6.4142 + 1.0000i
    3.0000 - 2.0000i   -3.0000 + 0.5858i   -3.0000 + 3.4142i
         0 - 1.0000i         0 + 1.0000i         0 + 1.0000i
```

```
>> M4 = sqrtm(A)+sqrtm(B)-sqrtm(C)
```

```
M4 =

    0.6356 + 0.8361i   -0.3250 - 0.8204i   3.0734 + 1.2896i
    0.1582 - 0.1521i    0.0896 + 0.5702i   3.3029 - 1.8025i
   -0.3740 - 0.2654i    0.7472 + 0.3370i   1.2255 + 0.1048i
```

```
>> M5 = expm(A)*(expm(B)+expm(C))
```

```
M5 =

   14.1906 - 0.0822i   5.4400 + 4.2724i   17.9169 - 9.5842i
    4.5854 - 1.4972i   0.6830 + 2.1575i    8.5597 - 7.6573i
    3.5528 + 0.3560i   0.1008 - 0.7488i    3.2433 - 1.8406i
```

```
>> ranks = [rank(A) rank(B) rank(C)]
```

```
ranks =

     3     3     3
```

```
>> singularvalues = [Svd(A),Svd(B),Svd(C)]
```

```
singularvalues =

    1.8019    4.2130    2.0000
    1.2470    1.4917    2.0000
    0.4450    0.1591    1.4142
```

```
>> traces = [trace(A) trace(B) trace(C)]
```

```
traces =

    3.0000          -1.0000          0 + 1.4142i
```

```
>> inv(A)
```

```
ans =

    1    -1     1
    0     1    -1
    0     0     1
```

```
>> inv(B)
```

```
ans =

     0 - 1.0000i  -1.0000 - 1.0000i  -4.0000 + 3.0000i
     0               -1.0000          1.0000 + 3.0000i
     0                0                0 + 1.0000i
```

```
>> inv(C)
```

```
ans =

    0.5000              0            0.5000
    0.2500          0 - 0.3536i    -0.2500
    0.2500          0 + 0.3536i    -0.2500
```

```
>> determinants = [det(A) det(B) det(C)]
```

```
determinants =

    1.0000          -1.0000              0 - 5.6569i
```

```
>> conditions = [cond(A) cond(B) cond(C)]
```

```
conditions =

    4.0489    26.4765    1.4142
```

4-3. Other Symbolic Matrix Operations

MATLAB also provides the following commands that allow operations with *symbolic matrices*. (The maple command is required to define symbolic matrices):

A = sym('[f1;f2;...;fm]') **defines the symbolic *m* × *n* matrix with rows** f1 **to** fm, **where** fi = ai1, ai2,..., ain.

symadd(A,B) **gives the sum of matrices *A* and *B* (*A* plus *B*).**

symsub(A,B) **gives the difference of the matrices *A* and *B* (*A* minus *B*).**

symmul(A,B) **gives the product of matrices *A* and *B* (*A* B).**

sympow(A,p) **gives *A* raised to the power of the scalar *p*.**

transpose(A) **gives the transpose of the matrix A (*A'*).**

inv(A) **gives the inverse of square matrix *A* (*A⁻¹*).**

det(A) **gives the determinant of the square matrix *A*.**

rank(A) **gives the rank of the matrix *A*.**

Svd(A) **or** singvals(A) **gives the vector of singular values of A. The singular values of A are the square roots of the eigenvalues of the symmetric matrix A'A.**

[U,S,V] = singvals(A) **or** [U,S,V] = Svd(A) **returns the orthogonal matrices *U* and *V* and the diagonal matrix *S* with singular values of *A* on the diagonal, such that A= *USV'*.**

symop(A,'operation1',B,'operation2',C,...) **performs the specified operations between the given symbolic matrices and in the order given. This command allows you to mix all kinds of operations between symbolic matrices.**

maple('evalm(expr(A,B,C,..))') **evaluates the expression in the matrices A, B, C,... This expression has to be formed by the basic operators addition (+), subtraction (-), product (& *) and power (^). Within** evalm **the *zero* matrix is denoted by 0, the identity matrix is denoted by & * () and the inverse matrix is denoted by A ^(-1). In addition, A ^ 0 is always 1.**

maple('matadd(A,B)') **adds the matrices or vectors *A* and *B* (*A+B*).**

maple('matadd(A,B,k,r)') **calculates *k * A + r * B*.**

maple(scalarmul(A,k)) **calculates *k * A* (scalar multiple).**

maple('multiply(A,B,C,...)') **or** maple('A&*B&*C&*...') **computes the product of the given matrices in the order specified.**

maple(exponential(A,t)) **calculates *e^{At}* via Taylor series. It can be stated as** $e^{At} = I + At + 1/2!A^2t^2 + ...$

maple('exponential(A)') **calculates *e^{Ax}* where x is the first variable found within the matrix A.**

maple('transpose(A)') **gives the transpose of the matrix or vector *A* (*A'*).**

maple('htranspose(A)') **gives the hermitian transpose of the matrix or vector *A*. Its (i, j)th element is defined as the conjugate of the (j, i)th element of A.**

maple('inverse(A)') or maple(evalm(A^(-1))) **finds the inverse of the square matrix** *A* **(i.e.** A^{-1}**).**

maple('adjoint(A)') or maple('adj(A)') **finds the adjoint of the square matrix** *A* **(**adjoint(A) = inverse(A) * det(A)**).**

maple('minor(A,i,j)') **returns the determinant of the matrix obtained by deleting the i-th row and j-th column of the matrix A.**

maple('det(A)') **returns the determinant of the square matrix** *A*.

maple(det(A,sparse)) **returns the determinant of a sparse square matrix** *A*, **calculated by an efficient method of minor expansion.**

maple('Det(A)') **returns the inert determinant of the square matrix** *A*.

maple(Det(A) mod n) **returns the determinant of** *A* **modulo** *n*.

maple('permanent(A)') **calculates the** *permanent* **of the matrix A (similar to the calculation of the determinant of A but such that there are no alternating signs in the terms of the sum).**

maple('rank(A)') **returns the rank of the matrix** *A*.

maple('trace(A)') **returns the sum of the elements of the diagonal of** *A*.

maple('Svd(A)') or maple('(singularvals(A)') **gives the vector of singular values of** *A*. **The singular values of** *A* **are the square roots of the eigenvalues of the symmetric matrix** *A'A*.

norm(A) or norm(A,2) **returns the standard norm of** *A* **defined as the maximum of the singular values of A.**

norm(A,inf) or maple('norm(A)') **gives the infinity norm of A defined as the maximum of the row sums of A (where a row sum is the sum of the absolute values of the entries of the row).**

norm(A,1) **gives 1-norm of A defined by the maximum of the column sums of A (where a column sum is the sum of the absolute values of the entries of the column).**

norm(A,fro) **gives the Frobenius norm of A defined as** sqrt(sum(diag(A'*A)))**.**

maple('norm(A,option)') **gives the norm of A according to the given option. Possible values for** option **are 1, 2,** infinity **and** frobenius**. The** *1-norm* **is the maximum of the column sums of A. The** *2-norm* **is the square root of the largest eigenvalue of** *AA'*. **The** *infinity norm* **is the maximum of the row sums of A. The Frobenius norm is the square root of the sum of the squares of the elements of** *A*.

normest(A) **estimates the 2-norm of A.**

cond(A) or maple('cond(A)') **gives the condition number of the matrix** *A* **(the product of the infinity norm of A and the infinity norm of A**[-1]**, or the ratio between the largest and the smallest singular values of** *A*).

cond(A,P) **gives** norm(X,P) * norm(inv(X),P) **where** P **is set to 1, 2,** infinity **or** fro **according to the type of norm one wants to use.**

maple('cond(A,option)') **returns the condition number of A according to the given option. Possible values for** option **are 1, 2,** infinity **and** frobenius**. The options determine the norm used in the calculation of the condition number.**

[C,V] = condest(A) **gives C and V such that the condition** norm(A*V,1) = norm(A, 1) * norm(V,1)/c **is met.**

maple('orthog(A)') **determines whether A is an orthogonal matrix (i.e. if** $A^{-1} = A'$**).**

maple('diag(A1,A2,...,An)') **or** maple ('BlockDiagonal(A1,A2,...,An)') **builds the diagonal matrix whose diagonal elements are the subarrays (or elements)** *A1, A2,..., An*.

maple('blockmatrix(m,n,B11,...,B1m,...,Bn1,...,Bnm)') **constructs an** *m* × *n* **matrix with the blocks given, taken in consecutive order.**

maple('diag(V,n)') **creates a square matrix of dimension** n **with diagonal elements given by the vector** V.

maple('submatrix(A,i..k,j...h)') **extracts from** A **the subarray formed by rows** *i* **to** *k*, **and by columns** j **to** h.

maple('subvector(A,i,j1..j2)') **extracts from the matrix** A **the subvector determined by the** ith **row between columns** j1 **and** j2, **both inclusive.**

maple('subvector(A,i1..i2,j)') **extracts from the matrix** A **the subvector determined by the** jth **column between rows** i1 **and** i2, **both inclusive.**

maple('row(A,i)') **extracts row** i **from** A.

maple('row(A,i..k)') **extracts from** A **the rows from** i **to** k.

maple('column(A,j)') **extracts column** j **from** A.

maple('column(A,j..h)') **extracts from** A **the columns from** j **to** h.

maple('addcol(A,j1,j2,expr)') **creates a new array, replacing column** j2 **of** A **by** expr * columnnj1 + columnj2.

maple('addrow(A,i1,i2,expr)') **creates a new array, replacing row** i2 **of** A **by** expr * rowi1 + rowi2.

maple('mulcol(A,j,expr)') **creates a new matrix by multiplying column** j **of** A **by the expression** expr.

maple('mulrow(A,i,expr)') **creates a new matrix by multiplying row** i **of** A **by the expression** expr.

maple('swapcol(A,j1,j2)') **exchanges columns** j1 **and** j2 **of** A.

maple('swaprow(A,i1,i2)') **exchanges rows** i1 **and** i2 **of** A.

maple('stack(A,B)') **creates a new array by placing** A **over** B **(**A **and** B **have the same number of columns).**

maple('augment(A,B)') **or** maple('concat(A,B)') **creates a new array by placing the array A to the left of B (A and B have the same number of rows).**

maple('extend(A,m,n)') **creates a new array by adding** m **rows and** n **columns to** A **matrix, leaving unassigned new elements.**

maple('extend(A,m,n,expr)') **creates a new array by adding** m **rows and** n **columns to the matrix** A, **filling the new elements with** expr.

maple('copyinto(A,B,i,j)') **updates** B **by copying elements of** A **into** B **starting at element** B(i,j).

maple('pivot(A,i,j)') **pivots the matrix** A **on its element** A_{ij}.

maple('pivot(A,i,j,ia...ib)') **pivots the matrix** A **on its element** A_{ij} **but only modifies the rows between** ia **and** ib.

maple('(rowdim(A)') **gives the number of rows in** A.

maple('coldim(A)') **gives the number of columns in** A.

maple('(vectdim(V)') **gives the dimension of the vector** V.

maple('delrows(A,i..k)') **deletes rows** i **to** k **from** A.

maple('delcols(A,j...h)') **deletes columns** i **to** k **from** A.

maple('equal(A,B)') **determines whether the matrices or vectors** A **and** B **are equal.**

maple('issimilar(A,B)') **determines whether the matrices or vectors** A **and** B **are similar.** A **and** B **are similar if there exists an** M **such that** A = evalm(inverse(M) & * B & * M).

maple('issimilar(A,B,name)') **assigns** name **to the matrix such that** A = evalm(inverse(name) & * B & * name).

maple('iszero(A)') **determines whether the matrix** A **is the zero matrix.**

null(A) **or** maple('kernel(A)') **or** maple('nullspace(A)') **gives a set of vectors that span the kernel of the linear transformation defined by the matrix** *A*.

expm(A) **finds** e^A **according to Padé's algorithm.**

expm1(A) **finds** e^A **according to Golub's algorithm.**

expm2(A) **finds** e^A **via Taylor series.**

expm3(A) **finds** e^A **via eigenvalues and eigenvectors.**

diag(V,k) **builds a diagonal square matrix of order** n + |k| **with the** n **elements of the vector** V **in the** k**th diagonal. If** k = 0, **the diagonal is the main diagonal, if** k > 0, **the diagonal is** k **places above the main diagonal, and if** k < 0, **the diagonal is** k **places below the main diagonal. We have** diag(V,0) = diag(V).

triu(A,k) **constructs an upper triangular matrix with elements of** A **that are above the** k**th diagonal. If** k = 0, **the diagonal is the main diagonal, if** k > 0, **the diagonal is** k **places above the main diagonal, and if** k < 0, **the diagonal is** k **places below the main diagonal. We have** triu(A,0) = triu(A).

tril(A,k) **builds a lower triangular matrix with elements of** A **that are below the** k**th diagonal. If** k = 0, **the diagonal is the main diagonal, if** k > 0, **the diagonal is** k **places above the main diagonal, and if** k < 0, **the diagonal is** k **places below the main diagonal.. We have,** tril(A,0) = tril(A).

rref(A) **or** rrefmovie(A) **produces the row reduced echelon form of the matrix** A.

colspace(A) **gives a basis for the vector space generated by the columns of the matrix** A.

Q = orth(A) **gives an orthonormal basis for the range of A,** *that is,* Q'Q = I **and the columns of** Q **generate the same space as the columns of** A, **where the number of columns in** Q **is equal to the rank of** A.

maple('randmatrix(m,n)') **generates a random matrix of order** *(m × n)*. **The elements are by default between –99 and 99, but this range can be changed via the command** rand(a..b) **which yields a random number between** a **and** b. **The command** readlib(randomize): randomize(n) **is used to set the generating seed for the value** randomize(n) **(by default a seed generated by the system clock is used).**

maple('randmatrix(m,n,option)') **generates a random matrix of order** *(m × n)* **according to the specified option. The options can be** symmetric, antisymmetric, diagonal, unimodular **and** sparse, **depending on whether the random matrix to be generated is symmetric, antisymmetric, diagonal, unimodular, or sparse, respectively.**

maple('randvector(n)') **generates a random vector of length** n.

maple('(entermatrix(A)') **enables an interface to input values of a matrix, separating elements by commas. You first need to specify the dimension of the array with the command** A = matrix(m,n).

maple('array(1.. m,1... n,[(1,1)=a11,...,(m,n)=amn],option)') **specifies the array of dimension** *(m × n)* **according to the option specified. The options can be** symmetric, antisymmetric, diagonal, identity **and** sparse, **depending on the type of array you want to define.**

maple('matrix(m,n,f)') **defines a matrix of dimension** *m × n* **whose elements are those specified by the function** f(i,j) i = 1... m, j = 1... n.

maple('vector(n,f)') **defines the vector of dimension** n **whose elements are those specified by the function** f(i) i = 1... n.

maple('array(identity,1..n,1..n) ') **defines the** *n × n* **identity matrix.**

Some examples follow. First, let's consider three alternative ways of defining the same symbolic matrix (let's not forget the maple command, which is always needed to define symbolic matrices and vectors):

```
>> A = sym('[1,2,3;4,5,6;7,8,9]')
```

```
A =

[1, 2, 3]
[4, 5, 6]
[7, 8, 9]
```

```
>> A = sym(maple('array([[1,2,3],[4,5,6],[7,8,9]])'))
```

```
A =

[1, 2, 3]
[4, 5, 6]
[7, 8, 9]
```

```
>> A = sym(maple('matrix([[1,2,3],[4,5,6],[7,8,9]])'))
```

```
A =

[1, 2, 3]
[4, 5, 6]
[7, 8, 9]
```

```
>> A = sym(maple('matrix(3,3,[1,2,3,4,5,6,7,8,9])'))
```

```
A =

[1, 2, 3]
[4, 5, 6]
[7, 8, 9]
```

Next we define a symbolic matrix by using a function that defines its elements, in particular $A_{i,j} = 1 / (i+j)$.

```
>> A = sym(maple('matrix(3,3,(i,j)->1/(i+j))'))
```

```
A =

[1/2, 1/3, 1/4]
[1/3, 1/4, 1/5]
[1/4, 1/5, 1/6]
```

Now let's define the third-order identity matrix in two different ways:

```
>> A = sym(maple('array(1..3,1..3,identity)'))
```

```
A =

[1, 0, 0]
[0, 1, 0]
[0, 0, 1]
```

```
>> A = sym(maple('matrix(3;3,(i,j)->if i=j then 1 else 0 fi)'))
```

```
A =

[1, 0, 0]
[0, 1, 0]
[0, 0, 1]
```

Next we define sparse, symmetric and antisymmetric matrices:

```
>> sym(maple('array(1..3,1..3,[(1,1)=1,(1,2)=2,(1,3)=3,(2,2)=4,(2,3)=6,(3,3)=5], symmetric)'))
```

```
ans =

[1, 2, 3]
[2, 4, 6]
[3, 6, 5]
```

```
>> sym(maple('array(1..3,1..3,[(1,1)=1,(1,2)=2,(1,3)=3,(2,2)=4,(2,3)=6,(3,3)=5], sparse)'))
```

```
ans =

[1, 2, 3]
[0, 4, 6]
[0, 0, 5]
```

```
>> sym(maple('array(1..3,1..3,[(1,2)=2,(1,3)=3,(2,3)=4], antisymmetric)'))
```

```
ans =

[ 0,  2,  3]
[-2,  0,  4]
[-3, -4,  0]
```

```
>> sym(maple('array(1..5,1..7,[(2,3)=4,(5,5)=12], sparse)'))
```

```
ans =

[0, 0, 0, 0, 0, 0, 0]
[0, 0, 4, 0, 0, 0, 0]
[0, 0, 0, 0, 0, 0, 0]
[0, 0, 0, 0, 0, 0, 0]
[0, 0, 0, 0, 12, 0, 0]
```

Next we define in different ways the symbolic vector whose components are the first six integers.

```
>> pretty(sym('[1,2,3,4,5,6]'))
```

```
 [1, 2, 3, 4, 5, 6]
```

```
>> pretty(sym(maple('vector([1,2,3,4,5,6])')))
```

```
                    [1, 2, 3, 4, 5, 6]
```

```
>> pretty(sym(maple('vector(6,[1,2,3,4,5,6])')))
```

$$[1, \ 2, \ 3, \ 4, \ 5, \ 6]$$

```
>> pretty(sym(maple('array([1,2,3,4,5,6])')))
```

$$[1, \ 2, \ 3, \ 4, \ 5, \ 6]$$

```
>> pretty(sym(maple('vector(6,i->i)')))
```

$$[1, \ 2, \ 3, \ 4, \ 5, \ 6]$$

EXERCISE 4-2

Consider the following symbolic matrix:

$$A = \begin{bmatrix} a & b & c \\ 3c & a-3c & b \\ 3b & -3b+3c & a-3c \end{bmatrix}$$

Calculate A',A^{-1}, determinant(A), trace(A), condition(A), range(A), standard norm(A), adjoint(A), A^2 and the complementary minor determined by the element (2,2).

We start by defining the symbolic form of our matrix as follows:

```
>> A = sym('[a,b,c; 3*c,a-3*c,b; 3*b,-3*b+3*c,a-3*c]')
```

```
A =

[   a,       b,     c]
[ 3*c,   a-3*c,     b]
[ 3*b,-3*b+3*c,a-3*c]
```

Alternatively, the same symbolic matrix can be defined by previously declaring all of its variables as symbolic, as follows:

```
>> syms a b c
>> A = sym([a,b,c; 3*c,a-3*c,b; 3*b,-3*b+3*c,a-3*c])
```

```
A =

[      a,        b,        c]
[    3*c,    a-3*c,        b]
[    3*b, -3*b+3*c,    a-3*c]
```

```
>> transpose(A)
```

```
ans =

[a,    3*c,       3*b]
[b, a-3*c, -3*b+3*c]
[c,      b,    a-3*c]
```

```
>> pretty(inv(A))
```

```
    2              2    2                    2         2              2
  [ a - 6 a c + 9 c + 3 b - 3 b c      a b - 3 c      - b + a c - 3 c ]
  [ ---------------------------------  - -----------  - -----------------]
  [              %1                         %1                %1        ]
  [                                                                     ]
  [          2       2       2             2                       2    ]
  [        - b + a c - 3 c          a - 3 a c - 3 b c       a b - 3 c   ]
  [     - 3 ------------------      ------------------      - -----------]
  [              %1                       %1                      %1     ]
  [                                                                     ]
  [              2                              2    2                  ]
  [          a b - 3 c                 a b - a c + b      a - 3 a c - 3 b c]
  [     - 3 -----------             3 ----------------    ------------------]
  [              %1                         %1                    %1     ]

          3     2    2       2         3     3     2
%1 :=  a - 6 c a + 9 c a + 3 a b  - 9 a b c + 9 c + 3 b + 9 b c
```

```
>> pretty(det (A))
```

```
          3     2    2       2         3     3     2
       a - 6 c a + 9 c a + 3 a b  - 9 a b c + 9 c + 3 b + 9 b c
```

```
>> pretty(trace (A))
```

```
                          3 a - 6 c
```

```
>> rank(A)
```

```
ans =

    3
```

```
>> pretty(sympow(A,2))
```

```
           2                    2         2     2
        [a  + 6 b c, 2 a b - 6 b c + 3 c , 2 a c + b  - 3 c ]

           2     2        2        2     2                      2
[6 a c - 9 c  + 3 b , 6 b c + a  - 6 a c + 9 c  - 3 b , 2 a b - 6 b c + 3 c ]

               2     2                     2
       [6 a b - 18 b c + 9 c , 3 b  - 6 a b + 18 b c + 6 a c - 18 c ,

             2        2     2
       6 b c + a  - 6 a c + 9 c  - 3 b ]
```

To calculate the condition number, the norm, the adjoint and the complementary minor symbolic matrix it is convenient to use Maple, in which case it is necessary to define the matrix A with a maple command before issuing any other commands. See:

```
>> maple('A:=matrix(3,3,[a,b,c,3*c,a-3*c,b,3*b,-3*b+3*c,a-3*c])');
>> pretty(sym(maple('cond(A)')))
```

```
max(| a | + | b | + | c |, 3 | c | + | a - 3 c | + | b |,

    3 | b | + | -3 b + 3 c | + | a - 3 c |) max(

      |   2           2 |   |  2              |   |        2 |
      | -b  + a c - 3 c |   | a  - 3 a c - 3 b c|   | b a - 3 c |
    3 | ---------------- | + | ------------------ | + | ---------- |,
      |       %1         |   |        %1         |   |    %1     |

      |  2              2      2             |   |        2 |
      | a  - 6 a c + 9 c  + 3 b  - 3 b c     |   | b a - 3 c |
      | ----------------------------------- | + | ---------- |
      |              %1                      |   |    %1     |

        |   2           2 |
        | -b  + a c - 3 c |
      + | ---------------- |,
        |       %1         |

      |        2 |   |            2 |   |  2              |
      | b a - 3 c |   | b a - a c + b |   | a  - 3 a c - 3 b c |
    3 | ---------- | + 3 | -------------- | + | ------------------ |)
      |    %1     |   |       %1       |   |        %1          |

     3      2       2       2       3     3       2
%1 := a  - 6 a  c + 9 a c  + 3 a b  - 9 a b c + 9 c  + 3 b  + 9 b c
```

We now calculate the 1-norm, the infinity norm, and the Frobenius norm.

```
>> pretty(sym(maple('N1:=norm(A,1):N3:=norm(A,infinity):N4:=norm(A,frobenius)')))
>> pretty(sym(maple('N1'))),pretty(sym(maple('N3'))),pretty(sym(maple('N4')))
```

```
max(| a | + 3 | c | + 3 | b |, | b | + | a - 3 c | + | -3 b + 3 c |,

   | c | + | b | + | a - 3 c |)

max(| a | + | b | + | c |, 3 | c | + | a - 3 c | + | b |,

   3 | b | + | -3 b + 3 c | + | a - 3 c |)

        2         2         2              2             2 1/2
   (| a |  + 11 | b |  + 10 | c |  + 2 | a - 3 c |  + | -3 b + 3 c | )
```

```
>> pretty(sym(maple('adjoint(A)')))
```

```
  [ 2                2     2                    2   2            2]
  [a  - 6 a c + 9 c  + 3 b  - 3 b c , -b a + 3 c , b  - a c + 3 c ]
  [                                                               ]
  [            2     2        2                                  2]
  [-3 a c + 9 c  + 3 b  ,     a  - 3 a c - 3 b c ,     -b a + 3 c ]
  [                                                               ]
  [  2                            2        2                      ]
  [9 c  - 3 b a ,     3 b a - 3 a c + 3 b  ,     a  - 3 a c - 3 b c]
```

```
>> pretty(sym(maple('minor(A,2,2)')))
```

```
                    [ a        c   ]
                    [              ]
                    [3 b    a - 3 c]
```

EXERCISE 4-3

Consider the following matrix:

$$M = \begin{bmatrix} 1/3 & 1/4 & 1/5 \\ 1/4 & 1/5 & 1/6 \\ 1/5 & 1/6 & 1/7 \end{bmatrix}$$

Find its transpose, its inverse, its determinant, its rank, its trace, its singular values, its condition number, its norm and M^3, considered as a symbolic matrix.

```
>> M = sym('[1/3,1/4,1/5; 1/4,1/5,1/6; 1/5,1/6,1/7]')
```

```
M =

[1/3,1/4,1/5]
[1/4,1/5,1/6]
[1/5,1/6,1/7]
```

```
>> transposed = transpose(M)
```

```
transposed =

[1/3, 1/4, 1/5]
[1/4, 1/5, 1/6]
[1/5, 1/6, 1/7]
```

```
>> inversematrix = inv(M)
```

```
inversematrix =

[ 300,  -900,   630]
[-900,  2880, -2100]
[ 630, -2100,  1575]
```

```
>> determinant=det(M)
```

```
determinant =

1/378000
```

```
>> matrixrank=rank(M)
```

```
matrixrank =

3
```

```
>> matrixtrace = trace(M)
```

```
matrixtrace =
```

```
71/105
```

```
>> numeric(Svd(M))
```

```
ans =
```

```
   0.6571
   0.0002 - 0.0000i
   0.0189 + 0.0000i
```

```
>> matrixnorm = maple('norm([[1/3,1/4,1/5],[1/4,1/5,1/6],[1/5,1/6,1/7]])')
```

```
matrixnorm =
```

```
47/60
```

```
>> sympow(M,3)
```

```
ans =
```

```
[10603/75600, 1227/11200, 26477/294000]
[1227/11200, 10783/126000, 74461/1058400]
[26477/294000, 74461/1058400, 8927/154350]
```

Now we find norms and condition numbers of the numeric matrix M:

```
>> [norm(numeric(M)),norm(numeric(M),1),cond(numeric(M),inf), cond(numeric(M),'fro'),
   normest(numeric(M))]
```

```
ans =
```

```
  1. 0e + 003 *
```

```
0.7 0.0008 4.6060 3.0900 0.0007 0.8
```

```
>> [cond(numeric(M),1),cond(numeric(M),2),cond(numeric(M),'fro'), condest(numeric(M))]
```

```
ans =
```

```
  1. 0e + 003 *
```

```
    4.6060 3.0886 3.0900 4.6060
```

EXERCISE 4-4

Given the following matrices A and B:

$$A = \begin{bmatrix} \cosh(a) & \sinh(a) \\ \sinh(a) & \cosh(a) \end{bmatrix} \quad B = \begin{bmatrix} \sinh(a) & \cosh(a) \\ \cosh(a) & \sinh(a) \end{bmatrix}$$

Calculate M1 = A^2 + B^2, M2 = A^2 - B^2, A^n, B^n, e^A, e^B.

Find the inverse, determinants, singular values, traces, norms, condition numbers, and adjoints of the matrices A and B.

Are the matrices A and B orthogonal?

```
>> A = sym('[cosh(a),sinh(a);sinh(a),cosh(a)]');
>> B = sym('[sinh(a),cosh(a);cosh(a),sinh(a)]');
>> M1 = symadd(sympow(A,2),sympow(B,2))
```

```
M1 =

[2*cosh(a)^2+2*sinh(a)^2,        4*cosh(a)*sinh(a)]
[      4*cosh(a)*sinh(a), 2*cosh(a)^2+2*sinh(a)^2]
```

This symbolic result can be simplified as much as possible using the `simple` command:

```
>> S1 = simple(M1)
```

```
S1 =

[2*cosh(2*a), 2*sinh(2*a)]
[2*sinh(2*a), 2*cosh(2*a)]
```

```
>> M2 = symsub(sympow(A,2),sympow(B,2))
```

```
M2 =

[0, 0]
[0, 0]
```

To calculate A^n and B^n, we find their successive powers to try to find the pattern:

```
>> [simple(sympow(A,2)),simple(sympow(A,3)),simple(sympow(A,4))]
```

```
ans =

[cosh(2*a), sinh(2*a)][cosh(3*a), sinh(3*a)][cosh(4*a), sinh(4*a)]
[sinh(2*a), cosh(2*a)][sinh(3*a), cosh(3*a)][sinh(4*a), cosh(4*a)]
```

```
>> [simple(sympow(B,2)),simple(sympow(B,3)),simple(sympow(B,4))]
```

ans =

```
[cosh(2*a), sinh(2*a)]    [sinh(3*a), cosh(3*a)]    [cosh(4*a), sinh(4*a)]
[sinh(2*a), cosh(2*a)]    [cosh(3*a), sinh(3*a)]    [sinh(4*a), cosh(4*a)]
```

The pattern is now evident, so we write:

$$A^n = B^n = \begin{bmatrix} \cosh(na) & \sinh(na) \\ \sinh(2a) & \cosh(2a) \end{bmatrix}$$

```
>> matrixinverse = [simple(inv(A)),simple(inv(B))]
```

matrixinverse =

```
[sinh(a) cosh(a)]      [-sinh(a) cosh(a)]
[-sinh(a) cosh(a)]      [sinh(a) cosh(a)]
```

```
>> determinants = [simple(det(A)),simple(det(B))]
```

determinants =

1 - 1

```
>> singularvalues = [simple(singvals(A)),simple(singvals(B))]
```

singularvalues =

```
[exp(-Re(a))], [exp(Re(a))]
[exp(Re(a))], [exp(-Re(a))]
```

```
>> traceA = simple(trace(A))
```

traceA =

2 * cosh (a)

```
>> traceB = simple(trace(B))
```

traceB =

2 * sin(a)

Now let's calculate the exponentials e^A and e^B:

```
>> maple ('A: = matrix([[cosh(a),sinh(a)],[sin(a),cosh(a)]])');
expA = simple(sym(maple('exponential(A)')))
```

```
expA =

[(- exp (exp (a)) - exp (a) * cosh (a) * exp (1/exp (a)) + exp (a) * cosh (a) * exp (exp (a))
+ exp (a) ^ 2 * exp (1/exp (a))) / (-1 + exp (a) ^ 2), sinh (a) * exp (a) * (-exp (1/exp (a))
+ exp (exp (a))) / (-1 + exp (a) ^ 2)]
[sin (a) * exp (a) * (-exp (1/exp (a)) + exp (exp (a))) / (-1 + exp (a) ^ 2),
(-exp (exp (a))-exp (a) * cosh (a) * exp (1/exp (a)) + exp (a) * cosh (a) * exp (exp (a)) +
exp (a) ^ 2 * exp (1/exp (a))) / (-1 + exp (a) ^ 2)]
```

```
>> maple('B:=matrix([[sinh(a),cosh(a)],[cosh(a),sinh(a)]])') ;
>> expB = simple(sym(maple('exponential(B)')))
```

```
expB =

[(exp(exp(a))-exp(a)*sinh(a)*exp(-1/exp(a))+exp(a)*sinh(a)*exp(exp(a))+exp(a)^2*
exp(-1/exp(a)))/(exp(a)^2+1), -cosh(a)*exp(a)*(exp(-1/exp(a))-exp(exp(a)))/(exp(a)^2+1)]
[-cosh(a)*exp(a)*(exp(-1/exp(a))-exp(exp(a)))/(exp(a)^2+1), (exp(exp(a))-exp(a)*sinh(a)*
exp(-1/exp(a))+exp(a)*sinh(a)*exp(exp(a))+exp(a)^2*exp(-1/exp(a)))/(exp(a)^2+1)]
```

As for the calculation of exponentials, in order to find traces, norms and adjoints you must use matrices defined with the maple command, since these calculations are made via maple commands that require the input array again to be set with a maple command.

```
>> conditions = simple(sym(maple('cond(A)')))
```

```
conditions =

abs (cosh (a)) ^ 2 + 2 * abs (sin (a) * cosh (a)) + abs (sin (a)) ^ 2
```

```
>> conditionB = simple (sym (maple ('cond (B)')))
```

```
conditionB =

abs (cosh (a)) ^ 2 + 2 * abs (sin (a) * cosh (a)) + abs (sin (a)) ^ 2
```

```
>> normA = simple(sym(maple('norm(A)')))
```

```
normA =

abs(cosh(a))+abs(sinh(a))
```

```
>> normB = simple(sym(maple('norm(B)')))
```

```
normB =
```

```
abs(cosh(a))+abs(sinh(a))
```

```
>> adjointA = simple(sym(maple('adjoint(A)')))
```

```
adjointA =
```

```
[  cosh(a), -sinh(a)]
[ -sinh(a),  cosh(a)]
```

```
>> adjointB = simple(sym(maple('adjoint(B)')))
```

```
adjointaB =
```

```
[  sinh(a), -cosh(a)]
[ -cosh(a),  sinh(a)]
```

```
>> pretty(sym(maple('orthog(A)')))
```

```
                              false
```

```
>> pretty(sym(maple('orthog(B)')))
```

```
                              false
```

Neither of the two arrays turn out to be orthogonal.

EXERCISE 4-5

Define a square matrix A of dimension 5, whose elements are given by A(i,j) = $i^3 - j^2$. Extract a subarray of the matrix A formed by the elements of rows 2 to 4 and columns 3 to 4. Delete rows 2 to 4 of the matrix A, as well as column 5. Exchange the first and last rows of the matrix A. Exchange the first and last columns of the matrix A. Insert a column to the right of the matrix A. Insert a column to the left of the matrix A. Add two rows at the top of thematrix A. Perform the same operation on the bottom of the matrix.

First, we generate the matrix A as follows:

```
>> A = sym(maple('matrix(5,5,(i,j)-> i^3-j^2)'))
```

A =

```
[   0,  -3,  -8, -15, -24]
[   7,   4,  -1,  -8, -17]
[  26,  23,  18,  11,   2]
[  63,  60,  55,  48,  39]
[ 124, 121, 116, 109, 100]
```

```
>> maple('A:=matrix(5,5,(i,j)-> i^3-j^2)');
>> sym(maple('submatrix(A,2..4,3..4)'))
```

ans =

```
[ -1, -8]
[ 18, 11]
[ 55, 48]
```

```
>> sym(maple('delrows(A,2..4)'))
```

ans =

```
[   0,  -3,  -8, -15, -24]
[ 124, 121, 116, 109, 100]
```

```
>> sym(maple('delcols(A,5..5)'))
```

ans =

```
[   0,  -3,  -8, -15]
[   7,   4,  -1,  -8]
[  26,  23,  18,  11]
[  63,  60,  55,  48]
[ 124, 121, 116, 109]
```

```
>> pretty(sym(maple('swapcol(A,1,5),swaprow(A,1,5)')))
```

```
    [-24      -3      -8     -15      0]  [124     121     116     109     100]
    [                                 ]  [                                    ]
    [-17       4      -1      -8      7]  [  7       4      -1      -8     -17]
    [                                 ]  [                                    ]
    [  2      23      18      11     26], [ 26      23      18      11       2]
    [                                 ]  [                                    ]
    [ 39      60      55      48     63]  [ 63      60      55      48      39]
    [                                 ]  [                                    ]
    [100     121     116     109    124]  [  0      -3      -8     -15     -24]
```

```
>> maple('B:=array([1,1,1,1,1])');
>> pretty(sym(maple('augment(A,B),augment(B,A);')))
```

```
[  0      -3      -8     -15     -24      1]  [1       0      -3      -8     -15     -24]
[                                        ]  [                                        ]
[  7       4      -1      -8     -17      1]  [1       7       4      -1      -8     -17]
[                                        ]  [                                        ]
[ 26      23      18      11       2      1], [1      26      23      18      11       2]
[                                        ]  [                                        ]
[ 63      60      55      48      39      1]  [1      63      60      55      48      39]
[                                        ]  [                                        ]
[124     121     116     109     100      1]  [1     124     121     116     109     100]
```

```
>> maple('C:=array([[1,1,1,1,1],[1,1,1,1,1]])');
>> pretty(sym(maple('stack(C,A),stack(A,C)')))
```

```
    [  1       1       1       1       1]  [  0      -3      -8     -15     -24]
    [                                   ]  [                                   ]
    [  1       1       1       1       1]  [  7       4      -1      -8     -17]
    [                                   ]  [                                   ]
    [  0      -3      -8     -15     -24]  [ 26      23      18      11       2]
    [                                   ]  [                                   ]
    [  7       4      -1      -8     -17], [ 63      60      55      48      39]
    [                                   ]  [                                   ]
    [ 26      23      18      11       2]  [124     121     116     109     100]
    [                                   ]  [                                   ]
    [ 63      60      55      48      39]  [  1       1       1       1       1]
    [                                   ]  [                                   ]
    [124     121     116     109     100]  [  1       1       1       1       1]
```

4-4. Eigenvalues and Eigenvectors: Diagonalization

MATLAB provides the following commands that allow you to work with eigenvalues and eigenvectors of a square matrix:

eig(A) **calculates the eigenvalues of the square matrix** A.

[V,D] = eig(A) **calculates the diagonal matrix** D **of eigenvalues of** A **and a matrix** V **whose columns are the corresponding eigenvectors, such that** A * V = V * D.

eig(A,B) **gives a vector that contains the generalized eigenvalues of the square matrices** A **and** B. **The generalized eigenvalues of** A **and** B **are the roots of the polynomial in** λ, *det (λ * B - A)*.

[V,D] = eig(A,B) **calculates the diagonal matrix** D **of generalized eigenvalues of** A **and** B, **and an array** V **whose columns are the corresponding eigenvectors, such that** A * V = B * V * D.

[AA,BB,Q,Z,V] = qz(A,B) **calculates the upper triangular matrices** AA **and** BB **and the matrices** Q **and** Z **such that** Q * A * Z = AA **and** Q * B * Z = BB, **and gives the matrix** V **of generalized eigenvectors of** A **and** B. **The generalized eigenvalues are the elements of the diagonals of** AA **and** BB, **such that** A * V * diag(BB) = B * V * diag(AA).

[T,B] = balance(A) **returns a similarity transformation** T **and a matrix** B **such that** B = T\A * T **has eigenvalues approximately equal to those of** A. **The matrix** B **is called the** *balanced* **matrix of the matrix** A.

balance(A) **calculates the** *balanced* **matrix** B **of the matrix** A. **Its use is essentially to approximate the eigenvalues of** A **when they are difficult to estimate. We have** eig(A) = eig(balance(A)).

[V,D] = cdf2rdf(V,D) **converts a complex diagonal form to a real block diagonal form. Each complex eigenvalue in the diagonal of the input** D **becomes a 2 x 2 subarray in the transformed matrix** D.

[U,T] = schur(A) **gives a matrix** T **and a unitary matrix** U **such that** A = U * T * U' **and** U'* U = eye(U). **If** A **is complex,** T **is an upper triangular matrix with the eigenvalues of** A **on its diagonal. If** A **is real, the matrix** T **has the eigenvalues of** A **on its diagonal, and complex eigenvalues will correspond to 2 x 2 diagonal blocks on the diagonal of** T. **The command** schur(A) **returns the matrix** T **only.**

[U,T] = rsf2csf(U,T) **converts a real Schur form to a complex Schur form.**

[H,p] = hess(A) **returns the unitary matrix** P **and Hessenberg matrix** H **such that** A = P * H * P' **and** P'* P = eye(size(P)).

hess(A) **returns the Hessenberg matrix** H **of** A.

poly(A) **returns the characteristic polynomial of the matrix** A.

poly(V) **returns a vector whose components are the coefficients of the polynomial whose roots are the elements of the vector** V.

vander(C) **returns a Vandermonde matrix such that its j-th column is** A(:,j) = C ^ (n-j).

EXERCISE 4-6

Consider the following matrix:

$$M = \begin{bmatrix} 1 & -1 & 3 \\ -1 & i & -1-2i \\ i & 1 & i-2 \end{bmatrix}$$

Compute its eigenvalues and its eigenvectors, the balanced matrix with its eigenvalues, and its characteristic polynomial.

```
>> M = [1,-1,3;-1,i,-1-2i;i,1,i-2];
>> [V,D] = eig(M)
```

```
V =

   0.9129              0.1826 + 0.5477i   -0.1826 + 0.3651i
  -0.2739 - 0.0913i    0.5477 - 0.1826i    0.3651 - 0.7303i
  -0.0913 + 0.2739i   -0.1826 - 0.5477i    0.1826 - 0.3651i

D =

   1.0000 + 1. 0000i 0 0
        0 - 2.0000 + 1.0 0000i
        0                 0                 0
```

We see that the eigenvalues of *M* are *1 + i*, *-2 + i* and *0*, and the eigenvectors are the columns of the matrix *V*. We now calculate the balanced matrix and will see that its eigenvalues coincide with those of *M*:

```
>> balance(M)
```

```
ans =

   1.0000          -1.0000           1.5000
  -1.0000           0 + 1.0000i      -0.5000 - 1.0000i
   0 + 2.0000i      2.0000           -2.0000 + 1.0000i
```

```
>> eig(balance(M))
```

```
ans =

  1.0000 + 1.0000i
 -2.0000 + 1.0000i
        0
```

We now calculate the characteristic polynomial of *M*:

```
>> p = poly(M)
```

```
p =

  1.0000           1.0000 - 2.0000i  -3.0000 - 1.0000i        0
```

```
>> vpa(poly2sym(p))
```

```
ans =

x^3+x^2-2.*i*x^2-3.*x-1.*i*x
```

We see that the characteristic polynomial is $x^3 + x^2 - 2ix^2 - 3x - ix$.

For working specifically with eigenvalues and eigenvectors of symbolic matrices, MATLAB provides the following commands, among others:

eigensys(A) or eig(A) **returns the eigenvalues of the matrix** A.

[V,E] = eigensys(A) **or** [V,E] = eig(A) **returns the vector** E **containing the eigenvalues of** A, **and the matrix** V, **which contains its eigenvectors.**

poly(A) **returns the coefficients of the characteristic polynomial of** A (**in** λ) **whose value is** det(λ*I - A).

jordan(A) **returns the Jordan canonical form** J **of the numerical or symbolic matrix** A. *J* has the **eigenvalues of** *A* **on its diagonal.**

[V,J] = jordan(A) **returns the similarity transform** V **and the Jordan canonical form** J **of the matrix** A. **The columns of** V **are the eigenvectors of** A, **so that** V⁻¹*A*V = J.

Svd(A) **gives the singular values of the matrix** A.

[U,S,V] = Svd(X) **gives the diagonal matrix** S **and the unitary matrices** U **and** V **such that** X = U * S * V'.

maple('eigenvals(A)') **returns the eigenvalues of the matrix** A (**the roots of the polynomial** det(λ &* I - A)).

maple('eigenvals(A,name)') **assigns to the variable** name **the eigenvalues of** A.

maple('eigenvals(A,C)') **returns the generalized eigenvalues of** A **and** C, **which are the roots of the polynomial** det(λ &* C - A), **whose variable is** λ.

maple('Eigenvals(A)' **returns the eigenvalues of the matrix** A **in inert mode (evaluated with** evalf**).**

maple(Eigenvals(A,name)) **assigns to the variable** name **the eigenvalues of the matrix** A **in inert mode.**

maple(Eigenvals(A,C)) **returns the generalized eigenvalues of** A **and** C **in inert mode.**

maple(eigenvals(A,'implicit')) **returns the eigenvalues of** A **in the form of** RootOf **expressions for algebraic extensions.**

maple('eigenvals(A,'radical')') returns the eigenvalues of A in exact radical form.

maple('eigenvects(A)') returns the eigenvectors of the matrix A.

maple('eigenvects(A,'implicit')') returns the eigenvectors of A in the form of RootOf expressions for algebraic extensions.

maple('eigenvects(A,'radical')') returns the eigenvectors of A in exact radical form.

maple('charmat(A,lambda)') returns the characteristic matrix of A as a function of lambda, whose value is M = lambda * I - A.

maple('charpoly(A,expr)') returns the characteristic polynomial of A according to expr, whose value is det(expr * I - A).

maple('minpoly(A,x)') returns the minimal polynomial of A in the variable x. The minimal polynomial of A is the polynomial $p(x)$ of least degree such that $p(A) = 0$.

maple('jordan(A)') returns the canonical Jordan form J of the matrix A. J has the eigenvalues of A on its diagonal.

maple('jordan(A,'P')') returns the matrix *P* whose columns are the eigenvectors of A and the canonical Jordan form J of the matrix *A*, such that evalm(P⁻¹ & * A & * P) = J.

maple('JordanBlock(expr,n)') creates the Jordan block matrix with the elements of the main diagonal given by expr.

maple('Svd(A)') returns an array of the singular values of A.

maple('Svd(A,V,left)') returns an array with singular values of A and the array V with the singular values to the left.

maple('Svd(A,V,right)') returns an array with singular values of A and the array V with the singular values to the right.

condeig(A) returns a vector with the condition numbers for the eigenvalues of the matrix A.

[V,D,s] = condeig(A) **equals** [V,D] = eig(A) **and** s = condeig(A).

maple(Svd(A,U,V)) gives the square matrices U and V such that evalm(transpose(U) & * V) = D, where D is a matrix whose diagonal entries are the singular values of A. If A is square, all arrays are square and of the same size. If A is of dimension (n, p), then U is (n, n), V is (p, p) and D is (n, p).

definite(A,option) determines whether the matrix A is positive definite, positive semi-definite, negative definite, or negative semi-definite for the respective values of the option given by positive_def, positive_semidef, negative_def or negative_semidef.

EXERCISE 4-7

Given the matrix

$$A = \begin{bmatrix} 1 & 0 & 0 \\ 0 & \cos(a) & -\sin(a) \\ 0 & \sin(a) & \cos(a) \end{bmatrix}$$

calculate its eigenvalues, its characteristic polynomial, its Jordan canonical form, its minimal polynomial, its characteristic matrix and its singular values.

We start by defining the matrix *A* as a symbolic matrix:

```
>> A = sym ('[1 0 0; 0 cos(a) -sin(a); 0 sin(a) cos(a)]')
```

```
A =

[ 1,     0,      0]
[ 0,cos(a),-sin(a)]
[ 0,sin(a), cos(a)]
```

```
>> eigensys(A)
```

```
ans =

[                               1]
[cos(a) + 1/2 * (- 4 * sin(a) ^ 2) ^(1/2)]
[cos(a) - 1/2 * (- 4 * sin(a) ^ 2) ^(1/2)]
```

```
>> pretty(simple(poly(A)))
```

```
            3        2           2
        x - 2 x cos (a) + x - x + 2 x cos (a) - 1
```

```
>> jordan(A)
```

```
ans =

[1, 0,                                         0]
[0, cos(a) + 1/2 * (- 4 * sin(a) ^ 2) ^ (1/2), 0]
[0, 0, cos(a) - 1/2 * (- 4 * sin(a) ^ 2) ^(1/2)]
```

```
>> simple(Svd(A))
```

```
ans =

[                                                        1]
[1/2 * (4 * cos(a-comp(a)) + 2 * (- 2 + 2 * cos(2 * a-2 * conj(a))) ^(1/2)) ^(1/2)]
[1/2 * (4 * cos(a-comp(a)) - 2 * (- 2 + 2 * cos(2 * a-2 * conj(a))) ^(1/2)) ^(1/2)]
```

```
>> pretty(simple(sym(maple('minpoly(matrix [[1, 0, 0], [0, cos(a), - sin(a)],
[0, sin(a), cos(a)]]), x)'))))
```

$$-1 + 2\,x\cos^2(a) + x^2 - 2\,x\cos^2(a) - x^3 + x^3$$

```
>> pretty(simple(sym(maple('charmat(matrix([[1, 0, 0], [0, cos(a), -sin(a)],
[0, sin(a), cos(a)]]), x)'))))
```

```
            [x - 1        0          0      ]
            [                               ]
            [0        x - cos(a)     sin(a) ]
            [                               ]
            [0         - sin(a) x   - cos(a)]
```

EXERCISE 4-8

Consider the symbolic fifth-order square matrix whose (i,j)th element is defined by $A_{ij} = 1/(i+j-1/2)$. Compute its eigenvalues, eigenvectors, characteristic polynomial, minimum polynomial, characteristic matrix, and singular values. Also find the vector of the condition numbers of the eigenvalues and analyze whether the matrix is positive definite, negative definite, positive semi-definite or negative semi-definite.

MATLAB enables you to define this type of symbolic matrix in the general form:

```
>> A = sym(maple('matrix(5,5,(i,j)-> 1/(i+j-1/2))'))
```

```
A =

[2/3, 2/5, 2/7, 2/9, 2/11]
[2/5, 2/7, 2/9, 2/11, 2/13]
[2/7, 2/9, 2/11, 2/13, 2/15]
[2/9, 2/11, 2/13, 2/15, 2/17]
[2/11, 2/13, 2/15, 2/17, 2/19]
```

```
>> [V,E] = eig(A)
```

```
V =

[-.1612e-1, -.6740e-2,   .3578,   2.482,  -288.7]
[   .2084,     .1400, -2.513, -15.01,   2298.]
[  -.7456,    -.6391,  3.482,  20.13,  -3755.]
[       1,         1,      1,      1,       1]
[  -.4499,    -.5011, -2.476, -8.914,   1903.]

E =

[  2/55*.4005e-4,              0,            0,            0,             0]
[              0, 2/55* .3991e-2,            0,            0,             0]
[              0,              0,  2/55* .1629,            0,             0]
[              0,              0,            0, 2/55* 3.420,             0]
[              0,              0,            0,            0, 2/55* 34.16]
```

As we know, the eigenvectors are the columns of the matrix *V*, and the eigenvalues are the elements of the diagonal of the matrix *E*.

```
>> pretty(simple(poly(A)))
```

```
 5    10042  4   362807509088   3    268537284608   2
x  - ----- x  + ------------- x  - --------------- x
      7315      2228304933855       285965799844725

         22809860374528               34359738368
     + -------------------- x  - ------------------------
       1699754375321798654375    1776243322211277388821875
```

We can approximate this output as follows:

```
>> pretty(simple(vpa(poly(A))))
```

```
  5        4        3           2          -6          -12
 x  - 1.373 x  + .1628 x  - .0009391 x  + .1342 10   x - .1934 10
```

The singular values are calculated in the following way:

```
>> pretty(simple(Svd (A)))
```

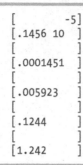

```
[           -5]
[.1456 10   ]
[           ]
[.0001451   ]
[           ]
[.005923    ]
[           ]
[.1244      ]
[           ]
[1.242      ]
```

The minimal polynomial and the characteristic matrix are calculated in the following way:

```
>> pretty(simple(sym(maple('minpoly(matrix(5,5,(i,j)-> 1/(i+j-1/2)),x)'))))
```

```
      34359738368                 22809860374528                268537284608   2
- ------------------------ + --------------------- x - -------------- x
  17762433222112773882187     1699754375321796543      285965799844725
  5                           75
      362807509088   3   10042   4    5
+ ------------- x  - ----- x  + x
  2228304933855       7315
```

```
>> pretty(simple(sym(vpa(maple('minpoly(matrix(5,5,(i,j)->1/(i+j-1/2)),x)')))))
```

```
          -12          -6            2          3         4    5
  -.1934 10    + .1342 10   x - .0009391 x  + .1628 x  - 1.373 x  + x
```

```
>> pretty(simple(sym(maple('charmat(matrix(5,5,(i,j)-> 1/(i+j-1/2)),x)'))))
```

```
       [                                              -2   ]
       [x - 2/3      -2/5         -2/7        -2/9     --   ]
       [                                              11   ]
       [                                                   ]
       [                                       -2     -2   ]
       [ -2/5      x - 2/7       -2/9          --     --   ]
       [                                      11     13   ]
       [                                                   ]
       [                                       -2     -2   ]
       [ -2/7       -2/9       x - 2/11        --     --   ]
       [                                      13     15   ]
       [                                                   ]
       [            -2          -2                    -2   ]
       [ -2/9       --          --        x - 2/15     --   ]
       [            11          13                    17   ]
       [                                                   ]
       [ -2        -2          -2          -2              ]
       [ --        --          --          --       x - 2/19]
       [ 11        13          15          17              ]
```

The vector of condition numbers of the eigenvalues is calculated as follows:

```
>> condeig(numeric(A))
```

```
ans =

    1.0000
    1.0000
    1.0000
    1.0000
    1.0000
```

In a more complete way, can calculate the matrix V whose columns are the eigenvectors of A, the diagonal matrix D whose diagonal elements are the eigenvalues of A, and the vector S of condition numbers of the eigenvalues of A, by using the command:

```
>> [V,D,s] = condeig(numeric(A))
```

V =

0.0102	0.0697	0.2756	-0.6523	0.7026
-0.1430	-0.4815	-0.7052	0.1593	0.4744
0.5396	0.6251	-0.2064	0.3790	0.3629
-0.7526	0.2922	0.2523	0.4442	0.2954
0.3490	-0.5359	0.5661	0.4563	0.2496

D =

0.0000	0	0	0	0
0	0.0001	0	0	0
0	0	0.0059	0	0
0	0	0	0.1244	0
0	0	0	0	1.2423

S =

```
1.0000
1.0000
1.0000
1.0000
1.0000
```

The matrix A is positive definite according to the command `definite`:

```
>> maple('definite(matrix(5,5,(i,j)-> 1/(i+j-1/2)),positive_def)')
```

ans =

true

4-5. Matrix Decomposition

MATLAB provides commands that allow you to decompose matrices as a product of special matrices in a number of different ways.

We have already seen how the command `[U,S,V] = Svd(A)` returns a diagonal matrix S of singular values of A (ordered in decreasing order of magnitude), and orthogonal matrices U and V such that $= U * S * V'$.

We have also seen that you can get the Jordan decomposition of a square matrix A via the command `[V,J] = jordan(A)`, which returns the canonical Jordan form J of A with the eigenvalues of A on its diagonal, and where the columns of V are the eigenvectors of A, so that $V^{-1} * A * V = J$.

On the other hand, we have also seen that you can obtain the Schur decomposition of a square matrix A via the command $[U,T]$ = schur(A), which returns an array T and an orthogonal matrix U such that A = U * T * U' and U'* U = eye(U). If A is complex, T is an upper triangular matrix with the eigenvalues of A on its diagonal. If A is real, the matrix T has real eigenvalues of A on its diagonal, and the corresponding complex eigenvalues correspond to diagonal 2 x 2 block submatrices of T. At the same time, we have also seen that a Hessenberg decomposition of a matrix A can be achieved through the command $[H, P]$ = hess(A), which gives the orthogonal matrix P and Hessenberg matrix H, such that $A = P * H * P'$ and $P'* P = eye (size (P))$.

In addition, MATLAB has other commands that also perform the decompositon of numerical (and sometimes symbolic) matrices. They include the following:

[L,U] = lu(A) **decomposes the matrix** *A* **into the product** A = L * U **(the** *LU* **decomposition of** A**), where** U **is an upper triangular matrix and** L **a lower pseudotriangular matrix (triangulizable via a permutation).**

[L,U,P] = lu(A) **returns a lower triangular matrix** L**, an upper triangular matrix** U**, and a permutation matrix** P **such that** P * A = L * U.

R = chol(A) **returns the upper triangular matrix** R **such that** R'* R = A **(the Cholesky decomposition), if** A **is positive definite. If** A **is not positive definite, it returns an error.**

[Q,R] = qr(A) **returns the upper triangular matrix** R **of the same dimension as** A**, and the orthogonal matrix** Q **such that** A = Q * R **(the** *QR* **decomposition of the matrix** A**). This decomposition can be applied to non-square matrices.**

[Q,R,E] = qr(A) **returns the upper triangular matrix** R **of the same dimension as** A**, where** E **is a permutation matrix and** Q **an orthogonal matrix such that** A * E = Q * R.

X = pinv(A) **returns the matrix** X **(the Moore-Penrose pseudoinverse of** *A)*, **of the same dimension as** A' **such that** A * X * A = A **and** X * A * X = X, **where** A * X **and** X * A **are hermitian.**

In addition, the following commands allow the decomposition of both numeric and symbolic matrices. All of them must be preceded by the maple command.

LUdecomp(A,P='p',L='l',U='u',U1='u1',R='r') **decomposes the matrix** A **into the product** A = evalm(P&*L&*U) **(the** *LU* **decomposition of** A**), where** U **is an upper triangular matrix and** L **a lower pseudotriangular matrix (that is, triangulizable via a permutation). In addition,** U= evalm(U1&*R) **with** U **upper triangular and** R **a reduced echelon form of** A**, so that** A = evalm(P&*L&*U1*R).

cholesky(A) **returns the lower triangular matrix** R **such that** A= evalm(R&*R') **(the Cholesky decomposition of** A**), provided** A **is positive definite.**

QRdecomp(A,Q='q') **returns the upper triangular matrix** R **of the same dimension as** A, **and the orthonormal matrix** Q **such that** A = evalm(Q&*R) **(the QR decomposition of** A**).**

companion(poly,var) **gives the matrix** C **associated with the given monic polynomial in the specified variable.** *If* poly = a0 + a1x +... +anx^n, **then:**

C(i,n)=-coeff(poly,var,i-1) i=1...n, C(i,i-1)=1 i=2...n,

C (i,j) = 0 **for the rest of the elements in the array.**

Frobenius(A) **or** ratform(A) **returns the canonical Frobenius form** F **of the matrix** A. F **is a block diagonal matrix (**F = diag(C1,C2,...,Cn)**), where the blocks are associated with polynomials** $p_1, p_2,..., p_k$ **so that** p_i **divides** p_{i-1} *for i = 2... k.*

Frobenius(A,'P') **returns the transformation matrix** P **and the canonical Frobenius form** F **of the matrix** *A*, **such that** evalm(P^{-1}& * A & * P) = F.

smith(A,var) **gives the diagonal matrix** S **corresponding to the Smith normal form of the square matrix** A **of polynomials in the variable** var.

smith(A,var,U,V) **gives the diagonal matrix** S **corresponding to the Smith normal form of the square matrix** A **of polynomials in the variable** var. **It also gives the matrices** U **and** V **such that** S = evalm(U&*A&*V).

ismith(A,var) **gives the diagonal matrix** S **corresponding to the integer Smith normal form of the square matrix** A **of polynomials in the variable** var.

ismith(A,var,U,V) **gives the diagonal matrix** S **corresponding to the integer Smith normal form of the square matrix** A **of polynomials in the variable** var. **It also gives the matrices** U **and** V **such that** S = evalm(U&*A&*V).

hermite(A,var) **computes the Hermite normal form of the square matrix** A **of polynomials in the variable** var **over the rational numbers**.

hermite(A,var,U) **computes the Hermite normal form of the square matrix** A **of polynomials in the variable** var **over the rational numbers. It also gives the matrix** U **such that** H = evalm(U&*A).

ihermite(A,var) **computes the Hermite normal form of the square matrix** A **of polynomials in the variable** var **over the integers.**

ihermite(A,var,U) **computes the Hermite normal form of the square matrix** A **of polynomials in the variable** var **over the integers. It gives also the matrix** U **such that** H= evalm(U&*A).

gaussjord(A) **gives an upper triangular matrix corresponding to the reduced row echelon form of the matrix** A. **This is used to facilitate the resolution of systems of linear equations whose coefficient matrix is the matrix** A.

gaussjord(A,j) **gives the row reduced echelon form of the matrix** A **terminating the elimination at column** j.

gaussjord(A,r,d) **gives the row reduced echelon form of the matrix** A **and assigns to the variable** r **the rank of** A **and the to the variable** d **the determinant of** submatrix(A,1..r,1..r). **This subarray is used for solving systems of linear equations whose coefficient matrix is** A.

gausselim(A) **performs Gaussian elimination on the matrix** A. **This is used to facilitate the solution of systems of linear equations whose coefficient matrix is the matrix** A.

gausselim(A,j) **performs Gaussian elimination on the matrix** A **terminating the elimination at the j-th column.**

gausselim(A,r,d) **performs Gaussian elimination on the matrix** A **and assigns to the variable** r **the rank of** A, **and to the variable** d **the determinant of** submatrix(A, 1..r,1..r). **This subarray is used for solving systems of linear equations whose coefficient matrix is** A.

backsub(A) **gives the vector** x **such that** A * x = V, **where** A **is an upper triangular matrix which is usually obtained with** gaussjord(A) **or** gausselim(A), **and where the vector** V **vector is the last column of the matrix** A.

backsub(A,V) **gives the vector** x **such that** A * x = V, **where** A **is an upper triangular matrix which is usually obtained with** gaussjord(A) **or** gausselim(A).

backsub(A,V,t) **gives the vector** x **such that** A * x = V, **where** A **is an upper triangular matrix which is usually obtained with** gaussjord(A) **or** gausselim(A) **and where the parameter** t **is used for a possible family of parametric system solutions.**

forwardsub(A,V) **gives the vector** x **such that** A * x = V, **where** A *is* **a lower row reduced matrix, which is usually obtained via the LU decomposition.**

forwardsub(A,V,t) **gives the vector** x **such that** A * x = V, **where** A *is* **a lower row reduced matrix, which is usually obtained via the LU decomposition, and where the parameter** t **is used for a possible family of parametric system solutions.**

forwardsub(A) **gives the vector** x **such that** A * x = V, **where** A *is* **a lower row reduced matrix, which is usually obtained via the LU decomposition, and where the vector** V **is the last column of** A.

forwardsub(A,B) **gives the matrix** X **such that** A * X = B, **where** A *is* **a lower row reduced matrix, which is usually obtained via the LU decomposition, and** B **is a matrix with the correct dimension and rank .**

geneqns(A,[x1,...,xn]) **generates linear equations equated to zero, in the variables given, corresponding to the coefficients of the matrix** A.

geneqns(A,[x1,...,xn],V) **generates linear equations equated to the elements of the vector** V, **in the variables given, corresponding to the coefficients of the matrix** A.

genmatrix([equation1,...,equationm],[x1,...,xn]) **generates the matrix corresponding to the given linear equations with respect to the specified variables.**

genmatrix([equation1,...,equationm],[x1,...,xn],flag) **generates the matrix corresponding to the given linear equations with respect to the specified variables, using the last column of the matrix as the right-hand sides of the equations.**

genmatrix([equation1,...,equationm],[x1,..,xn],name) **generates the matrix corresponding to the given linear equations with respect to the specified variables, and assigns to** name **the vector defining the right-hand sides of the equations.**

EXERCISE 4-9

Consider the 3 × 3 matrix A whose rows are the vectors (1,5,-2), (-7,3,1) and (2,2,-2). Perform the Schur, LU, QR, Cholesky, Hessenberg and singular value decompositions of A. Verify that the results are correct. Also find the pseudoinverse of A.

First, we find the Schur decomposition, checking that the result is correct:

```
>> A = [1,5,-2;-7,3,1;2,2,-2];
>> [U,T] = schur(A)
```

U =

```
   -0.0530   -0.8892   -0.4544
   -0.9910   -0.0093    0.1337
    0.1231   -0.4573    0.8807
```

T =

```
    2.4475   -5.7952   -4.6361
    5.7628    0.3689    2.4332
         0         0   -0.8163
```

Now, we check that U * T * U' = A and that U * U' = eye(3):

```
>> [U * T * U', U * U']
```

ans =

```
    1.0000 5.0000 - 2.0000 1.0000 0.0000 0.0000
   -7.0000 3,0000    1.0000 0.0000 1.0000 0.0000
    2.0000 2.0000 - 2.0000 0.0000 0.0000 1.0000
```

Now we find the LU, QR, Cholesky, Hessenberg and singular value decompositions, checking the results for each case:

```
>> [L,U,P] = lu(A)
```

L =

```
    1.0000         0         0
   -0.1429    1.0000         0
   -0.2857    0.5263    1.0000
```

U =

```
   -7.0000    3.0000    1.0000
         0    5.4286   -1.8571
         0         0   -0.7368
```
P =

```
    0    1    0
    1    0    0
    0    0    1
```

>> [P * A, L * U]

```
   -7    3    1   -7    3    1
    5    1   -2    1    5   -2
    2    2   -2    2    2   -2
```
*we have that   P * A = L * U*

>> [Q, R, E] = qr(A)

Q =

```
   -0.1361   -0.8785   -0.4579
    0.9526   -0.2430    0.1831
   -0.2722   -0.4112    0.8700
```

R =

```
   -7.3485    1.6330    1.7691
         0   -5.9442    2.3366
         0         0   -0.6410
```

E =

```
    1    0    0
    0    1    0
    0    0    1
```

>> [A * E, Q * R]

ans =

```
    1.0000 5.0000 - 2.0000    1.0000 5.0000 - 2.0000
   -7.0000 3,0000    1.0000 - 7.0000 3,0000    1.0000
    2.0000 2.0000 - 2.0000    2.0000 2.0000 - 2.0000
```

Then, A * E = Q * R.

```
>> R = chol(A)
```

```
??? Error using ==> chol
Matrix must be positive definite.
```

This returns an error message because the matrix is not positive definite.

```
>> [P,H] = hess(A)
```

```
P =

    1.0000         0         0
         0   -0.9615    0.2747
         0    0.2747    0.9615
```

```
H =

    1.0000   -5.3571   -0.5494
    7.2801    1.8302   -2.0943
         0   -3.0943   -0.8302
```

```
>> [P*H*P', P'*P]
```

```
ans =

    1.0000 5.0000 - 2.0000 1.0000 0        0
   -7.0000 3.0000    1.0000 0     1.0000 0
    2.0000 2.0000 - 2.0000 0        0     1.0000
```

Then we solve for PHP' = A and P'P = I.

```
>> [U,S,V] = svd(A)
```

```
U =
   -0.1034 - 0.8623    0.4957
   -0.9808    0.0056 - 0.1949
    0.1653 - 0.5064 - 0.8463
```

```
S =

    7.8306 0        0
    0       6.2735  0
    0       0        0.5700
```

```
V =

    0.9058 - 0.3051 0.2940
   -0.3996 - 0.8460 0.3530
   -0.1411   0.4372 0.8882
```

```
>> U * S * V'
```

```
ans =

    1.0000 5.0000 - 2.0000
   -7.0000 3.0000   1.0000          we see that   USV'= A
    2.0000 2.0000 - 2.0000
```

Now, we calculate the pseudoinverse of *A*:

```
>> X' = pinv(A)
```

```
X =

    0.2857 - 0.2143 - 0.3929
    0.4286 - 0.0714 - 0.4643
    0.7143 - 0.2857 - 1.3571
```

```
>> [A * X * A, X * A * X]
```

```
ans =

    1.0000 5.0000 - 2.0000 0.2857 - 0.2143 - 0.3929
   -7.0000 3,0000   1.0000 0.4286 - 0.0714 - 0.4643
    2.0000 2.0000 - 2.0000 0.7143 - 0.2857 - 1.3571
```

Thus, it follows that *AXA = A*, *XAX = X*.

EXERCISE 4-10

Consider the fifth-order square matrix whose (i,j)th element is defined by $A_{ij} = 1/(i+j-1/2)$. Calculate its Jordan canonical form (verifying the result). Also find its LU, QR, Frobenius, Smith and Hermite decompositions, calculating the matrices involved and verifying that the results are correct.

```
>> A = sym(maple('matrix(5,5,(i,j)-> i+j-1/2)'))
```

A =

```
[  3/2,  5/2,  7/2,  9/2, 11/2]
[  5/2,  7/2,  9/2, 11/2, 13/2]
[  7/2,  9/2, 11/2, 13/2, 15/2]
[  9/2, 11/2, 13/2, 15/2, 17/2]
[ 11/2, 13/2, 15/2, 17/2, 19/2]
```

```
>> [V,J] = Jordan(A);
>> pretty(sym(V))
```

```
       [                   1/2                 1/2        22   19]
       [8/9 ,  - 9/170 17     + 3/10 ,  9/170 17    + 3/10 , -- , --]
       [                                               45   45]
       [                                                        ]
       [-71           1/2               1/2           -7        ]
       [--- ,  - 2/85 17    + 1/5 ,  2/85 17    + 1/5 , -- , -2/9]
       [90                                            18        ]
       [                                                        ]
       [-67          1/2                1/2          -49  -14]
       [--- , 1/170 17    + 1/10 ,  - 1/170 17    + 1/10 , --- , ---]
       [90                                            90   45 ]
       [                                                        ]
       [                1/2               1/2                   ]
       [3/10 ,   3/85 17    ,    - 3/85 17    ,   3/10 ,   -2/5]
       [                                                        ]
       [31    11   1/2            11   1/2            13   23]
       [-- ,  --- 17   - 1/10 ,  - --- 17   - 1/10 ,  -- , --]
       [90    170               170               90   45]
```

```
>> pretty(sym(J))
```

```
[0          0              0        0   0]
[                                       ]
[          1/2                           ]
[0   55/4 + 15/4 17        0        0   0]
[                                       ]
[                        1/2            ]
[0          0       55/4 - 15/4 17  0   0]
[                                       ]
[0          0              0        0   0]
[                                       ]
[0          0              0        0   0]
```

```
>> pretty(simple(sym(symmul(symmul(V,J),inv(V)))))
```

```
[3/2     5/2     7/2     9/2     11/2]
[                                    ]
[5/2     7/2     9/2     11/2    13/2]
[                                    ]
[7/2     9/2     11/2    13/2    15/2]
[                                    ]
[9/2     11/2    13/2    15/2    17/2]
[                                    ]
[11/2    13/2    15/2    17/2    19/2]
```

We have calculated the transformation matrix V and the diagonal matrix J. We have also verfied that V * J * V⁻¹= A. Now we will calculate the LU decomposition of A and the matrices involved, checking the result. Because it is a symbolic matrix, we will use the `maple` command.

```
>> maple('A:=matrix(5,5,(i,j)-> i+j-1/2)');
>> pretty(sym(maple('LUdecomp(A,P=p,L=l,U=u,U1=u1,R=r)')))
```

```
[3/2     5/2     7/2     9/2     11/2]
[                                    ]
[ 0     -2/3    -4/3     -2     -8/3]
[                                    ]
[ 0      0       0       0       0  ]
[                                    ]
[ 0      0       0       0       0  ]
[                                    ]
[ 0      0       0       0       0  ]
```

```
>> pretty(sym(maple('print(p,l)')))
```

```
[1   0   0   0   0]  [ 1     0   0   0   0]
[                 ]  [                     ]
[0   1   0   0   0]  [5/3    1   0   0   0]
[                 ]  [                     ]
[0   0   1   0   0], [7/3    2   1   0   0]
[                 ]  [                     ]
[0   0   0   1   0]  [ 3     3   0   1   0]
[                 ]  [                     ]
[0   0   0   0   1]  [11/3   4   0   0   1]
```

```
>> pretty(sym(maple('print(u1,r)')))
```

```
[3/2   5/2    0   0   0]  [1   0   -1   -2   -3]
[                      ]  [                    ]
[ 0   -2/3    0   0   0]  [0   1    2    3    4]
[                      ]  [                    ]
[ 0    0     1   0   0], [0   0    0    0    0]
[                      ]  [                    ]
[ 0    0     0   1   0]  [0   0    0    0    0]
[                      ]  [                    ]
[ 0    0     0   0   1]  [0   0    0    0    0]
```

```
>> pretty(sym(maple('evalm(p&*l&*u1&*r),evalm(p&*l&*u)')))
```

```
[3/2    5/2    7/2    9/2    11/2]  [3/2    5/2    7/2    9/2    11/2]
[                                ]  [                                ]
[5/2    7/2    9/2    11/2   13/2]  [5/2    7/2    9/2    11/2   13/2]
[                                ]  [                                ]
[7/2    9/2    11/2   13/2   15/2], [7/2   9/2    11/2   13/2   15/2]
[                                ]  [                                ]
[9/2    11/2   13/2   15/2   17/2]  [9/2    11/2   13/2   15/2   17/2]
[                                ]  [                                ]
[11/2   13/2   15/2   17/2   19/2]  [11/2   13/2   15/2   17/2   19/2]
```

We see that p * l * u1 * r = A and that p * l * u = A. We now calculate the QR decomposition of A and the matrices involved, checking the result.

```
>> pretty(sym(maple('print(R)')))
```

```
[          1/2     71    1/2    85     1/2    33    1/2    113    1/2]
[1/2 285      , --- 285      , --- 285      , -- 285      , --- 285   ]
[             114           114          38          114            ]
[                                                                    ]
[          1/2              1/2              1/2               1/2   ]
[0 ,   2/57 570      , 4/57 570      , 2/19 570      , 8/57 570      ]
[                                                                    ]
[0 ,          0 ,           0 ,           0 ,             0]
[                                                                    ]
[0 ,          0 ,           0 ,           0 ,             0]
[                                                                    ]
[0 ,          0 ,           0 ,           0 ,             0]
```

```
>> pretty(sym(maple('print(q)')))
```

```
[        1/2              1/2              1/2                          ]
[1/95 285     ,    3/95 570     ,   1/5 10     ,        0    ,       0 ]

[        1/2       11    1/2              1/2              1/2          ]
[1/57 285     ,    --- 570     , - 1/5 10     ,   1/10 30     ,     0 ]
[                 570                                                  ]

[        1/2              1/2              1/2              1/2     1/2 ]
[7/285 285     ,  2/285 570     , - 1/10 10     , - 2/15 30     , 1/6 6 ]

[        1/2              1/2                         1/2         1/2  ]
[3/95 285     , - 1/190 570     ,       0     , - 1/30 30     ,- 1/3 6 ]

[11     1/2               1/2              1/2              1/2     1/2]
[--- 285      , - 1/57 570     ,   1/10 10     , 1/15 30     , 1/6 6 ]
[285                                                                  ]
```

```
>> pretty(sym(maple('evalm(q&*R)')))
```

```
[3/2     5/2     7/2     9/2     11/2]
[                                    ]
[5/2     7/2     9/2     11/2    13/2]
[                                    ]
[7/2     9/2     11/2    13/2    15/2]
[                                    ]
[9/2     11/2    13/2    15/2    17/2]
[                                    ]
[11/2    13/2    15/2    17/2    19/2]
```

We see that q * R = A. Next we will calculate the Smith decomposition of the matrix A and the matrices involved, checking the result.

```
>> pretty(sym(maple('smith(A,X,U,V)')))
```

$$
\begin{bmatrix}
1 & 0 & 0 & 0 & 0 \\
0 & 1 & 0 & 0 & 0 \\
0 & 0 & 0 & 0 & 0 \\
0 & 0 & 0 & 0 & 0 \\
0 & 0 & 0 & 0 & 0
\end{bmatrix}
$$

```
>> pretty(sym(maple('print(U,V)')))
```

$$
\begin{bmatrix}
0 & 0 & 0 & 0 & 2/11 \\
0 & 0 & 0 & 11/2 & -9/2 \\
-1 & 2 & -1 & 0 & 0 \\
0 & 1 & -2 & 1 & 0 \\
0 & 0 & 1 & -2 & 1
\end{bmatrix},
\begin{bmatrix}
1 & \dfrac{-13}{11} & 1 & 2 & 3 \\
0 & 1 & -2 & -3 & -4 \\
0 & 0 & 1 & 0 & 0 \\
0 & 0 & 0 & 1 & 0 \\
0 & 0 & 0 & 0 & 1
\end{bmatrix}
$$

```
>> pretty(sym(maple('evalm(U&*A&*V)')))
```

$$
\begin{bmatrix}
1 & 0 & 0 & 0 & 0 \\
0 & 1 & 0 & 0 & 0 \\
0 & 0 & 0 & 0 & 0 \\
0 & 0 & 0 & 0 & 0 \\
0 & 0 & 0 & 0 & 0
\end{bmatrix}
$$

We see that U * A * V = Smith matrix. Next we will calculate the Hermite decomposition of A and the matrices involved, verifying the result.

```
>> pretty(sym(maple('H:=hermite(A,x,V); V:=evalm(V)')))
>> pretty(sym(maple('print(H,V)')))
```

```
    [1    0    -1    -2   -3]  [-7/2    5/2    0    0    0]
    [                      ]  [                          ]
    [0    1     2     3    4]  [ 5/2   -3/2    0    0    0]
    [                      ]  [                          ]
    [0    0     0     0    0], [  2     -4     2    0    0]
    [                      ]  [                          ]
    [0    0     0     0    0]  [  4     -6     0    2    0]
    [                      ]  [                          ]
    [0    0     0     0    0]  [  6     -8     0    0    2]
```

```
>> pretty(sym(maple('evalm(V&*A)')))
```

```
        [1    0    -1    -2   -3]
        [                      ]
        [0    1     2     3    4]
        [                      ]
        [0    0     0     0    0]
        [                      ]
        [0    0     0     0    0]
        [                      ]
        [0    0     0     0    0]
```

Thus we see that V * A = H. Finally, we will calculate the Frobenius decomposition of A, checking the result.

```
>> pretty(sym(maple('F:=frobenius(A,P); P:=evalm(P)')))
>> pretty(sym(maple('print(F,P)')))
```

```
                              [ 67                  22     19 ]
                              [ --    3/2   285/4   --     -- ]
                              [ 45                  45     45 ]
                              [                             ]
    [0    0    0    0    0]   [ -7                  -7        ]
    [                    ]   [ --    5/2   355/4   --    -2/9]
    [1    0    50   0    0]   [ 18                  18        ]
    [                    ]   [                             ]
    [0    1   55/2   0    0], [-49                  -49   -14 ]
    [                    ]   [---    7/2   425/4   ---   --- ]
    [0    0    0    0    0]   [90                   90    45  ]
    [                    ]   [                             ]
    [0    0    0    0    0]   [3/10   9/2   495/4   3/10  -2/5]
                              [                             ]
                              [ 13                  13     23 ]
                              [ --   11/2   565/4   --     -- ]
                              [ 90                  90     45 ]
```

```
>> pretty(sym(maple('evalm(P^(-1)&*A&*P)')))
```

$$
\begin{bmatrix}
0 & 0 & 0 & 0 & 0 \\
1 & 0 & 50 & 0 & 0 \\
0 & 1 & 55/2 & 0 & 0 \\
0 & 0 & 0 & 0 & 0 \\
0 & 0 & 0 & 0 & 0
\end{bmatrix}
$$

Thus we see that $P^{-1} * A * P = F$.

EXERCISE 4-11

Consider the 3 x 3 matrix A whose rows are the vectors (1,5,-2), (-7,3,1) and (2,2,-2). Let V be the vector of ones and solve the system L * x = V based on the LU decomposition. Solve the system G * x = V by performing Gaussian elimination on A. Solve the system J * x = V by transforming A into its Jordan canonical form. Represent the matrix system in the form of equations, and perform the Hermite and Smith decompositions for the integer matrix A.

First, we define the matrix *A* and vector *V* using maple commands as follows:

```
>> maple ('A: = matrix(3,3,[1,5,-2,-7,3,1,2,2,-2]);) V: = array([1,1,1])');
```

Then we find an LU decomposition, solving the system A * x = V using the command backsub.

```
>> pretty(sym(maple('L:=LUdecomp(A)')))
>> pretty(sym(maple('backsub(L,V)')))
```

$$
\begin{bmatrix}
\dfrac{253}{532} & \dfrac{-233}{532} & \dfrac{-19}{14}
\end{bmatrix}
$$

Thus we have solved the system L * x = V, which can be expressed in the form of equations using the command geneqns as follows:

```
>> pretty(sym(maple('geneqns(L,[x1,x2,x3],V)')))
```

$$
\{x1 + 5\ x2 - 2\ x3 = 1,\ 38\ x2 - 13\ x3 = 1,\ -\frac{14}{19}\ x3 = 1\}
$$

Now, we solve the system G * x = V, transforming *A* via Gaussian elimination to G.

```
>> pretty(sym(maple('G:=gausselim(A)')))
>> pretty(sym(maple('backsub(G,V)')))
```

$$\begin{bmatrix} 79 & -11 & \\ -- & --- & -2/7 \\ 56 & 56 & \end{bmatrix}$$

The system of equations is found by:

```
>> pretty(sym(maple('geneqns(G,[x1,x2,x3],V)')))
```

$$\{x\,1 + 5\,x\,2 - 2\,x\,3 = 1,\ 8\,x\,2 + 2\,x\,3 = 1,\ -7/2\,x\,3 = 1\}$$

Now, we need to solve the system J * x = V, transforming *A* to its canonical Jordan form and then using the command forwardsub.

```
>> pretty(sym(maple('J:=gaussjord(A)')))
>> pretty(sym(maple('forwardsub(J,V)')))
```

$$[1\ 1\ 1]$$

Finally, we find the Smith and Hermite decompositions of *A*.

```
>> pretty(sym(maple('ihermite(A,x)')))
```

$$\begin{bmatrix} 1 & 1 & 6 \\ 0 & 2 & 3 \\ 0 & 0 & 14 \end{bmatrix}$$

```
>> pretty(sym(maple('ismith(A)')))
```

$$\begin{bmatrix} 1 & 0 & 0 \\ 0 & 1 & 0 \\ 0 & 0 & 28 \end{bmatrix}$$

4-6. Similar Matrices and Diagonalization

Two matrices, A and B, of dimensions $(M \times N)$ are equivalent if there exist invertible U and V such that $A = UBV$. The MATLAB command [U, S, V] = svd (A) calculates a diagonal matrix S, which is equivalent to A.

Two square matrices A and B of order n are said to be congruent if there is an invertible matrix P such that $A = PBP^t$.

The MATLAB command [U, T] = schur(A) calculates an array T which is congruent with A. Congruence implies equivalence, and two congruent matrices must always have the same rank.

Two square matrices of order n, A and B, are similar if there is an invertible matrix P, called the transformation matrix, such that $A = PBP^{-1}$.

Two similar matrices are equivalent.

A matrix A is diagonalizable if it is similar to a diagonal matrix D, that is, if there is an invertible matrix P such that $A = PDP^{-1}$.

The process of calculating the diagonal matrix D and the matrix P is known as diagonalization.

Given a real square matrix A, if all the eigenvalues of A are real and distinct, then A is diagonalizable. The diagonal matrix D will have the eigenvalues of A as its diagonal elements.

The matrix P consists of columns that are the eigenvectors of A corresponding to the eigenvalues appearing on the diagonal of D.

If an n×n matrix A has eigenvalues r with multiplicity greater than 1, then A is diagonalizable if, and only if, the kernel of the matrix $A - r * I_n$ has dimension equal to the degree of multiplicity of the eigenvalue r.

The MATLAB command [V,J] = jordan(A) diagonalizes the matrix A, returning the transformation matrix V and the diagonal matrix J.

EXERCISE 4-12

Diagonalize the symmetric matrix whose rows are the vectors:

(3, - 1, 0), (- 1, 2 - 1), (0, - 1, 3)

Find the transformation matrix V and the diagonal matrix J, check the result, and verify that the eigenvalues of the initial matrix are the elements of the diagonal of J.

We calculate the diagonal matrix J of A, which will have the eigenvalues of A on its diagonal, and the transformation matrix V. To do this, we use the command [V,J] = jordan(A):

```
>> A = [3, 0, - 1, - 1, 2, - 1; 0 - 1, 3]
```

```
A =

    3 -1  0
   -1 -2 -1
    0 -3 -1
```

```
>> [V,J] = jordan(A)
```

V =

```
[1/6, 1/2, 1/3]
[1/3, 0,  -1/3]
[1/6,-1/2, 1/3]
```

J =

```
[1, 0, 0]
[0, 3, 0]
[0, 0, 4]
```

We now show that the diagonal matrix J has the eigenvalues of A on its diagonal:

```
>> eigensys(A)
```

ans =

```
[1]
[3]
[4]
```

The matrices *A* and *J* are similar, because we have $V^1 * A * V = J$:

```
>> symmul(symmul(inv(V),A),V)
```

ans =

```
[1, 0, 0]
[0, 3, 0]
[0, 0, 4]
```

EXERCISE 4-13

Find a diagonal matrix similar to each of the following matrices:

$$A = \begin{bmatrix} 0 & -r & q \\ r & 0 & -p \\ -q & p & 0 \end{bmatrix}, \quad B = \begin{bmatrix} 0 & 1 & -\sin(a) \\ -1 & 0 & \cos(a) \\ -\sin(a) & \cos(a) & 0 \end{bmatrix}, \quad C = \begin{bmatrix} \cos(a) & -\sin(a) \\ \sin(a) & \cos(a) \end{bmatrix}.$$

Find the transformation matrices and verify the results. Find the characteristic polynomial and the minimal polynomial for each of the three matrices.

```
>> A = sym('[0,-r,q;r,0,-p;-q,p,0]');
>> [V,J] = jordan(A)
```

V =

```
[1 /(q^2+r^2+p^2) * p ^ 1/2, 2, 1/2 /(q^2+r^2+p^2) *(q^2+r^2) /(q^2+r^2+p^2) *(q^2+r^2)]
[1 /(q^2+r^2+p^2) * q * p, 1/2 * i * (i * *(q^2+r^2+p^2) ^(1/2) p * q+r * p ^ 2 + r *
q ^ 2 + r ^ 3) /(q^2+r^2+p^2) ^(3/2), 1/2 * i * (i * *(q^2+r^2+p^2) ^(1/2) p * q-r *
p ^ 2-r * q ^ 2-r ^ 3) /(q^2+r^2+p^2) ^(3/2)]
[1 /(q^2+r^2+p^2) * r * p, 1/2 * i * (i * p *(q^2+r^2+p^2) ^(1/2) * r-p ^ 2 * q-q ^ 3-q * r ^ 2)
/(q^2+r^2+p^2) ^(3/2), 1/2 * i * (i * p *(q^2+r^2+p^2) ^(1/2) * r + p ^ 2 * q + q ^ 3 +
q * r ^ 2) /(q^2+r^2+p^2) ^(3/2)]
```

J =

```
[0,                    0,                          0]
[0,     -(-q^2-r^2-p^2) ^(1/2),                    0]
[0,                    0,      (-q ^ 2-r ^ 2 p ^ 2) ^(1/2)]
```

Thus we have found the diagonal matrix *J*, similar to the matrix *A*, and the transformation matrix *V*. Now, we analyze the matrix *B*:

```
>> B = sym ('[0, 1, -sin(a); - 1, 0, cos (a); -sin(a), cos(a), 0]')
>> J = simple(jordan(B))
```

J =

```
[0, 0, 0]
[0, 0, 0]
[0, 0, 0]
```

We see that the matrix B has a single eigenvalue zero and its multiplicity is 3. In addition, the kernel of $B - 0 * eye(3) = B$ has dimension less than three, as the determinant of B is zero. In particular, it has dimension one (as we see by calculating a basis with the command `nullspace(B)`). As the multiplicity and the dimension of the kernel differ, we conclude that the matrix B is not diagonalizable:

```
>> null(B)
```

```
ans =

[cos(a)]
[sin(a)]
[     1]
```

We have calculated a basis of the kernel of B, which is formed by a single vector. It follows that the dimension of the kernel of B is 1:

```
>> det (B)
```

```
ans =

0
```

We now analyze the matrix C:

```
>> C = sym ('[cos(a) - sin(a); sin(a), cos(a)]');
>> [V,J] = jordan(C)
```

```
V =

[1/2, 1/2]
[(-1/2*4^(1/2)/abs(sin(a))/(-1-signum(-sin(a)^2)-i+i*signum(-sin(a)^2))*sin(a),
1/2*4^(1/2)/abs(sin(a))/(-1-signum(-sin(a)^2)-i+i*signum(-sin(a)^2))*sin(a)]

J =

[cos(a) + 1/2 * (- 4 * sin(a) ^ 2) ^ (1/2), 0]
[0, cos(a) - 1/2 * (- 4 * sin(a) ^ 2) ^(1/2)]
```

We can try to simplify the Jordan matrix J.

```
>> simple(J)
```

```
ans =

[exp(i*a),          0]
[0,        1/exp(i*a)]
```

We already have the diagonal matrix *J* similar to the matrix *C* and the transformation matrix *V*. We now calculate the characteristic and minimal polynomials of the three matrices:

```
>> pretty(poly(A))
```

$$x^3 + x^2 p^2 + r^2 x + q^2 x$$

```
>> pretty(sym(maple('minpoly(array([[0,-r,q],[r,0,-p],[-q,p,0]]),x)')))
```

$$(r^2 + q^2 + p^2) x + x^3$$

```
>> pretty(simple(sym(poly(B))))
```

$$x^3$$

```
>> pretty(simple(sym(maple('minpoly(array([[0,1,-sin(a)],[-1,0,cos(a)],
[-sin(a),cos(a),0]]), x)'))))
```

$$x^3$$

```
>> pretty(simple(sym(poly(C))))
```

$$x^2 - 2 x \cos(a) + 1$$

```
>> pretty(simple(sym(maple('minpoly(array([[cos(a),-sin(a)],[sin(a),cos(a)]]),x)'))))
```

$$x^2 - 2 x \cos(a) + 1$$

4-7. Sparse Matrices

A matrix is called *sparse* if it has sufficiently many zero elements that one can take advantage of. Sparse matrix algorithms do not store null elements in memory, so when working on matrix processing with sparse matrices one gains time and efficiency. There are specialized commands that can be used to deal with sparse matrices. Some of these commands are listed below.

S = sparse(i,j,s,m,n,nzmax), i = vector, j = vector, s = vector. **Creates a sparse matrix** S **of dimension** m×n **with space for** nzmax **non-zero elements given by** s. **The vector** i **contains the** *i*-**input components of the non-null elements and the vector** j **contains the corresponding** j-**input components.**

S=sparse(i,j,s,m,n) **creates the sparse matrix** S **using** nzmax=length(s).

S = sparse(i,j,s) **creates a sparse matrix** S **with** m = max (i) **and** n = max (j).

S = sparse(A) **converts the matrix** A **into sparse form.**

A = full(S) **converts the sparse matrix** S **into full matrix form** A.

S = spconvert(D) **converts an external ASCII file read with name** D **into a sparse matrix** S.

(i,j) = find(A) **returns the row and column indices of the non-zero entries of the matrix** A.

B = spdiags(A,d) **builds a sparse matrix by extracting the diagonal elements of** A **specified by the vector** d.

S = speye(m,n) **creates the sparse** m×n **matrix with ones on the main diagonal.**

S = speye(n) **creates the sparse square identity matrix of order** n.

R = sprandn(S) **generates a random sparse matrix with non-zero values normally distributed in (0,1) with the same structure as the sparse matrix** S.

R = sprandsym(S) **generates a sparse random symmetric matrix with non-zero entries normally distributed in (0,1) whose lower diagonal triangle has the same structure as** S.

r = sprank(S) **gives the structural rank of the sparse matrix** S.

n = nnz(S) **gives the number of non-zero elements in the sparse matrix** S.

k = nzmax(S) **returns the amount of storage occupied by the non-zero elements in the sparse matrix** S. **If** S **is a full matrix then** nzmax(S) = prod(size(S)).

s=spalloc(m,n,nzmax) **creates space in memory for a sparse matrix of dimension** m×n.

R = spones(S) **replaces the zero entries of the sparse matrix** S **with ones.**

n = condest(S) **computes a lower bound for the 1-norm condition number of a square matrix** S.

m = normest(S) **returns an estimate of the 2-norm of the matrix** S.

issparse(A) **returns 1 if the matrix** A **is sparse, and 0 otherwise.**

Here are some examples:

```
>> sparse([1,1,2,2,3,4],[4,2,3,1,2,3],[-7,12,25,1,-6,8],4,4,10)
```

ans =

```
    (2,1)        1
    (1,2)       12
    (3,2)       -6
    (2,3)       25
    (4,3)        8
    (1,4)       -7
```

Now, we convert this sparse matrix into complete form:

```
>> full(ans)
```

ans =

```
    0    12     0    -7
    1     0    25     0
    0    -6     0     0
    0     0     8     0
```

Next, we define a sparse matrix whose full form is a diagonal matrix:

```
sparse(1:5,1:5,-6)
```

ans =

```
    (1,1)       -6
    (2,2)       -6
    (3,3)       -6
    (4,4)       -6
    (5,5)       -6
```

```
>> full(ans)
```

ans =

```
   -6     0     0     0     0
    0    -6     0     0     0
    0     0    -6     0     0
    0     0     0    -6     0
    0     0     0     0    -6
```

4-8. Special Numeric and Symbolic Matrices

MATLAB provides commands to define certain special types of matrices. These include the following:

H = hadamard(n) **returns the Hadamard matrix of order n, a matrix with values 1 or - 1 such that** H' * H = n * eye(n).

Hankel(V) **returns the square Hankel matrix whose first column is the vector V and whose elements are zero below the first anti-diagonal. The matrix** hankel(C,R) **has first column vector C and last row vector R.**

Hilb(n) **returns the Hilbert matrix of order n, a matrix whose ij-th element is** *1 /(i+j-1)*.

invhilb(n) **returns the inverse of the Hilbert matrix of order n.**

magic(n) **returns a magic square of order n. Its elements are integers from 1 to n² with equal sums of rows and columns.**

pascal(n) **returns the Pascal matrix of order n (symmetric, positive definite with integer entries taken from Pascal's triangle).**

Rosser **returns the Rosser matrix, an 8 × 8 matrix with a double eigenvalue, three nearly equal eigenvalues, dominant eigenvalues of the opposite sign, a zero eigenvalue and a small non-zero eigenvalue.**

toeplitz(C,R) **returns a Toeplitz matrix (not symmetric, with the vector C in the first column and R as the first row vector).**

vander(C) **returns a Vandermonde matrix A whose penultimate column is the vector C. In addition,** A(:,j) = C^(n-j).

wilkinson(n) **returns the Wilkinson matrix of order n (symmetric tridiagonal with pairs of eigenvalues close but not the same).**

compan(P) **returns the corresponding companion matrix whose first row is** -P(2:n)/P(1), **where** P **is a vector of polynomial coefficients.**

maple('hadamard(n)') **returns the Hadamard matrix of order n, a matrix with values 1 or - 1 such that** H'* H = n * eye(n).

maple('hilbert(n)') **returns the Hilbert matrix of order n, a matrix whose ij-th element is** *1 /(i+j-1)*.

maple('hilbert(n,exp)') **returns the matrix of order n with ij-th entry equal to** *1 /(i+j-exp)*.

maple('bezout(poly1,poly2,x)') **constructs the Bézout matrix of the given polynomials in x, with dimension** max(m,n), **where** m = degree(poly1) **and** n = degree(poly2). **The determinant of this matrix is the resultant of the two polynomials (**resultant(poly1,poly2,x)**).**

maple('sylvester(p1,p2,x)') **constructs the Sylvester matrix of the given polynomials in x, with dimension** n+m, **where** m = degree(p1) **and** n =degree(p2). **The determinant of this matrix is the resultant of the two polynomials.**

maple('fibonacci(n)') **returns the** n **th Fibonacci matrix** F(n) **whose size is the sum of the dimensions of** F(n-1) **and** F(n-2).

maple('toeplitz([ex1,...,exn])') **returns the symmetric Toeplitz matrix whose elements are the specified expressions.**

maple('vandermonde([expr1,..., exprn])') **returns the Vandermonde matrix whose** (i,j)**th element is** expri^{j-1}.

maple('wronskian(V,x)') **returns the Wronskian matrix of the vector** V =(f1,...,fn) **with respect to the variable** x. **The ij-th element is** diff(fj, x\$(i-1)).

maple('jacobian([expr1,...,exprm],[x1,..., xn])') **returns the** m×n **Jacobian matrix with ij-th element** diff(expri,xj).

maple('hessian(exp,[x1,...,xn])') **returns the** m×n **Hessian matrix with ij-th element** diff(exp,xi,xj).

EXERCISE 4-14

Find the eigenvalues of the Wilkinson matrix of order 8, a magic square of order 8 and the Rosser matrix.

```
>> [eig(wilkinson(8)), eig(rosser), eig(magic(8))]
```

ans =

1.0e+003 *

0.0042	1.0000	0.2600
0.0043	1.0000	0.0518
0.0028	1.0200	-0.0518
0.0026	1.0200	0.0000
0.0017	1.0199	0.0000 + 0.0000i
0.0011	0.0001	0.0000 - 0.0000i
0.0002	0.0000	0.0000 + 0.0000i
-0.0010	-1.0200	0.0000 - 0.0000i

Observe that the Wilkinson matrix has pairs of eigenvalues which are close, but not equal. The Rosser matrix has a double eigenvalue, three nearly equal eigenvalues, dominant eigenvalues of the opposite sign, a zero eigenvalue and a small non-zero eigenvalue.

EXERCISE 4-15

Find the Smith and Hermite forms of the inverse of the Hilbert matrix of order 2 in the variable x. Also find the corresponding transformation matrices.

```
>> maple('with(linalg):H:= inverse(hilbert(2,x))');
>> pretty(simple(sym(maple('H'))))
```

```
         [              2                                        ]
         [   -(-3 + x)  (-2 + x)        (-3 + x) (-2 + x) (-4 + x)]
         [                                                        ]
         [                                          2             ]
         [(-3 + x) (-2 + x) (-4 + x)      -(-3 + x)  (-4 + x)      ]
```

```
>> maple ('B: = smith(H,x,U,V);)U: = eval (U); V: = eval (V)');
>> pretty(simple(sym(maple('B'))))
```

```
         [-3 + x                0            ]
         [                                   ]
         [                      2            ]
         [  0        (-2 + x) (x  - 7 x + 12)]
```

```
>> pretty(simple(sym(maple('U'))))
```

```
         [       -1                   -1        ]
         [                                      ]
         [              2                    2]
         [10 - 13/2 x + x      - 13/2 x + 9 + x ]
```

```
>> pretty(simple(sym(maple('V'))))
```

```
         [- 7/2 + x    -4 + x]
         [                   ]
         [- 3/2 + x    -2 + x]
```

```
>> maple('HM:=hermite(H,x,Q);Q:=evalm(Q)');
>> pretty(simple(sym(maple('HM'))))
```

```
          [ 2                        ]
          [x  - 5 x + 6        0     ]
          [                          ]
          [                 2        ]
          [    0           x  - 7 x + 12]
```

```
>> pretty(simple(sym(maple('Q'))))
```

```
          [-x + 3     -x + 2]
          [                 ]
          [-x + 4     -x + 3]
```

EXERCISE 4-16

Confirm that the functions x, x^2 and x^3 are linearly independent.

```
>> maple('v:=[x,x^2,x^3]:w:=wronskian(v,x)');
>> pretty(simple(sym(maple('w'))))
```

```
          [        2       3 ]
          [x      x       x  ]
          [                  ]
          [                 2]
          [1     2 x     3 x ]
          [                  ]
          [0      2      6 x ]
```

```
>> pretty(simple(sym(maple('det(w)'))))
```

```
              3
          2 x
```

Since the determinant of the Wronskian is non-zero, the functions are linearly independent.

EXERCISE 4-17

Find the Jacobian matrix and the Jacobian determinant of the transformation:

$x = e^u \sin(v)$, $y = e^u \cos(v)$.

```
>> pretty(sym(maple('jacobian(vector([exp(u) * sin(v), exp(u) * cos(v)]), [u,v])')))
```

```
                    [exp(u) sin(v)    exp(u) cos(v) ]
                    [                                ]
                    [exp(u) cos(v)   -exp(u) sin(v)]
```

```
>> pretty(simple(sym(maple('det(")')))))
```

```
                              2
                      -exp(u)
```

EXERCISE 4-18

Find the Bézout and Sylvester matrices B and T for the functions $p = a + bx + cx^2$ and $q = d + ex + fx^2$. Verify that the determinants of B and T coincide with the resultant of p and q.

```
>> maple('p:=a+b*x+c*x^2:q:= d+e*x+f*x^2:B:=bezout(p, q, x);T:=sylvester(p, q, x)')
>> pretty(sym(maple('B')))
```

```
                    [d c - a f    d b - a e]
                    [                       ]
                    [e c - b f    d c - a f]
```

```
>> pretty(sym(maple('T')))
```

```
                    [c    b    a    0]
                    [                ]
                    [0    c    b    a]
                    [                ]
                    [f    e    d    0]
                    [                ]
                    [0    f    e    d]
```

```
>> pretty(sym(maple('det(B)'))),pretty(sym(maple('det(T)'))),
pretty(sym(maple('resultant(p,q,x)')))
```

$$d^2 c^2 - 2 d c a f + a^2 f^2 - d b e c + d b^2 f + a e^2 c - a e b f$$

$$d^2 c^2 - 2 d c a f + a^2 f^2 - d b e c + d b^2 f + a e^2 c - a e b f$$

$$d^2 c^2 - 2 d c a f + a^2 f^2 - d b e c + d b^2 f + a e^2 c - a e b f$$

CHAPTER 5

■ ■ ■

Equations and Systems

MATLAB offers certain commands that allow you to solve equations and systems. Among them are the following:

solve('equation','x') **solves the equation in the variable** x.

syms x; solve(equ(x),x) **solves the equation** equ(x)**in the variable** x.

solve('eq1,eq2,...,eqn','x1,x2,...,xn') **solves** n **simultaneous equations** eq1,...,eqn **(in the variables** x1,..., xn**).**

syms x1 x2 ... xn; solve(eq1,eq2,...,eqn,x1,x2,...,xn) **solves** n **simultaneous equations** eq1,...,eqn **(in the variables** x1,..., xn**).**

X = linsolve(A,B) **solves** A * X = B **for a square matrix** A, **where** B **and** X **are matrices.**

x = nnls(A,b) **solves** A * x = b **in the least-squares sense, where** x **is a vector** (x³0)**.**

x = lscov(A,b,V) **gives the vector** x **that minimizes** (A * x-b)'* inv(V) *(A*x-b)**.**

roots(V) **gives the roots of the polynomial whose coefficients are the components of the vector** V**.**

X = A\B **solves the system** A * X = B**.**

X = a/b **solves the system** X * A = B**.**

5-1. Special Commands

In addition, equations and systems can be solved using the following commands (all of them must be preceded by the maple command):

solve(equation,variable) **solves the given equation in the specified variable.**

solve(expression,variable) **solves the equation** expression = 0 **in the given variable.**

solve({expr1,..,exprn},{var1,..,varn}) **solves the system given by the specified equations in the given variables.**

solve(equation) **solves the equation for all of its variables.**

solve(expr1,...,exprn) **solves the specified system of equations for all possible variables.**

solve(inequality,variable) **solves the inequality for the specified variable.**

solve(s,var) **solves the set of equations** s **for the specified variable.**

LHS(equation) **returns the left-hand side of the equation.**

LHS(inequality) **returns the left-hand side of the inequality.**

RHS(equation) **returns the right-hand side of the equation.**

RHS(inequality) **returns the right-hand side of the inequality.**

readlib(isolate): isolate(equation,expression) **isolates the specified expression in the given equation.**

readlib(isolate): isolate(expr1,expr2) **isolates the subexpression** expr2 **in the equation** expr1 = 0.

reablib(isolate): isolate(equation,expression,n) **isolates the specified expression in the given equation by running at least** n **transformations or steps in the calculations.**

testeq(expr1=expr2) **or** testeq(expr1,expr2) **tests whether the expressions are equivalent. The purpose may be to eliminate redundant equations in a system.**

eliminate(setequ,setvar) **eliminates the given set of variables in the specified set of equations.**

isolve(equation) **returns the set of integer solutions of the given equation for all of its variables.**

isolve(expression) **returns the set of integer solutions of the equation** expression = 0 **for all of its variables.**

isolve({equ1,..,equn}) **gives the set of integer solutions of the specified system of equations for all variables.**

isolve(equation,variable) **returns the integer solutions of the specified equation in the given variable.**

isolve({equ1,...,equn},{var1,...,varn}) **finds the integer solutions of the specified system in the given variables.**

isolve(equation,{var1,...,varn}) **finds the set of integer solutions of the given equation for the specified variables.**

fsolve(equation,variable) **solves the equation for the given variable, by Newton's method.**

fsolve(expression,variable) **solves the equation** expression = 0 **for the given variable, by Newton's method.**

fsolve({equ1,...,equn},{var1,...,varn}) **solves the system of equations for the variables given, by numerical methods (the number of equations is equal to the number of unknowns).**

fsolve(expr) **or** fsolve({equ1,...,equn}) **solves the equation** expr = 0 **or the system of equations in the given variables by numerical methods.**

fsolve(equation,var,a..b) **solves the equation in the variable** var **by numerical methods, obtaining solutions in the interval** [a,b].

fsolve({equ1,...,equn},{var1,...,varn},{var1=a1..B1,..., varn=an...BN}) **finds real solutions of the system in the given variables that are in the specified intervals (by numerical methods).**

`fsolve(equation,variable,complex)` **finds all the complex solutions of the given equation.**

`fsolve(equation,variable,'maxsols'=m)` **finds only the** `m` **least solutions of the equation.**

`fsolve(equation,variable,'fulldigits')` **ensures an optimum value of digits for computing the largest number of possible solutions of the given equation in the specified variable.**

`msolve(equation,m)` **solves the equation modulo** `m` **in all its variables.**

`msolve(expression,m)` **solves the equation** `expression` = 0 **modulo** `m` **in all its variables.**

`msolve({equ1,...,equn},m)` **solves the given system modulo** `m` **in all its variables.**

`msolve(equation,variable,m)` **or** `msolve(equation,{var1,...,varn},m)` **solves the equation modulo** `m` **in the variable or variables specified.**

`msolve({equ1,...,equn},{var1,...,varn},m)` **solves the given system modulo** `m` **in the specified variables.**

`RootOf(Equation,variable)` **represents the roots of the given equation in the variable given in the form of** `RootOf` **expressions. The solution of certain transcendental equations and systems are usually given in terms of** `RootOf` **expressions.**

`RootOf(expression,variable)` **presents the solutions of the equation** `expression` = 0 **in terms of** `RootOf` **expressions.**

`RootOf(equation)` **presents in the form of** `RootOf` **expressions the solutions of the given univariate equation.**

`allvalues(expr)` **gives all the possible values of the specified RootOf expression. This command uses** *solve* **to calculate the exact roots of the expression, and if this is not possible, uses** *fsolve* **to calculate the approximate roots.**

`allvalues(expr,d)` **ensures that identical** `RootOfs` **in the expression are only evaluated once, thus avoiding redundant calculations and increasing efficiency.**

`convert(ineq,equality)` **converts the given inequality to an equality by replacing the signs < or < = by =.**

`convert(equ,lessequal)` **converts the given equation or strict inequality into a non-strict inequality, by replacing < or = with < =.**

`convert(equ,lessthan)` **converts the equation or non-strict inequality into the corresponding strict inequality, replacing the symbols = or < = with the symbol <.**

`with(student):equate(list1,list2)` **creates a set of equations of the form** `(list1[1] = list2[1],...,list1[n] = list2[n])`.

`equate(list)` **creates set of equations of the form** `{list[1] = 0,..., list[n] = 0}`.

`equate(array1,array2)` **converts the two arrays to a set of equations.**

`equate(Table1,Table2)` **converts the two tables to a set of equations.**

`equate(expr1,expr2)` **converts the two expressions to the equation** `expr1 = expr2`.

Here are some examples. First, we solve an equation in exact and approximate form and check one of the solutions.

```
>> pretty(sym(maple('eq := x^4-5*x^2+6*x=2: solve(eq,x)')))
```

```
      1/2          1/2
-1 + 3     , -1 - 3    , 1, 1
```

```
>> pretty(sym(maple('sols := [solve(eq,x)] : evalf(sols,10)')))
```

```
[.732050808    -2.732050808    1.    1.]
```

```
>> pretty(simple(sym(maple('subs(x=sols[1],eq )'))))
```

```
2 = 2
```

The previous equation also can be solved as follows:

```
>> solve('x^4-5*x^2+6*x=2')
```

```
ans =

[- 1 + 3 ^(1/2)]
[^(1/2) - 1-3]
[           1]
[           1]
```

Another way to solve the same equation would be as follows:

```
>> syms x
>> solve(x^4-5*x^2+6*x-2)
```

```
ans =

[- 1 + 3 ^(1/2)]
[^(1/2) - 1-3]
[           1]
[           1]
```

Next we solve a system and check its solutions.

```
>> maple('eqns:= {u+v+w=1, 3*u+v=3, u-2*v-w=0}:sols:= solve(eqns)')
```

```
ans =
sols := {w = -2/5, v = 3/5, u = 4/5}
```

```
>> maple('subs(sols,eqns)')
```

```
ans =
{1 = 1, 0 = 0, 3 = 3}
```

The previous system can also be solved in the following way:

```
>> syms u v w
>> [u,v,w] = solve(u+v+w-1, 3*u+v-3, u-2*v-w, u, v, w)
```

```
u =

4/5

v =

3/5

w =

-2/5
```

The same system can also be solved in another way:

```
>> [u,v,w] = solve('u+v+w=1', '3*u+v=3', 'u-2*v-w=0', 'u','v','w')
```

```
u =

4/5

 v =

3/5

 w =

-2/5
```

Finally, we can solve the system in the following way:

```
>> [u,v,w] = solve('u+v+w=1, 3*u+v=3, u-2*v-w=0', 'u,v,w')
```

u =

4/5

v =

3/5

w =

-2/5

Next we solve some systems, subject to certain conditions.

```
>> pretty(sym(maple('solve({x^2*y^2=0, x-y=1})')))
```

{x = 0, y = - 1}, {x = 0, y = - 1}, {x = 1, y = 0}, {x = 1, y = 0}

```
>> pretty(sym(maple('solve({x^2*y^2=0, x-y=1, x<>0})')))
```

{x = 1, y = 0}, {x = 1, y = 0}

```
>> pretty(sym(maple('solve({x^2*y^2-b, x^2-y^2-a},{x,y})')))
>> pretty(sym(maple('solve({x^2*y^2-b, x^2-y^2-a},{x,y})')))
```

{y = 1/2 %4, x = 1/2 %3}, {y = 1/2 %4, x = - 1/2 %3},

    {y = - 1/2 %4, x = 1/2 %3}, {y = - 1/2 %4, x = - 1/2 %3},

    {y = 1/2 %1, x = 1/2 %2}, {x = - 1/2 %2, y = 1/2 %1},

    {y = - 1/2 %1, x = 1/2 %2}, {x = - 1/2 %2, y = - 1/2 %1}

$$\%1 := (-2\,a - 2\,(a^2 + 4\,b)^{1/2})^{1/2}$$

$$\%2 := (2\,a - 2\,(a^2 + 4\,b)^{1/2})^{1/2}$$

$$\%3 := (2\,a + 2\,(a^2 + 4\,b)^{1/2})^{1/2}$$

$$\%4 := (-2\,a + 2\,(a^2 + 4\,b)^{1/2})^{1/2}$$

Next we find the integer solutions of an equation:

```
>> pretty(sym(maple('isolve(3*x-4*y=7)')))
```

$$\{y = 2 + 3 \_N1, \; x = 5 + 4 \_N1\}$$

Now we solve system and an equation approximately.

```
>> maple('f: = sin(x + y) - exp(x) * y = 0: ' g: = x ^ 2 - y = 2:');
>> pretty(sym(maple('fsolve({f,g},{x,y},{x=-1..1,y=-2..0})')))
```

$$\{y = -1.552838698, \; x = -.6687012050\}$$

```
>> maple('f:=10-(ln(v+(v^2-1)^(1/2))-ln(3+(3^2-1)^(1/2)))');
>> pretty(sym(maple('fsolve(f,v)')))
```

$$64189.82535$$

```
>> pretty(sym(maple('fsolve(f,v,1..infinity)')))
```

$$64189.82535$$

In the two following equations, instead of solving for x, we solve for $sin(x)$ in the first and x^2 in the second.

```
>> pretty(sym(maple('readlib(isolate):isolate(4*x*sin(x)=3,sin(x))')))
```

$$sin(x) = 3/4 \; x$$

```
>> pretty(sym(maple('isolate(x^2-3*x-5,x^2)')))
```

$$x^2 = 3 x + 5$$

Now we test whether two expressions are not equal but probabilistically equivalent.

```
>> maple('a: = (sin(x) ^ 2 - cos(x) * tan(x)) * (sin(x) ^ 2 + cos(x) * tan(x)) ^ 2:)
         b: = 1/4 * sin(2*x) ^ 2 - 1/2 * sin(2*x) * cos(x) - 2 * cos(x) ^ 2
              (+ 1/2 * sin(2*x) * cos(x) ^ 3 + 3 * cos(x) ^ 4 - cos(x) ^ 6:');
>> pretty(sym(maple('evalb(a = b)')))
```

$$false$$

```
>> pretty(sym(maple('evalb(expand(a) = expand(b))')))
```

---

                                false

```
>> pretty(sym(maple('testeq(a = b)')))
```

---

                                 true

In the following example, we eliminate a variable from a system:

```
>> pretty(sym(maple('readlib(eliminate):eliminate({x^2+y^2-1,x^3-y^2*x+x*y-3},x)')))
```

$$[\{x = -\frac{3}{2y^2 - y - 1}\}, \{4y^6 - 7y^4 - 4y^5 + 6y^3 + 4y^2 - 2y + 8\}]$$

EXERCISE 5-1

Find solutions to the following equations:

sin(x) cos(x) = 0, sin(x) = acos(x), ax ^ 2 + bx + c = 0 and sin(x) + cos(x) = sqrt(3) / 2

```
>> solve('sin(x) * cos(x) = 0')
```

```
ans =

[      0]
[1/2 * pi]
[-1/2 * pi]
```

```
>> solve('sin(x) = a * cos(x)','x')
```

```
ans =

atan (a)
```

```
>> solve('a*x^2+b*x+c=0','x')
```

```
ans =

[1/2/a * (-b + (b ^ 2-4 * a * c) ^(1/2))]
[1/2/a * (-b-(b^2-4*a*c) ^(1/2))]
```

```
>> solve('sin(x)+cos(x)=sqrt(3)/2')
```

```
ans =

[1/2 * 3 ^(1/2)]
[1/2 * 3 ^(1/2)]
```

EXERCISE 5-2

Find at least two solutions for each of the following trigonometric and exponential equations:

$x \sin (x) = 1/2$ and $2^{x \wedge 3} = 4 \ (2^{3x})$

Initially, we use the fsolve command:

```
>> maple ('fsolve(x * sin(x) = 1/2)')
```

```
ans =
-.74084095509549062101093540994313
```

```
>> maple('fsolve(2^(x^3)=4*2^(3*x))')
```

```
ans =
2.0000000000000000000000000000000000
```

For both equations we get a single solution. For more solutions, we can plot a graphical representation of the functions (see Figure 5-1) to determine the approximate intervals where possible solutions fall:

```
>> fplot('[x * sin (x) - 1/2.0]', [0, 4 * pi])
```

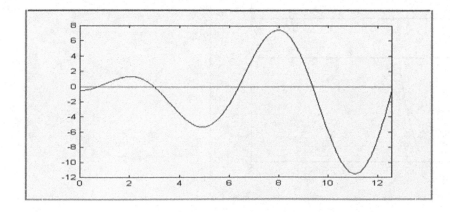

Figure 5-1.

We can see that there is a solution between 0 and 2, another between 2 and 4, another between 4 and 8, and so on. We can calculate three of them as follows:

```
>> (('s1=maple('fsolve(x*sin(x)=1/2,x,0..2)')
```

```
s1 =
.7408409550954906
```

```
>> s2=maple('fsolve(x*sin(x)=1/2,x,2..4)')
```

```
s2 =
2.972585490382360
```

```
>> s3=maple('fsolve(x*sin(x)=1/2,x,4..8)')
```

```
S3 =
6.361859813361645
```

We repeat the process for the second equation, starting with the plotted graph (see Figure 5-2):

```
>> subplot(2,1,1)
>> fplot('[2^(x^3),4*2^(3*x)]',[-3,1,-1/4,3/2])
>> subplot(2,1,2)
>> fplot('[2^(x^3),4*2^(3*x)]',[1,3,100,400])
```

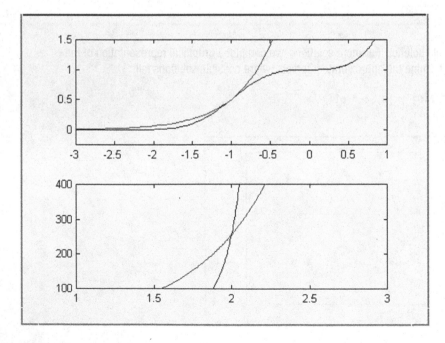

Figure 5-2.

Two areas where there are intersections for different values of the variables *x* and *y* have been represented on the same graph. There are possible solutions between −4 and 0, and between 0 and 3. We try to find these solutions:

```
>> maple('fsolve(2 ^(x^3) = 4 * 2 ^(3*x), x, -4.. 0)')
```

ans =

-1.00000000000

```
>> maple('fsolve(2^(x^3)=4*2^(3*x),x,0..3)')
```

ans =

2.00000000000

We see that *x =-1* and *x = 2* are exact solutions of the equation.

EXERCISE 5-3

Solve each of the two following logarithmic and surd equations:

$x^{3/2} \log(x) = x \log(x^{3/2})$, sqrt[1-x]+sqrt[1+x] = a

```
>> maple('fsolve(x^(3/2)*log(x)=x*log(x)^(3/2))')
```

ans =

1.

We first generate the corresponding graphs (see Figure 5-3) to determine the intervals in which possible solutions are found. This reveals that *x = 1* is the only real solution.

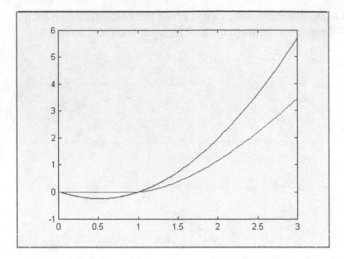

Figure 5-3.

```
>> fplot('[x^(3/2) * log(x), x * log(x^(3/2))]', [0,3,-1,6])
```

Now, let's solve the surd equation:

```
>> pretty(sym(solve('sqrt(1-x)+sqrt(1+x)=a','x')))
```

```
                         2      1/2
            [- 1/2 a (-a  + 4)     ]
            [                      ]
            [             2     1/2 ]
            [ 1/2 a (-a  + 4)      ]
```

EXERCISE 5-4

Solve the following two equations:

$x^5 + 16 x^4 + 7 x^3 + 17 x^2 + 11 x + 5 = 0$ and $x^4 - 1 = 0$

In addition, solve the first equation modulo 19 and the second modulo 5.

```
>> s1=solve('x^5 +16*x^4+7*x^3+17*x^2+11*x+5=0')
```

```
[                    -15.61870451719182]
[-.3867059805744952-.3977796861292117*i]
[-.3867059805744952+.3977796861292117*i]
[ .1960582391704047-1.000858165543796*i]
[ .1960582391704047+1.000858165543796*i]
```

```
>> s2=solve('x^4-1=0')
```

```
s2 =

[1]
[-1]
[i]
[-i]
```

Now, we solve the first equation modulo 19:

```
>> maple('msolve(x^5 +16*x^4+7*x^3+17*x^2+11*x+5=0,19)')
```

```
ans =

{x = 1}, {x = 18}, {x = 3,} {x = 7}, {x = 12}
```

Next, we solve the second equation modulus 5:

```
>> maple('msolve(x^4-1=0,5)')
```

```
ans =

{x = 1}, {x = 2}, {x = 3}, {x = 4}
```

Because we have two polynomial equations, there is also the option of solving the two equations with the roots command, as shown here:

```
>> roots([5,11,17,7,16,5])
```

```
ans =

  -1.2183 + 1.3164i
  -1.2183 - 1.3164i
   0.2827 + 0.9302i
   0.2827 - 0.9302i
  -0.3289
```

```
>> roots([-1,0,0,0,1])
```

```
ans =

  -1.0000
   0.0000 + 1.0000i
   0.0000 - 1.0000i
   1.0000
```

EXERCISE 5-5

Solve the following system of two equations:

$\cos(x/12) / \exp(x^2/16) = y$

$-5/4 + y = \sin(x^{3/2})$

```
>> [x,y] = solve('cos(x/12)/exp(x^2/16) = y','- 5/4 + y = sin(x^(3/2))')
```

```
x =

2.412335896593778

y =

.6810946557469383
```

EXERCISE 5-6

Find the intersection of the hyperbolas of equations $x^2 - y^2 = r^2$ and $a^2x^2 - b^2y^2 = a^2b^2$ with the parabola $z^2 = 2px$.

```
>> [x,y,z] = solve('a^2*x^2-b^2*y^2=a^2*b^2','x^2-y^2=r^2','z^2=2*p*x', 'x,y,z')
```

```
x =

[1/2*RootOf((a^2-b^2)*_Z^4+4*b^2*r^2*p^2-4*a^2*b^2*p^2)^2/p]
[1/2*RootOf((a^2-b^2)*_Z^4+4*b^2*r^2*p^2-4*a^2*b^2*p^2)^2/p]

y =

[1/2*(RootOf((a^2-b^2)*_Z^4+4*b^2*r^2*p^2-4*a^2*b^2*p^2)^4-4*r^2*p^2)^(1/2)/p]
[-1/2*(RootOf((a^2-b^2)*_Z^4+4*b^2*r^2*p^2-4*a^2*b^2*p^2)^4-4*r^2*p^2)^(1/2)/p]
```

```
z =

[RootOf((a^2-b^2)*_Z^4+4*b^2*r^2*p^2-4*a^2*b^2*p^2)]
[RootOf((a^2-b^2)*_Z^4+4*b^2*r^2*p^2-4*a^2*b^2*p^2)]
```

Now, we simplify the RootOf expressions in the above solutions:

```
>> [simple(allvalues(x)), simple(allvalues(y)), simple(allvalues(z))]
```

ans =

```
[b*(-r^2+a^2) ^(1/2) /(a^2-b^2) ^(1/2) b]  [a *(b^2-r^2) ^(1/2) /(a^2-b^2) ^(1/2)]
[2 ^(1/2) * b ^(1/2) * p ^(1/2) *(-r^2+a^2) ^(1/4) /(a^2-b^2) ^(1/4)]
[b*(-r^2+a^2) ^(1/2) /(a^2-b^2) ^(1/2) b]  [a *(b^2-r^2) ^(1/2) /(a^2-b^2) ^(1/2)]
[- 2 ^(1/2) * b ^(1/2) * p ^(1/2) *(-r^2+a^2) ^(1/4) /(a^2-b^2) ^(1/4)]
[-b *(-r^2+a^2) ^(1/2) /(a^2-b^2) ^(1/2)]  [a *(b^2-r^2) ^(1/2) /(a^2-b^2) ^(1/2)]
[i * 2 ^(1/2) * b ^(1/2) * p ^(1/2) *(-r^2+a^2) ^(1/4) /(a^2-b^2) ^(1/4)]
[-b*(-r^2+a^2)^(1/2)/(a^2-b^2)^(1/2)]  [ a*(b^2-r^2)^(1/2)/(a^2-b^2)^(1/2)]
[-i*2^(1/2)*b^(1/2)*p^(1/2)*(-r^2+a^2)^(1/4)/(a^2-b^2)^(1/4)]
[ b*(-r^2+a^2)^(1/2)/(a^2-b^2)^(1/2)]  [-a*(b^2-r^2)^(1/2)/(a^2-b^2)^(1/2)]
[2^(1/2)*b^(1/2)*p^(1/2)*(-r^2+a^2)^(1/4)/(a^2-b^2)^(1/4)]
[b*(-r^2+a^2)^(1/2)/(a^2-b^2)^(1/2)]  [-a*(b^2-r^2)^(1/2)/(a^2-b^2)^(1/2)]
[-2^(1/2)*b^(1/2)*p^(1/2)*(-r^2+a^2)^(1/4)/(a^2-b^2)^(1/4)]
[-b*(-r^2+a^2)^(1/2)/(a^2-b^2)^(1/2)]  [-a*(b^2-r^2)^(1/2)/(a^2-b^2)^(1/2)]
[i*2^(1/2)*b^(1/2)*p^(1/2)*(-r^2+a^2)^(1/4)/(a^2-b^2)^(1/4)]
[-b*(-r^2+a^2)^(1/2)/(a^2-b^2)^(1/2)]  [-a*(b^2-r^2)^(1/2)/(a^2-b^2)^(1/2)]
[-i*2^(1/2)*b^(1/2)*p^(1/2)*(-r^2+a^2)^(1/4)/(a^2-b^2)^(1/4)]
```

Each line of this output (a set of three values) is a solution of the system, that is, a point of intersection of the three curves.

EXERCISE 5-7

Solve the inequality $x^2 + x > 5$.

```
>> maple('solve(x^2+x>5,x)')
```

ans =

```
RealRange(-inf,Open(-1/2-1/2*21^(1/2))),RealRange(Open(-1/2+1/2*21^(1/2)),inf)
```

CHAPTER 6

███

Series, Continuity, Derivatives, Integrals and Differential Equations

6-1. Predefined Symbolic Functions

MATLAB provides a group of predefined special symbolic functions, whose syntax is presented in the following table:

`cosint(x)`	*Cosine integral,* $Ci(x) = \gamma + \ln(x) + \int_0^x \frac{\cos(t)-1}{t} dt$ $\gamma = 0.57\ldots$
`sinint(x)`	*Sine integral,* $Si(x) = \int_0^x \frac{\sin(t)}{t} dt.$
`hypergeom(n,d,z)`	*Generalized hypergeometric function.*
`lambertw(x)`	*Solves the equation* $\lambda(x)e^{\lambda(x)} = x.$
`Zeta(x)`	*Riemann zeta function, defined as* $Z(x) = \sum_{k=1}^{\infty} \frac{1}{k^x}.$
`Zeta (n,x)`	*nth derivative of zeta (x).*

As a first example, we find the sum of the series $\sum_{k=1}^{\infty} \frac{1}{k^4}$., whose value will be $Z(4)$.

```
>> zeta(4)
```

```
ans =

    1.0823
```

Then to solve the integral $\int_0^2 \frac{\sin(t)}{t} dt$ we use the sine integral function:

```
>> sinint(2)
```

```
ans =
    1.6054
```

6-2. Functions for Mathematical Analysis: Limits, Continuity and Series

MATLAB's symbolic mathematics module enables you to explore mathematical analysis with ease. You can calculate limits, obtain derivatives, find the sum of series, expand functions as Taylor series, calculate integrals, and work with equations.

When calculating limits and working with numerical series, the same functions are used to calculate limits of sequences, limits of functions, and limits of sequences of functions, and of course, to analyze the continuity of functions and convergence of numerical series and power series. The analysis for single and multiple variables is similar. This group of functions includes the following.

`limit(sequence,inf)`	*Calculates the limit of the sequence, indicated by its general term, as n tends to infinity*
`limit(function,x,a)`	*Calculates the limit of the function of the variable x, indicated by its analytical expression, as the variable x tends towards the value a.*
`limit(function,a)`	*Calculates the limit of the function of the variable x, indicated by its analytical expression, as the variable x tends toward the value a.*
`limit(function,x,a,'right')`	*Calculates the limit of the function of the variable x, indicated by its analytical expression, as the variable x tends toward the value from the right.*
`limit(function,x,a,'left')`	*Calculates the limit of the function of the variable x, indicated by its analytical expression, as the variable x tends toward the value from the left.*
`symsum(S,v,a,b)`	*Sums the series S with respect to the variable v varying from a to b.*
`symsum(S,v)`	*Sums the series S with respect to the variable v varying from 0 to v-1.*
`r = symsum(S)`	*Sums the series S with respect to its symbolic variable k (as determined by* `findsym`*) from 0 up to k-1.*
`symsum(S,a,b)`	*Sums the series S with respect to its symbolic variable k (determined by* `findsym`*), varying between a and b.*

As a first example we calculate the limits of the following sequences:

$$\lim_{n\to\infty}\left(\frac{-3+2n}{-7+3n}\right)^4, \ \lim_{n\to\infty}\frac{1+7n^2+3n^3}{5-8n+4n^3}, \ \lim_{n\to\infty}\left(\frac{1+n}{2}\right)^4\frac{1+n}{n^5}, \ \lim_{n\to\infty}\sqrt[n]{\frac{1+n}{n^2}}$$

We have:

```
>> syms n
>> limit(((2*n-3)/(3*n-7))^4,inf)
```

```
ans =

16/81
```

```
>> limit((3*n^3+7*n^2+1)/(4*n^3-8*n+5),n,inf)
```

ans =

3/4

```
>> limit(((n+1)/2) * ((n^4+1)/n^5),inf)
```

ans =

1/2

```
>> limit(((n+1)/n^2)^(1/n),inf)
```

ans =

1

Next we calculate the limits of the following functions:

$$\lim_{x\to 1}\frac{-1+x}{-1+\sqrt{x}}, \ \lim_{x\to 2}\frac{x-\sqrt{2+x}}{-3+\sqrt{1+4x}}, \ \lim_{x\to 0}\sqrt[x]{1+x}, \ \lim_{x\to 0}\frac{\sin[(ax)^2]}{x^2}$$

We have:

```
>> syms x a
>> limit((x-1)/(x^(1/2)-1),x,1)
```

ans =

2

```
>> limit((x-(x+2)^(1/2))/((4*x+1)^(1/2)-3),2)
```

ans =

9/8

```
>> limit((1+x)^(1/x))
```

ans =

exp (1)

```
>> limit(sin(a*x)^2/x^2,x,0)
```

ans =

a^2

In the following example, we calculate the limit function of the sequence of functions defined by $g_n(x) = (x^2+nx)/n$ with $x \in R$.

```
>> limit((x^2+n*x)/n,n,inf)
```

ans =

x

We have obtained the limit function, which is the diagonal of the first and third quadrants. We illustrate this graphically (Figure 6-1) as follows:

```
>> fplot('[(x^2+x),(x^2+2*x)/2,(x^2+3*x)/3,(x^2+4*x)/4,
(x^2+5*x)/5,(x^2+5*x)/5,(x^2+6*x)/6,(x^2+7*x)/7,(x^2+8*x)/8,
(x^2+9*x)/9]',[-2,2,-2,2])
```

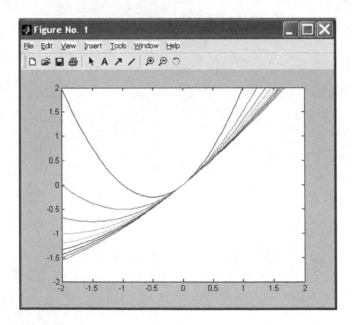

Figure 6-1.

The following example checks the continuity in R-{0} of the function $f(x) = sin(x)/x$. This will verify that $\lim_{x \to a} f(x) = f(a)$.

```
>> syms x a
>> limit(sin(x)/x, x, a)
```

ans =

```
sin(a)/a
```

We then confirm that the function $f(x) = \sqrt[x]{e}$ is not continuous at the point $x = 0$, because the lateral limits do not match (one is zero and the other infinite).

```
>> syms x
>> limit((exp(1/x)),x,0,'right')
```

ans =

```
inf
```

```
>> limit((exp(1/x)),x,0, 'left')
```

ans =

```
0
```

In the following example we test whether the numerical series $\sum_{n=1}^{\infty} \dfrac{n}{2^n}$ is convergent by applying the ratio test $\left(\lim_{n \to \infty} \dfrac{a(n+1)}{a(n)} < 1 \right)$ and, if so, we calculate its sum.

```
>> syms n
>> f = n/2^n
```

f =

```
n/(2^n)
```

```
>> limit(subs(f,n,n+1)/f, n, inf)
```

ans =

```
1/2
```

We can see that the limit is less than 1, so we conclude that the series converges. We calculate the sum in the following way:

```
>> symsum(f,n,1,inf)
```

ans =

2

6-3. Derivatives, Integrals and Differential Equations

MATLAB provides the following functions for mathematical analysis, a group that includes commands relating to derivatives, integrals, and differential equations. We will begin with the functions related to differentiation.

`diff('f','x')`	*Returns the derivative of the function* f *with respect to* x.
`syms x, diff(f,x)`	*Returns the derivative of the function* f *with respect to* x.
`diff('f', 'x', n)`	*Returns the* nth *derivative of* f *with respect to* x.
`syms x, diff(f,x,n)`	*Returns the* nth *derivative of* f *with respect to* x.
`r = taylor(f,n,v)`	*Returns the MacLaurin series up to order* n-1 *of the function* f *in the variable* v.
`r = taylor(f)`	*Returns the MacLaurin series up to order* 5 *of the function* f *in the default variable.*
`r = taylor(f,n,v,a)`	*Returns the Taylor series up to order* n-1 *of the function* f *in the variable* v *in a neighbourhood of the point* a.
`R = jacobian(w,v)`	*Returns the Jacobian matrix of* w *with respect to* v.

The following are the integration-related functions:

`syms x, int(f(x),x) or int('f(x)', 'x')`	*Computes the indefinite integral* $\int f(x)dx$.
`int(int('f(x,y)', 'x'), 'y')`	*Calculates the double integral* $\int \int f(x,y)dxdy$
`syms x y, int(int(f(x,y),x),y)`	*Calculates the double integral* $\int \int f(x,y)dxdy$.
`int(int(int(... int('f(x,y...z)', 'x'), 'y'),..., 'z')`	*Calculates* $\int \int \cdots \int f(x,y,\cdots,z)\,dxdy\cdots dz$.
`syms x y z,` `int(int(int(... int(f(x, y,...,z), x), y)..., z)`	*Calculates* $\int \int \cdots \int f(x,y,\cdots,z)\,dxdy\cdots dz$.
`syms x a b, int(f(x),x,a,b)`	*Calculates the definite integral* $\int_a^b f(x)dx$.
`int('f(x)', 'x', 'a', 'b')`	*Calculates the definite integral* $\int_a^b f(x)dx$.
`int(int('f(x,y)', 'x', 'a', 'b'), 'y', 'c', 'd')`	*Computes the integral* $\int_a^b \int_c^d f(x,y)dxdy$

syms x y a b c d, int (int (f(x,y), x, a, b), y, c, d)	Calculates $\int_a^b \int_c^d f(x,y)\,dxdy$.
int(int(int(...int('f(x,y,...,z)', 'x', 'a', 'b'), 'y', ' it, ' from),...)), 'z', 'e', 'f')	Finds $\int_a^b \int_c^d \cdots \int_e^f f(x,y,\cdots,z)\,dxdy\cdots dz$
Syms x y z a b c d e f, int (int (int (... int(f(x,y,...,z), x, a, b), y, c, d),...), z, e, f)	Finds $\int_a^b \int_c^d \cdots \int_e^f f(x,y,\cdots,z)\,dxdy\cdots dz$

The following table summarizes the functions related to differential equations:

dsolve('e', 'v')	Solves the differential equation where v is the independent variable (if you don't specify 'v', the independent variable is assumed by default to be x). It returns only explicit solutions.
dsolve('e', 'c', 'v')	Solves the differential equation subject to the specified initial condition c.
dsolve('e','c1','c2',...,'cn','v')	Solves the differential equation e subject to the specified initial conditions c_i.
dsolve('e','c1,c2,...,cn','v')	Solves the differential equation subject to the specified initial conditions.
dsolve('e1', 'e2',..., 'en',) ('c1', 'c2',..., 'cn', 'v')	Solves the given system of differential equations (explicitly) subject to the specified initial conditions.
dsolve('e1, e2,..., en',) ('c1, c2,..., cn', 'v')	Solves the given system of differential equations subject to the specified initial conditions.

As a first example, we calculate the derivative of the function $log(sin(2x))$.

```
>> pretty(diff('log(sin(2*x))','x'))
```

```
      cos(2 x)
   2  ---------
      sin(2 x)
```

We can then find the fully simplified derivative:

```
>> pretty(simple(diff('log(sin(2*x))','x')))
```

```
      2
   --------
   tan (2 x)
```

217

In the following example, we calculate the first four derivatives of the function $f(x) = 1/x$.

```
>> f='1/x';
 [diff(f),diff(f,2),diff(f,3),diff(f,4),diff(f,5)]
```

ans =

```
[-1/x ^ 2, 2/x ^ 3, - 6/x ^ 4, 24/x ^ 5, - 120/x ^ 6]
```

Next, given the function $f(x,y) = sin(xy) + cos(xy^2)$, we calculate the following:

$$\frac{\partial f}{\partial x}, \frac{\partial f}{\partial y}, \frac{\partial^2 f}{\partial x^2}, \frac{\partial^2 f}{\partial y^2}, \frac{\partial^2 f}{\partial x \partial y}, \frac{\partial^2 f}{\partial y \partial x}, \frac{\partial^4 f}{\partial^2 x \partial^2 y}$$

```
>> syms x y
>> f = sin(x*y) + cos(x*y^2)
```

f =

```
sin(x*y) + cos(x*y^2)
```

```
>> diff(f,x)
```

ans =

```
cos(x*y) *-sin(x*y^2) * y ^ 2
```

```
>> diff(f,y)
```

ans =

```
cos(x*y) * x-2 * sin(x*y^2) * x * y
```

```
>> diff(diff(f,x),x)
```

ans =

```
-sin(x*y) * y ^ 2-cos(x*y^2) * y ^ 4
```

```
>> diff (diff(f,y), y)
```

ans =

-sin(x*y) * x ^ 2-4 * cos(x*y^2) * x ^ 2 * y ^ 2-2 * sin(x*y^2) * x

```
>> diff(diff(f,x),y)
```

ans =

-sin(x*y) * x * y + cos(x*y)-2 * cos(x*y^2) * x * y ^ 3-2 * sin(x*y^2) * y

```
>> diff(diff(f,y),x)
```

ans =

-sin(x*y) * x * y + cos(x*y)-2 * cos(x*y^2) * x * y ^ 3-2 * sin(x*y^2) * y

```
>> diff(diff(diff(diff(f,x),x),y,y))
```

ans =

sin(x*y) * y ^ 3 * x-3 * cos(x*y) * y ^ 2 + 2 * cos(x*y^2) * y ^ 7 * x + 6 * sin(x*y^2) * y ^ 5

Next we find the Taylor series up to order 10 of the function $1/(2-x)$ in a neighborhood of the point $x = 1$

```
>> syms x
>> f=1/(2-x)
```

f =

1/(2-x)

```
>> pretty(taylor(f,11,x,1))
```

```
          2         3         4         5         6         7
 x + (x - 1)  + (x - 1)  + (x - 1)  + (x - 1)  + (x - 1)  + (x - 1)

            8         9          10
   + (x - 1)  + (x - 1)  + (x - 1)
```

The following example computes the integral $\int \dfrac{1}{x^2-1}\,dx$.

```
>> int('1/(x^2-1)','x')
```

ans =

-atanh (x)

The following example finds the integral $\int aLn(1-bx)dx$, where a and b are parameters.

```
>> syms x a b, pretty(simple(int(a*log(1+b*x),x)))
```

```
           a (log(1 + b x) - 1) (1 + b x)
           -------------------------------
                          b
```

The following example computes the double integral $\iint aLn(1-bx)dxdb,$ where a is a parameter.

```
>> syms x a b, pretty(simple(int(int(a*log(1+b*x),x),b)))
```

```
a (-dilog(1 + b x) + log(1 + b x) + log(1 + b x) x b - 1 - 2 b x - log(b))
```

The following example computes the triple integral $\iiint aLn(1-bx)dxdbda$.

```
>> syms x a b, pretty(simple(int(int(int(a*log(1+b*x),x),b),a)))
```

```
    2
1/2a(-dilog(1 + b x) + log(1 + b x) + log(1 + b x) x b - 1 - 2 b x - log(b))
```

Next we calculate $\int_0^1 aLn(1-bx)dx$

```
>> syms x a b, pretty(simple(int(a * log(1+b*x), x, 0, 1)))
```

```
           a log(1 + b)
           ------------ - a + a log(1 + b)
                b
```

The following example computes $\int_0^1 \int_2^3 aLn(1-bx)dxdb$

```
>> syms x a b, pretty(simple(int(int(a*log(1+b*x),x,0,1),b,2,3)))
```

$$(- 2 + 8 \log(2) - dilog(4) - 3 \log(3) + dilog(3)) \; a$$

The following example solves the first-order, first-degree differential equation $y'(t) = ay(t)$ with a = parameter.

```
>> pretty(dsolve('Dy = a*y'))
```

$$C1 \; exp \; (a \; t)$$

The family of solutions turns out to be $y(t) = c_1 e^{at}$.
Next we solve the above differential equation with the initial condition $y(0) = b$.

```
>> pretty(dsolve('Dy = a*y', 'y(0) = b'))
```

$$b \; exp \; (a \; t)$$

Now we solve the second-degree, first-order differential equation $y'^2(s) + y^2(s) = 1$ with the initial condition $y(0) = 0$.

```
>> y = dsolve ('(Dy) ^ 2 + y ^ 2 = 1', 'y(0) = 0', 's')
```

```
y =

[-sin(s)]
[sin(s)]
```

Now we solve the differential equation of second order and first degree $y''(t) = -a^2 y'(t)$ with the initial conditions $y(0) = 1$ and $y'(p/a) = 0$.

```
>> pretty(dsolve('D2y = - a ^ 2 * y', 'y(0) = 1, Dy(pi/a) = 0'))
```

$$cos(a \; t)$$

Therefore, the solution is the function $y(t) = cos(at)$.

The following example solves the system: $x'(t) = y(t)$, $y'(t) = -x(t)$.

```
>> [x, y] = dsolve('Dx = y', 'Dy =-x')
```

```
x =

cos (t) * C1 + sin (t) * C2


y =

-sin (t) * C1 + cos (t) * C2
```

We then calculate the solution of the previous system of differential equations subject to the initial conditions $x(0) = 0$ and $y(0) = 1$.

```
>> [x, y] = dsolve('Dx = y, Dy = - x', 'x(0) = 0, y(0) = 1')
```

```
x =

sin(t)


y =

cos(t)
```

EXERCISE 6-1

Consider the following symbolic matrix A:

$$\begin{bmatrix} a & b & c \\ 3c & a-3c & b \\ 3b & -3b+3c & a-3c \end{bmatrix}$$

Calculate A', A⁻¹, determinant(A), trace(A), rank(A) and A².

We start by defining the symbolic form of our problem matrix as follows:

```
>> A=sym('[a,b,c; 3*c,a-3*c,b; 3*b,-3*b+3*c,a-3*c]')
```

```
A =
[   a,       b,      c]
[ 3*c,    a-3*c,     b]
[ 3*b, -3*b+3*c,a-3*c]
```

Alternatively, the same symbolic matrix can be defined by previously declaring all variables as symbolic, as follows:

```
>> syms a b c
>> A=sym([a,b,c; 3*c,a-3*c,b; 3*b,-3*b+3*c,a-3*c])
```

```
A =
[        a,        b,        c]
[      3*c,     a-3*c,       b]
[      3*b, -3*b+3*c,     a-3*c]
```

```
>> transpose(A)
```

```
ans =

[a, 3 * c, * 3B]
[b, a-3*c, -3*b+3*c]
[c,      b,    a-3*c]
```

```
>> pretty(inv(A))
```

```
     2                    2     2                 2             2           2
  [ a  - 6 a c + 9 c  + 3 b  - 3 b c       a b - 3 c        - b  + a c - 3 c ]
  [ --------------------------------     - ---------      - -----------------]
  [               %1                          %1                   %1        ]
  [                                                                          ]
  [          2            2     2             2                            2  ]
  [        - b  + a c - 3 c          a  - 3 a c - 3 b c       a b - 3 c      ]
  [     - 3 -----------------        -------------------     - ----------    ]
  [               %1                       %1                     %1         ]
  [                                                                          ]
  [              2                         2     2           2               ]
  [        a b - 3 c               a b - a c + b       a  - 3 a c - 3 b c    ]
  [     - 3 ----------           3 ----------------    -------------------   ]
  [             %1                       %1                   %1             ]
```

```
         3       2     2       2          3     3     2
%1 :=  a  - 6 c a  + 9 c  a + 3 a b  - 9 a b c + 9 c  + 3 b  + 9 b c
```

```
>> pretty(det(A))
```

```
       3       2     2       2          3     3     2
      a  - 6 c a  + 9 c  a + 3 a b  - 9 a b c + 9 c  + 3 b  + 9 b c
```

```
>> pretty(trace(A))
```

$$3\,a\, -\, 6\,c$$

```
>> rank(A)

ans =

    3
```

```
>> A^2

ans =

[           a^2+6*b*c,               a*b+b*(a-3*c)+c*(-3*b+3*c),              a*c+b^2+c*(a-3*c)]
[ 3*a*c+3*c*(a-3*c)+3*b^2,          3*b*c+(a-3*c)^2+b*(-3*b+3*c),              3*c^2+2*b*(a-3*c)]
[ 3*a*b+3*c*(-3*b+3*c)+3*b*(a-3*c),   3*b^2+2*(-3*b+3*c)*(a-3*c),    3*b*c+(a-3*c)^2+b*(-3*b+3*c)]
```

EXERCISE 6-2

Find the intersection of the hyperbolas with equations $x^2 - y^2 = 1$ and $a^2x^2 - b^2y^2 = 16$ with the parabola $z^2 = 2x$.

We can solve the system formed by the three equations as follows:

```
>> [x, y, z] = solve('a^2*x^2-b^2*y^2=16','x^2-y^2=1','z^2=2*x','x,y,z')
```

```
x =

[   1/2*(((b^2-16)/(a^2-b^2))^(1/4)+i*((b^2-16)/(a^2-b^2))^(1/4))^2]
[   1/2*(((b^2-16)/(a^2-b^2))^(1/4)+i*((b^2-16)/(a^2-b^2))^(1/4))^2]
[  1/2*(-((b^2-16)/(a^2-b^2))^(1/4)+i*((b^2-16)/(a^2-b^2))^(1/4))^2]
[  1/2*(-((b^2-16)/(a^2-b^2))^(1/4)+i*((b^2-16)/(a^2-b^2))^(1/4))^2]
[   1/2*(((b^2-16)/(a^2-b^2))^(1/4)-i*((b^2-16)/(a^2-b^2))^(1/4))^2]
[   1/2*(((b^2-16)/(a^2-b^2))^(1/4)-i*((b^2-16)/(a^2-b^2))^(1/4))^2]
[  1/2*(-((b^2-16)/(a^2-b^2))^(1/4)-i*((b^2-16)/(a^2-b^2))^(1/4))^2]
[  1/2*(-((b^2-16)/(a^2-b^2))^(1/4)-i*((b^2-16)/(a^2-b^2))^(1/4))^2]

y =

[   1/(a^2-b^2)*(-(a^2-b^2)*(a^2-16))^(1/2)]
[  -1/(a^2-b^2)*(-(a^2-b^2)*(a^2-16))^(1/2)]
[   1/(a^2-b^2)*(-(a^2-b^2)*(a^2-16))^(1/2)]
[  -1/(a^2-b^2)*(-(a^2-b^2)*(a^2-16))^(1/2)]
```

```
[   1/(a^2-b^2)*(-(a^2-b^2)*(a^2-16))^(1/2)]
[  -1/(a^2-b^2)*(-(a^2-b^2)*(a^2-16))^(1/2)]
[   1/(a^2-b^2)*(-(a^2-b^2)*(a^2-16))^(1/2)]
[  -1/(a^2-b^2)*(-(a^2-b^2)*(a^2-16))^(1/2)]


z =

[   ((b^2-16)/(a^2-b^2))^(1/4)+i*((b^2-16)/(a^2-b^2))^(1/4)]
[   ((b^2-16)/(a^2-b^2))^(1/4)+i*((b^2-16)/(a^2-b^2))^(1/4)]
[  -((b^2-16)/(a^2-b^2))^(1/4)+i*((b^2-16)/(a^2-b^2))^(1/4)]
[  -((b^2-16)/(a^2-b^2))^(1/4)+i*((b^2-16)/(a^2-b^2))^(1/4)]
[   ((b^2-16)/(a^2-b^2))^(1/4)-i*((b^2-16)/(a^2-b^2))^(1/4)]
[   ((b^2-16)/(a^2-b^2))^(1/4)-i*((b^2-16)/(a^2-b^2))^(1/4)]
[  -((b^2-16)/(a^2-b^2))^(1/4)-i*((b^2-16)/(a^2-b^2))^(1/4)]
[  -((b^2-16)/(a^2-b^2))^(1/4)-i*((b^2-16)/(a^2-b^2))^(1/4)]
```

EXERCISE 6-3

Solve the following integrals:

$$\int_{-3}^{3}\frac{1}{3}\frac{\sin(2t)}{t}dt, \ \int_{0}^{5}\frac{\cosh(x)-1}{x}dx$$

For the first integral the integrand is an even function, so the integral will be double the integral of the function between the limits 0 and 3. Then, we make the change of variable $2t = v$, and arrive at the integral:

$$\int_{-3}^{3}\frac{1}{3}\frac{\sin(2t)}{t}dt=2\int_{0}^{3}\frac{1}{3}\frac{\sin(2t)}{t}dt=\frac{2}{3}\int_{0}^{6}\frac{\sin(v)}{v}dv$$

whose solution is given by MATLAB as follows:

```
>> (2/3) * (sinint(6))
```

```
ans =

    0.9498
```

To calculate the second integral we have in mind the following:

$$Ci(x)=\gamma+\ln(x)+\int_{0}^{x}\frac{\cos(t)-1}{t}dt \ \Rightarrow \ \int_{0}^{5}\frac{\cos(x)-1}{x}dx=Ci(5)-\gamma+\ln(5)$$

which can be calculated in MATLAB as follows:

```
>> cosint(5) - 0.577215664 - log(5)
```

ans =

   -2.3767

EXERCISE 6-4

Given the function h defined by $h(x,y) = (\cos(x^2-y^2), \sin(x^2-y^2))$, calculate h(1,2), h(-Pi,Pi) and h(cos(a²), cos(1-a²)).

We create a two-dimensional vector function as follows:

```
>> syms x y a.
>> h = [cos(x^2-y^2), sin(x^2-y^2)]
```

h =

[cos(x^2-y^2), sin(x^2-y^2)]

Now we calculate the requested values:

```
>> subs(h,{x,y},{1,2})
```

ans =

   -0.9900-0.1411

```
>> subs(h,{x,y},{-pi,pi})
```

ans =

    1 0

```
>> subs(h, {x,y}, {cos(a^2), cos(1-a^2)})
```

ans =

[cos(cos(a^2) ^ 2-cos(-1+a^2) ^ 2), sin(cos(a^2) ^ 2-cos(-1+a^2) ^ 2)]

EXERCISE 6-5

Given the function f defined by

$f(x,y) = 3 (1-x)^2 e^{-(y+1)^2-x^2} -10(x/5-x^3-y/5) e^{-x^2-y^2}-1/3e^{-(x+1)^2-y^2}$

find f(0,0) and represent the function graphically.

In this case, since it is necessary to represent the function, we define it via the M-file shown in Figure 6-2.

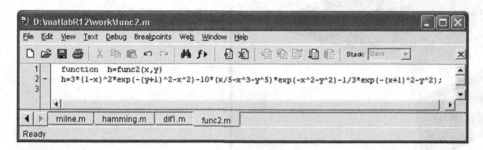

Figure 6-2.

Now, we calculate the value of *f* at *(0,0)*:

```
>> func2 (0,0)
```

ans =

   0.9810

To graph the function, use the command meshgrid to draw the graph on screen (in a neighborhood of the origin), and the command surf to generate the surface graph:

```
>> [x,y] = meshgrid(-0.5:.05:0.5,-0.5:.05:0.5);
>> z = func2(x,y);
>> surf(x,y,z)
```

The result is the graph shown in Figure 6-3.

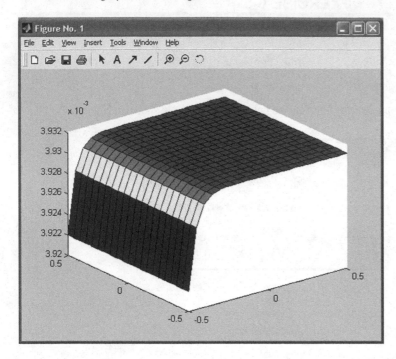

Figure 6-3.

EXERCISE 6-6

Given functions f(x) = sin(cos(x^{1/2}) and g(x) = sqrt(tan(x²)), calculate the composite of f and g and the composite of g and f. Also calculate the inverse of the functions f and g.

```
>> syms x, f = (cos(x^(1/2)));
>> g=sqrt(tan(x^2));
>> simple(compose(f,g))
```

```
ans =

sin(cos(tan(x^2)^(1/4)))
```

```
>> simple(compose(g,f))
```

```
ans =

tan(sin(cos(x^(1/2))))^2)^(1/2)
```

```
>> F = finverse(f)
```

```
F =
```

```
acos(asin(x))^2
```

```
>> G = finverse(g)
```

```
G =
```

```
atan(x^2)^(1/2)
```

EXERCISE 6-7

Given the function defined as

$$f(x)=\frac{1}{1+\sqrt[x]{e}} \ \ if \ \ x\neq 0 \ \ and \ \ f(x)=1 \ \ if \ \ x=0$$

study its continuity on the real line.

Except at the point $x = 0$, the continuity is clear. To analyze the function at the point $x = 0$ we calculate the lateral limits as $x \to 0$:

```
>> syms x
limit(1/(1+exp(1/x)),x,0,'right')
```

```
ans =
```

```
0
```

```
>> limit(1/(1+exp(1/x)),x,0,'left')
```

```
ans =
```

```
1
```

The limit of the function as $x \rightarrow 0$ does not exist, because the lateral limits are different. But because the lateral limits are both finite, the discontinuity at $x = 0$ is a finite jump. We can illustrate this result with the plot shown in Figure 6-4.

```
>> fplot('1/(1+exp(1/x))',[-5,5])
```

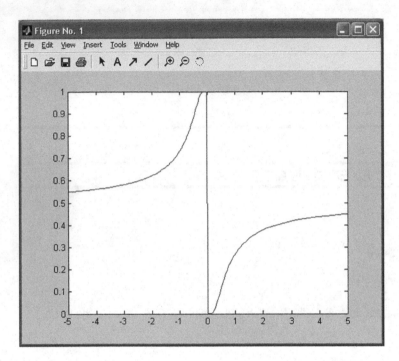

Figure 6-4.

EXERCISE 6-8

Calculate the continuity of the function f: $R^2 \rightarrow R$ defined by:

$$f(x,y) = \frac{(x-1)^2 y^2}{(x-1)^2 + y^2} \ \textit{if } (x,y) \neq (1,0) \ \textit{and if } (1,0) = 0.$$

The only problem is at (1,0). To confirm that the function is continuous at this point, we need to check that

$$\lim_{(x,y) \to (1,0)} f(x,y) = 0.$$

```
>> syms x y m a r
>> limit(limit(y ^ 2 *(x-1) ^ 2 / (y ^ 2 +(x-1) ^ 2), x, 0), y, 0)
```

```
ans =

0
```

```
>> limit(limit(y ^ 2 *(x-1) ^ 2 / (y ^ 2 + (x-1) ^ 2), y, 0), x, 0)
```

```
ans =

0
```

```
>> limit((m*x)^2*(x-1)^2/((m*x)^2+(x-1)^2),x,0)
```

```
ans =

0
```

```
>> limit ((m*x) *(x-1)^2/((m*x) +(x-1)^2),x,0)
```

```
ans =

0
```

It turns out that the iterated and directional limits (as calculated along a straight line $y = mx$) coincide, which leads us to believe in the existence of the limit and that its value is zero. To corroborate this, we can calculate the limit in polar coordinates:

```
>> limit(limit((r ^ 2 * sin(a) ^ 2) * (r * cos(a) - 1) ^ 2 / ((r ^ 2 * sin(a) ^ 2) + (r *
cos(a) - 1) ^ 2), r, 1), a, 0)
```

```
ans =

0
```

We find that the limit is zero at the point (1,0), which ensures the continuity of the function. Figure 6-5 shows the surface, and in particular the continuity and the tendency toward 0 in a neighborhood of the point (1,0).

```
>> [x, y] = meshgrid(0:0.05:2,-2:0.05:2);
z=y.^2.*(x-1).^2./(y.^2+(x-1).^2);
mesh(x,y,z), view ([- 23, 30])
```

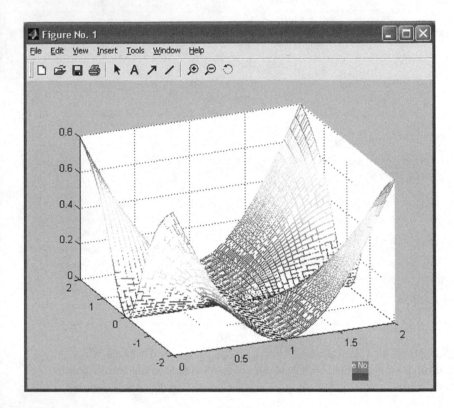

Figure 6-5.

EXERCISE 6-9

Find the sum of the following series:

$$\sum_{n=2}^{\infty} \frac{3+2n}{7^n\,n(n+1)}, \quad \sum_{n=1}^{\infty} \frac{n}{p^n}, \quad p=parameter.$$

Before attempting to find the sums we first need to show that the sums are indeed convergent. We apply the ratio test for the first series:

```
>> syms n
>> f=(3+2*n)/((1-n)*n*7^n);
>> pretty(f)
```

```
                    3 + 2 n
                 ------------
                            n
                 (1 - n) n 7
```

```
>> limit(subs(f,n,n+1)/f,n,inf)
```

```
ans =

1/7
```

As the limit is less than 1, the series is convergent. We will calculate its sum. MATLAB tries to return the result, which can be complicated. Often, the result returned depends on certain special functions defined by the program. Here's an example:

```
>> S1 = symsum(f,n,2,inf)
```

```
S1 =

-6 * log(6/7)-22/21 + 13/343 * hypergeom([2, 2],[3],1/7)
```

Now we apply the ratio test to the second series:

```
>> syms n p
>> g=n/p^n;
>> pretty(g)
```

```
                    n
                 ----
                    n
                 p
```

```
>> limit(subs(g,n,n+1)/g,n,inf)
```

```
ans =

1/p
```

Thus, if $p > 1$, the series converges; if $p < 1$, the series diverges; and if $p = 1$, we get the series of general term n, which diverges. When p is greater than 1, we find the sum of the series:

```
>> S2=symsum(g,n,2,inf)
```

```
S2 =

2/p^2*(1/2/(-1+p)^3*p^4*(-1/p+1)-1/2*p)
```

```
>> pretty(simple(S2))
```

```
                    -1 + 2 p
                 -----------
                          2
                 p (- 1 + p)
```

EXERCISE 6-10

Find the MacLaurin series up to order 13 of the function sinh(x). Also find the Taylor series up to order 6 of the function $1/(1+x)$ in a neighborhood of the point $x = 1$.

```
>> pretty(taylor(sinh(x),13))
```

```
          3          5           7            9             11
 x + 1/6 x  + 1/120 x  + 1/5040 x  + 1/362880 x  + 1/39916800 x
```

```
>> pretty(taylor(1/(1+x),6,1))
```

```
                    2            3            4            5
 3/4 - 1/4 x + 1/8 (x - 1)  - 1/16 (x - 1)  + 1/32 (x - 1)  - 1/64 (x - 1)
```

EXERCISE 6-11

Conduct a full study of the function

$$f(x) = \frac{x^3}{x^2 - 1}$$

calculating the asymptotes, maximum, minimum, inflection points, intervals of growth and decrease, and intervals of concavity and convexity.

```
>>  f='x ^ 3 /(x^2-1)'
```

```
f =

x^3 /(x^2-1)
```

```
>> syms x, limit (x^3 /(x^2-1), x, inf)
```

```
ans =

NaN
```

We can see that there are no horizontal asymptotes. To see if there are any vertical asymptotes, let's look at the values of *x* that make *y* infinite:

```
>> solve('x^2-1')
```

```
ans =

[1]
[-1]
```

The vertical asymptotes are the straight lines $x = 1$ and $x = -1$. Now let's see if there are any oblique asymptotes:

```
>> limit(x^3/(x^2-1)/x,x,inf)
```

```
ans =

1
```

```
>> limit(x^3/(x^2-1)-x,x,inf)
```

```
ans =

0
```

The straight line $y = x$ is an oblique asymptote. Now, the maximum and minimum, inflection points and intervals of concavity and growth will be analyzed:

```
>> solve(diff(f))
```

```
ans =

[          0]
[          0]
[3 ^(1/2)   ]
[^(1/2) - 3]
```

The first derivative vanishes at the points with x-coordinates $x = 0$, $x = \sqrt{3}$ and $x = -\sqrt{3}$. These include maximum and minimum candidates. To test whether they are maxima or minima, we find the value of the second derivative at those points:

```
>> [numeric(subs(diff(f,2),0)),numeric(subs(diff(f,2),sqrt(3))),
   numeric(subs(diff(f,2),-sqrt(3)))]
```

```
ans =

     0 2.5981 - 2.5981
```

Therefore, at the point with abscissa $x = -\sqrt{3}$ there is a maximum and at the point with abscissa $x = \sqrt{3}$ there is a minimum. At $x = 0$ we know nothing:

```
>> [numeric(subs(f, sqrt(3))), numeric(subs(f, -sqrt(3)))]
```

```
ans =

   2.5981 - 2.5981
```

236

Therefore, the highest point is (-$\sqrt{3}$,-2.5981) and the minimum point is ($\sqrt{3, 2.5981}$).

We will now analyze the points of inflection:

```
>> solve(diff(f,2))
```

ans =

```
[          0]
[  i*3^(1/2)   ]
[-i * 3 ^(1/2)]
```

The only possible turning point occurs at $x = 0$, and because $f(0) = 0$, this possible turning point is (0,0):

```
>> subs(diff(f,3), 0)
```

ans =

-6

As the third derivative at $x = 0$ is non-zero, the origin really is a turning point:

```
>> pretty(simple(diff(f)))
```

$$\frac{x^2 (x^2 - 3)}{(x^2 - 1)^2}$$

The curve is increasing when $y' > 0$, that is, in the intervals $(-\infty,-\sqrt{3})$ and $(\sqrt{3},\infty)$.

The curve is decreasing when $y' < 0$, that is, in the intervals

$(-\sqrt{3},-1)$, $(-1,0)$, $(0,1)$ and $(1, \sqrt{3})$.

```
>> pretty(simple(diff(f,2)))
```

$$2 \frac{x (x^2 + 3)}{(x^2 - 1)^3}$$

The curve is concave when $y''> 0$, that is, in the intervals *(-1,0)* and *(1, ∞)*.

The curve is convex when $y''< 0$, that is, in the intervals *(0,1)* and *(-∞ ,-1)*.

The curve has horizontal tangents at the three points at which the first derivative is zero. The equations of the horizontal tangents are $y = 0$, $y = 2.5981$ and $y = -2.5981$.

The curve has vertical tangents at the points that make the first derivative infinite. These include $x = 1$ and $x =-1$. Therefore, the vertical tangents coincide with the two vertical asymptotes.

We can then represent the curve along with its asymptotes as shown in Figure 6-6.

```
>> fplot('[x^3/(x^2-1),x]',[-5,5,-5,5])
```

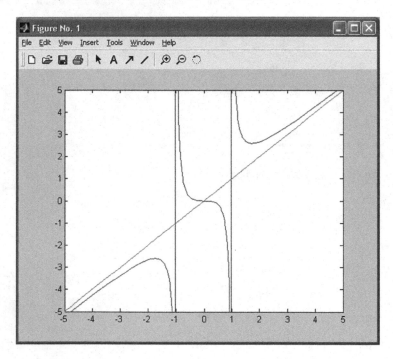

Figure 6-6.

We can also represent the curve, its asymptotes, and their horizontal and vertical tangents in the same graph (see Figure 6-7).

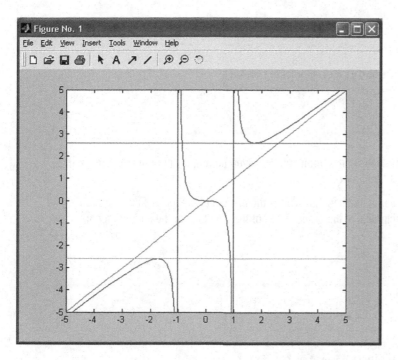

Figure 6-7.

```
>> fplot('[x^3/(x^2-1),x,2.5981,-2.5981]',[-5,5,-5,5])
```

EXERCISE 6-12

Given the vector function (u(x,y), v(x,y)), where:

$$u(x,y)=\frac{x^4+y^4}{x},\ v(x,y)=\sin(x)+\cos(y)$$

find the conditions under which there is an inverse vector function (x(u,v), y(u,v)) with x = x(u,v) and y = y(u,v) and find the derivative and the Jacobian of the inverse transformation. Find its value at the point ($\pi/4$,-$\pi/4$).

The conditions that must be met are the hypotheses of the inverse function theorem. The functions are differentiable with a continuous derivative, except perhaps at x= 0. Now let's consider the Jacobian of the direct transformation ∂(u(x,y), v(x,y)) /∂(x,y):

```
>> syms x y
>> J = simple((jacobian ([(x^4+y^4)/x, sin(x) + cos(y)], [x, y])))
```

```
J =
[3 * x^2 - 1/x^2 * y^4, 4 * y^3/x]
[cos(x),-sin(y)]
```

```
>> pretty(det(J))
```

$$
-\frac{3\,\sin^4(y)\,x - \sin^4(y)\,y + 4\,y\,\cos^3(x)\,x}{x^2}
$$

Therefore, at the points where this expression is non-zero, it can be solved for *x* and *y* in terms of *u* and *v*. In addition, it must also meet the requirement that $x \neq 0$.

We next calculate the derivative of the inverse function. Its value is the inverse of the initial Jacobian matrix, and the determinant of the Jacobian is the reciprocal of the determinant of the Jacobian of the initial function:

```
>> I=simple(inv(J));
>> pretty(simple(det(I)))
```

$$
-\frac{x^2}{3\,\sin^4(y)\,x - \sin^4(y)\,y + 4\,y\,\cos^3(x)\,x}
$$

Next we are going to find the value of this function at the point *(π/4, -π/4)*:

```
>> numeric(subs(subs(determ(I),pi/4,'x'),-pi/4,'y'))
```

```
ans =

   0.38210611216717
```

```
>> numeric(subs(subs(symdiv(1,determ(J)),pi/4,'x'),-pi/4,'y'))
```

```
ans =
   0.38210611216717
```

These results corroborate that the determinant of the Jacobian of the inverse function is the reciprocal of the determinant of the Jacobian of the original function.

EXERCISE 6-13

Given the function $f(x,y)=e^{-(x+y)}$ and the transformation u = u(x,y) = x + y, v = v(x,y) = x, find f(u,v).

We calculate the inverse transformation and its Jacobian to apply the change of variables theorem:

```
>> syms x y u v
>> [x, y] = solve('u=x+y,v=x','x','y')
```

```
x =

v

y =

u-v
```

```
>> jacobian([v,u-v],[u,v])
```

```
ans =

[0, 1]
[1, - 1]
```

```
>> f = exp(x-y);
>> pretty(simple(subs(f,{x,y},{v,u-v}) * abs(det(jacobian([v, u-v], [u, v])))))
```

$$exp(2\ v-u)$$

The requested function is $f(u,v) = e^{2v-u}$.

EXERCISE 6-14

Solve the following integrals:

$$\int \frac{dx}{x^3\sqrt{x^2+3x-1}}, \ \int \frac{\sqrt{9-4x^2}}{x}dx, \ \int x^8(3+5x^3)^{1/4}dx$$

```
>> syms x
>> pretty(simple(int(x^(-3)*(x^2+3*x-1)^(-1/2),x)))
```

```
        2          1/2       2          1/2
     (x + 3 x - 1)         (x + 3 x - 1)
  1/2 ----------------- + 9/4 -----------------
           2                        x
          x

                        -2 + 3 x
       + 31/8 tie 1/2 (-)
                     2          1/2
                   (x. + 3 x - 1)
```

```
>> pretty(simple(int(x^(-1)*(9-4*x^2)^(1/2), x)))
```

```
              2 1/2                    3
          (9 - 4 x )    - 3 atanh(-------------)
                                     2 1/2
                                  (9 - 4 x )
```

```
>> pretty(simple(int(x^8*(3+5*x^3)^(1/4),x)))
```

```
                     3         6         9        3 1/4
       4/73125 (288 - 120 x + 125 x + 1875 x) (3 + 5 x)
```

EXERCISE 6-15

Consider the curve given in polar coordinates by r = 3-3cos(a). Calculate the length of the arc corresponding to one complete revolution (0≤a≤2π).

```
>> r='3-3*cos(a)';
>> diff(r,'a')
```

ans =

3 * sin (a)

```
>> R = simple(int('((3-3 * cos(a))^2 + (3 * sin(a))^2)^(1/2)','a', '0','2 * pi'))
```

R =

24

EXERCISE 6-16

Calculate the value of the following integral

$$\int_{-1.96}^{1.96} \frac{e^{-x^2/2}}{\sqrt{2\pi}} dx$$

which represents the area under the normal curve between the specified limits.

```
>> numeric(int('exp(-x^2/2)/(2*pi)^(1/2)','x',-1.96,1.96))
```

ans =
    0.95000420970356

EXERCISE 6-17

Find the intersection of the paraboloid $ax^2 + y^2 = z$ and the cylinder $z = a^2 - y^2$ and calculate the volume enclosed by the intersection. Also find the volume of the intersection of the cylinder $z = x^2$ and $4 - y^2 = z$.

The first volume is calculated by means of the integral:

```
>> pretty(simple(int(int(int('1','z','a*x^2+y^2',
  'a^2-y^2'),'y',0,'sqrt((a^2-a*x^2)/2)'),'x',0,'sqrt(a)')))
```

```
     /
     |                2     2        2 1/2
 1/24 |    lim      3 a  x (2 a  - 2 a x )
     |        1/2
     \x -> (a   )-

                           1/2  1/2
          7/2  1/2       2    a   x              2        2 1/2   |
    + 3 a    2    atan(-------------- ) + x (2a - 2ax )           |
                          2        2 1/2                          |
                       (2 a  - 2 a x )                            /
```

To calculate the second volume we graph the requested intersection, as shown in Figure 6-8, with the aim of clarifying the limits of integration, using the following syntax:

```
>> [x, y] = meshgrid(-2:.1:2);
z = x ^ 2;
mesh(x,y,z)
hold on;
z = 4 - y. ^ 2;
mesh (x, y, z)
```

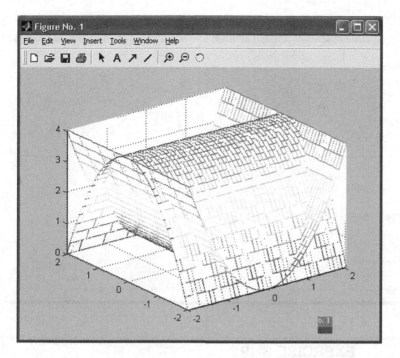

Figure 6-8.

Now we can calculate the volume requested via the following integral:

```
>> pretty(simple(int(int(int('1','z','x^2','4-y^2'),
   'y',0,'sqrt(4-x^2)'),'x',0,2)))
```

$$2\ pi$$

EXERCISE 6-18

Solve the following differential equation:

$$\frac{dy}{dx} = \frac{xy}{y^2 - x^2}$$

```
>> pretty(simple(dsolve('Dy =(x*y)/(y^2-x^2)')))
```

```
                              t + C1
                      exp (-2)--------
                                 x
          -1/2 lambertw(- ------------------) x - t - C1
                                 2
                                x
      exp(-----------------------------------------------)
                                x
```

EXERCISE 6-19

Solve the following equations:

$$9y'''' - 6y''' + 46y'' - 6y' + 37y = 0$$

$$3y'' + 2y' - 5y = 0$$

$$2y'' + 2y' + 5y = 0, \ y(0) = 0, \ y'(0) = 1/2.$$

```
>> pretty(simple(dsolve('9*D4y-6*D3y+46*D2y-6*Dy+37*y=0')))
```

```
C1 sin(t) + cos(t) C2 + C3 exp(1/3 t)sin(2t) + C4 exp(1/3 t)cos(2t)
```

```
>> pretty(dsolve('3*D2y+2*Dy-5*y=0'))
```

```
          exp(t) C1 + C2 exp(-5/3 t)
```

```
>> pretty(dsolve('2 * D2y + 5 * Dy + 5 * y = 0', 'y (0) = 0 Dy (0) = 1/2 '))
```

```
            1/2                         1/2
      2/15 15 exp(-5/4 t) sin(1/4 15 t)
```

EXERCISE 6-20

With the initial conditions x(0) = 1 and y(0) = 2, solve the following system of equations:

$$x' - y' = e^{-t}$$

$$y' + 5x + 2y = \sin(3t)$$

```
>> [x,y] = dsolve('Dx-Dy = exp(-t), Dy+5 * x + 2 * y = sin(3 + t)','x(0) = 1, y(0) = 2')
```

x =

(-7/50 * sin(3) + 1/50 * cos(3) + 7/6) * exp(-7*t) + 7/50 * sin(3+t)-1/50 * cos(3+t)-1/6 * exp(-t)

y =

(-7/50 * sin(3) + 1/50 * cos(3) + 7/6) * exp(-7*t) + 5/6 * exp(-t) + 7/50 * sin(3+t)-1/50 * cos(3 + t)

Get the eBook for only $10!

> Now you can take the weightless companion with you anywhere, anytime. Your purchase of this book entitles you to 3 electronic versions for only $10.

This Apress title will prove so indispensible that you'll want to carry it with you everywhere, which is why we are offering the eBook in 3 formats for only $10 if you have already purchased the print book.

Convenient and fully searchable, the PDF version enables you to easily find and copy code—or perform examples by quickly toggling between instructions and applications. The MOBI format is ideal for your Kindle, while the ePUB can be utilized on a variety of mobile devices.

Go to www.apress.com/promo/tendollars to purchase your companion eBook.